Cambridge International
AS & A Level Mathematics:
Pure Mathematics 1

Practice Book

CAMBRIDGE
UNIVERSITY PRESS

CAMBRIDGE
UNIVERSITY PRESS

Shaftesbury Road, Cambridge CB2 8EA, United Kingdom

One Liberty Plaza, 20th Floor, New York, NY 10006, USA

477 Williamstown Road, Port Melbourne, VIC 3207, Australia

314–321, 3rd Floor, Plot 3, Splendor Forum, Jasola District Centre, New Delhi – 110025, India

103 Penang Road, #05-06/07, Visioncrest Commercial, Singapore 238467

Cambridge University Press is part of the University of Cambridge.

It furthers the University's mission by disseminating knowledge in the pursuit of education, learning and research at the highest international levels of excellence.

www.cambridge.org
Information on this title: www.cambridge.org/9781108444880

© Cambridge University Press & Assessment 2018

First published 2018

20 19 18 17 16 15 14 13 12 11 10 9 8

Printed in Spain by GraphyCems

A catalogue record for this publication is available from the British Library

ISBN 978-1-108-44488-0 Paperback

This Practice Book has been compiled and authored by Muriel James, using some questions from:

Cambridge International AS and A Level Mathematics: Pure Mathematics 1 Coursebook (*Revised edition*) by Hugh Neill, Douglas Quadling and Julian Gilbey, that was originally published in 2016.

A Level Mathematics for OCR A Student Book 1 (*AS/ Year 1*) by Vesna Kadelburg, Ben Woolley, Paul Fannon and Stephen Ward

A Level Mathematics for OCR A Student Book 2 (*Year 2*) by Vesna Kadelburg, Ben Woolley, Paul Fannon and Stephen Ward

Cover image: iStock/Getty Images

Contents

How to use this book   iv

1   Quadratics   1

2   Functions   23

3   Coordinate geometry   49

4   Circular measure   63

5   Trigonometry   71

6   Series   91

7   Differentiation   104

8   Further differentiation   113

9   Integration   126

Answers   148

How to use this book

Throughout this book you will notice particular features that are designed to help your learning. This section provides a brief overview of these features.

- Find the equation of a straight line given sufficient information.
- Interpret and use any of the forms $y = mx + c$, $y - y_1 = m(x - x_1)$, $ax + by + c = 0$ in solving problems.
- Understand that the equation $(x - a)^2 + (y - b)^2 = r^2$ represents the circle with centre (a, b) and radius r.

Learning objectives indicate the important concepts within each chapter and help you to navigate through the practice book.

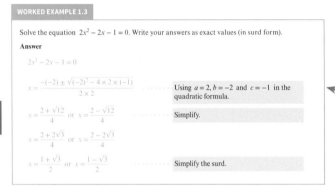

WORKED EXAMPLE 1.3

Solve the equation $2x^2 - 2x - 1 = 0$. Write your answers as exact values (in surd form).

Answer

$2x^2 - 2x - 1 = 0$

$x = \dfrac{-(-2) \pm \sqrt{(-2)^2 - 4 \times 2 \times (-1)}}{2 \times 2}$ ...... Using $a = 2, b = -2$ and $c = -1$ in the quadratic formula.

$x = \dfrac{2 + \sqrt{12}}{4}$ or $x = \dfrac{2 - \sqrt{12}}{4}$ ...... Simplify.

$x = \dfrac{2 + 2\sqrt{3}}{4}$ or $x = \dfrac{2 - 2\sqrt{3}}{4}$

$x = \dfrac{1 + \sqrt{3}}{2}$ or $x = \dfrac{1 - \sqrt{3}}{2}$ ...... Simplify the surd.

END-OF-CHAPTER REVIEW EXERCISE 7

1 Find the gradient of the graph of $y = \dfrac{1}{2\sqrt{x}}$ at the point where the y-coordinate is 3.

2 $f(x) = ax^3 + bx^{-2}$ where a and b are constants. $f'(1) = 18$ and $f''(1) = 18$. Find a and b.

3 $f(x) = \sqrt{x^3} + 15\sqrt{x}$. Find the values of x for which the gradient of $f(x)$ is 9.

The **End-of-chapter review exercise** contains exam-style questions covering all topics in the chapter. You can use this to check your understanding of the topics you have covered.

 TIP

Substitute the value of r that minimises the quantity back into the **original expression** to find the minimum value of that quantity.

Tip boxes contain helpful guidance about calculating or checking your answers.

Worked examples provide step-by-step approaches to answering questions. The left side shows a fully worked solution, while the right side contains a commentary explaining each step in the working.

Throughout each chapter there are multiple exercises containing practice questions. The questions are coded:

PS These questions focus on problem-solving.

P These questions focus on proofs.

M These questions focus on modelling.

You should not use a calculator for these questions.

iv

Chapter 1
Quadratics

- Carry out the process of completing the square for a quadratic polynomial $ax^2 + bx + c$ and use a completed square form.
- Find the discriminant of a quadratic polynomial $ax^2 + bx + c$ and use the discriminant.
- Solve quadratic equations, and quadratic inequalities, in one unknown.
- Solve by substitution a pair of simultaneous equations of which one is linear and one is quadratic.
- Recognise and solve equations in x that are quadratic in some function of x.
- Understand the relationship between a graph of a quadratic function and its associated algebraic equation, and use the relationship between points of intersection of graphs and solutions of equations.

1.1 Solving quadratic equations by factorisation

WORKED EXAMPLE 1.1

Lim walked $12\,$km from A to B at a steady speed of $x\,$km/h.

His average speed for the return was $2\,$km/h slower.

    a   Write down, in terms of x, the total time taken for the complete journey.

    b   If the total time he took was $3.5\,$hours, write an equation in x and solve it to find his speed from A to B.

Answer

a $\dfrac{12}{x} + \dfrac{12}{x-2}$ hours   From using $\text{speed} = \dfrac{\text{distance}}{\text{time}}$.

b $\dfrac{12}{x} + \dfrac{12}{x-2} = 3.5$ Multiply both sides by $x(x-2)$.

    $12(x-2) + 12x = 3.5x(x-2)$ Expand brackets and rearrange.

    $12x - 24 + 12x = 3.5x^2 - 7x$ Multiply both sides by 2 and rearrange.

    $7x^2 - 62x + 48 = 0$ Factorise.

    $(7x - 6)(x - 8) = 0$ Solve.

    $x = \dfrac{6}{7}$ or $x = 8$

    The value of $x = \dfrac{6}{7}$ is a solution to the equation, but it gives a negative speed for the return journey.

    Lim's speed from A to B is $8\,$km/h.

1 By factorising, solve the following equations:

   a **i** $3x^2 + 2x = x^2 + 3x + 6$ **ii** $2x^2 + 3 = 17x - 7 - x^2$

   b **i** $9x^2 = 24x - 16$ **ii** $18x^2 = 2x^2 - 40x - 25$

   c **i** $(x - 3)(x + 2) = 14$ **ii** $(2x + 3)(x - 1) = 12$

   d **i** $2x = 11 + \dfrac{6}{x}$ **ii** $3x + \dfrac{4}{x} = 7$

2 Solve the following equations. (In most cases, multiplication by an appropriate expression will turn the equation into a form you should recognise.)

   a $x = 3 + \dfrac{10}{x}$ **b** $x + 5 = \dfrac{6}{x}$

   c $2t + 5 = \dfrac{3}{t}$ **d** $x = \dfrac{12}{x + 1}$

   e $x - \dfrac{2}{x + 2} = \dfrac{1}{3}$ **f** $\dfrac{20}{x + 2} - 1 = \dfrac{20}{x + 3}$

   g $\dfrac{12}{x + 1} - \dfrac{10}{x - 3} = -3$ **h** $\dfrac{15}{2x + 1} + \dfrac{10}{x} = \dfrac{55}{2}$

3 Solve algebraically:

   $(2x - 3)(x - 5) = (x - 3)^2$

4 Solve the equation $x^2 + 8k^2 = 6kx$, giving your answer in terms of k.

5 Find the exact solutions of the equation $x^2\sqrt{2} + 2x\sqrt{5} - 3\sqrt{2} = 0$.

6 Solve the equation $\dfrac{49}{(5x + 2)^2} - \dfrac{14}{5x + 2} + 1 = 0$

PS **7** The product of two positive, consecutive even integers is 168. Use this information to form a quadratic equation and solve it to find the two integers.

PS **8** Two men A and B working together can complete a task in 4 days. If B completes the task on his own, he takes 6 more days than if A did the task on his own.

   Use the information to form an equation.

   Solve the equation to find the time that A takes to complete the task on his own.

9 Solve by factorisation.

   a $\dfrac{3x + 2}{2x - 1} = \dfrac{5x + 6}{x + 4}$ **b** $\dfrac{2}{3x + 1} + \dfrac{3}{1 - x} = \dfrac{1}{2}$

   c $\dfrac{5}{x + 3} + \dfrac{7}{x - 1} = 8$ **d** $\dfrac{x^2 - 5x - 6}{x^2 - 1} = 0$

10 If 5 is a root of the equation $2x^2 - 3x + c = 0$, find the value of c and the second root of the equation.

1.2 Completing the square

WORKED EXAMPLE 1.2

a Write $x^2 + 6x - 5$ in completed square form.

b Complete the square $2x^2 + 12x - 5$.

c Express $1 - 4x - 2x^2$ in the form $p - q(x + r)^2$.

d **i** Express $x^2 - 7x + 15$ in the form $(x - a)^2 + b$ where a and b are constants.

ii Hence, state the maximum value of $\dfrac{1}{x^2 - 7x + 15}$.

Answer

a $(x^2 + 6x) - 5$ Halve the coefficient of x and complete the square.

$\left\{(x + 3)^2 - 3^2\right\} - 5$ Remove the brackets {}.

$(x + 3)^2 - 3^2 - 5$ Simplify.

$(x + 3)^2 - 14$

b $2x^2 + 12x - 5$ Take out the factor of 2 from the terms that involve x.

$2(x^2 + 6x) - 5$ Complete the square.

$2\left\{(x + 3)^2 - 3^2\right\} - 5$ Simplify.

$2(x + 3)^2 - 18 - 5$ Simplify.

$2(x + 3)^2 - 23$

c $1 - 4x - 2x^2$ Rearrange.

$-2x^2 - 4x + 1$ Take out the factor of -2 from the terms that involve x.

$-2(x^2 + 2x) + 1$ Complete the square.

$-2\left\{(x + 1)^2 - 1^2\right\} + 1$ Simplify.

3

$$-2(x+1)^2 + 2 + 1 \quad \cdots \cdots \text{Simplify.}$$

$$-2(x+1)^2 + 3 \quad \cdots \cdots \text{Rearrange.}$$

$$3 - 2(x+1)^2$$

d   i $x^2 - 7x + 15$ $\cdots \cdots$ Complete the square.

$$= \left(x - \frac{7}{2}\right)^2 - \left(\frac{7}{2}\right)^2 + 15 \quad \cdots \text{Simplify.}$$

$$= \left(x - \frac{7}{2}\right)^2 + \frac{11}{4}$$

$$a = \frac{7}{2},\ b = \frac{11}{4}$$

ii $\dfrac{1}{\left(x - \dfrac{7}{2}\right)^2 + \dfrac{11}{4}}$ $\cdots \cdots$ The **maximum** value of this fraction is when the denominator has the **minimum** value. This occurs when $x = \dfrac{7}{2}$.

$$= \dfrac{1}{\left(\dfrac{7}{2} - \dfrac{7}{2}\right)^2 + \dfrac{11}{4}} \quad \cdots \cdots \text{Evaluate the expression.}$$

$$= \frac{4}{11}$$

EXERCISE 1B

1   Express the following in completed square form.

a $x^2 + 2x + 2$ b $x^2 - 8x - 3$ c $x^2 + 3x - 7$

d $5 - 6x + x^2$ e $x^2 + 14x + 49$ f $2x^2 + 12x - 5$

g $3x^2 - 12x + 3$ h $7 - 8x - 4x^2$ i $2x^2 + 5x - 3$

2   Use the completed square form to factorise the following expressions.

a $x^2 - 2x - 35$ b $x^2 - 14x - 176$ c $x^2 + 6x - 432$

d $6x^2 - 5x - 6$ e $14 + 45x - 14x^2$ f $12x^2 + x - 6$

3   Solve the following quadratic equations. Leave surds in your answer.

a $(x - 3)^2 - 3 = 0$ b $(x + 2)^2 - 4 = 0$ c $2(x + 3)^2 = 5$

d $(3x - 7)^2 = 8$ e $(x + p)^2 - q = 0$ f $a(x + b)^2 - c = 0$

4 A recycling firm collects aluminium cans from a number of sites. It crushes them and then sells the aluminium back to a manufacturer.

The profit from processing t tonnes of cans each week is $\$p$, where

$$p = 100t - \frac{1}{2}t^2 - 200.$$

By completing the square, find the greatest profit the firm can make each week, and how many tonnes of cans it has to collect and crush each week to achieve this profit.

 5 By writing the left-hand side in the form $a(x + p)^2 + q$, show that the equation $-2x^2 + 8x - 13 = 0$ has no real roots.

6 The quadratic function $y = a(x - b)^2 + c$ passes through the points $(-2, 0)$ and $(6, 0)$. Its maximum y value is 48. Find the values of a, b and c.

7 a Write $x^2 - 10x + 35$ in the form $(x - p)^2 + q$.

b Hence, or otherwise, find the maximum value of $\dfrac{1}{(x^2 - 10x + 35)^3}$.

 8 Two cars are travelling along two straight roads that are perpendicular to each other and meet at the point O, as shown in the diagram. The first car starts 50 km west of O and travels east at the constant speed of 20 km/h. At the same time, the second car starts 30 km south of O and travels north at the constant speed of 15 km/h.

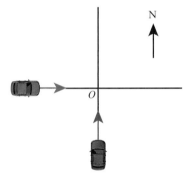

a Show that at time t (hours) the distance d (km) between the two cars satisfies
$$d^2 = 625t^2 - 2900t + 3400.$$

b Hence find the closest distance between the two cars.

1.3 The quadratic formula

WORKED EXAMPLE 1.3

Solve the equation $2x^2 - 2x - 1 = 0$. Write your answers as exact values (in surd form).

Answer

$2x^2 - 2x - 1 = 0$ — Using $a = 2, b = -2$ and $c = -1$ in the quadratic formula.

$x = \dfrac{-(-2) \pm \sqrt{(-2)^2 - 4 \times 2 \times (-1)}}{2 \times 2}$ — Simplify.

$x = \dfrac{2 + \sqrt{12}}{4}$ or $x = \dfrac{2 - \sqrt{12}}{4}$

$x = \dfrac{2 + 2\sqrt{3}}{4}$ or $x = \dfrac{2 - 2\sqrt{3}}{4}$ — Simplify the surd.

$x = \dfrac{1 + \sqrt{3}}{2}$ or $x = \dfrac{1 - \sqrt{3}}{2}$

6

EXERCISE 1C

1 Use the quadratic formula to find the exact solutions of the following equations:

a i $2x^2 + x = x^2 + 4x - 1$ ii $x^2 - 3x + 5 = 6 - 2x$

b i $3x^2 - 4x + 1 = 5x^2 + 2x$ ii $9x - 2 = 5x^2 + 1$

c i $(x + 1)(x + 3) = 5$ ii $(3x + 2)(x - 1) = 2$

d i $2x + \dfrac{1}{x} = 6$ ii $x = 4 + \dfrac{3}{x}$

2 Use the quadratic formula to solve the following equations. Leave irrational answers in surd form. If there is no solution, say so.

a $x^2 + 3x - 5 = 0$ b $x^2 - 4x - 7 = 0$ c $x^2 + 6x + 9 = 0$

d $x^2 + 5x + 2 = 0$ e $x^2 + x + 1 = 0$ f $3x^2 - 5x - 6 = 0$

g $2x^2 + 7x + 3 = 0$ h $8 - 3x - x^2 = 0$ i $5 + 4x - 6x^2 = 0$

 3 A rectangular garden measures 12 m by 16 m. A path is to be constructed around the perimeter of the garden (see diagram). The area of the garden plus path will be 285 m².

What will be the width of the path?

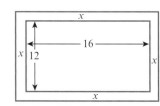

PS 4 A square has sides of length $x + 2$ cm.

A right-angled isosceles triangle has its two equal sides of length $2x + 1$ cm.

The area of the square is equal to the area of the triangle.

By writing and solving a quadratic equation, find the perimeter of the square to 3 significant figures.

PS 5 The height of an object in metres above the ground is given by: $h = -16t^2 + 64t + 190, t \geqslant 0$ where t is the time in seconds.

Find the time it takes for the object to fall to the ground. Give your answer to 3 significant figures.

1.4 Solving simultaneous equations (one linear and one quadratic)

WORKED EXAMPLE 1.4

A 160 cm length of wire has to be bent to form three small square shapes together with one larger square shape.

The total area of the four square shapes is 508 cm².

The smaller squares have side length x cm and the large square has side length y cm. Use this information to form two equations.

Hence find the dimensions of each square.

Answer

The total perimeter of the 4 squares is equal to 160 cm.

So $12x + 4y = 160$ ----------(1)

The total area of the 4 squares is 508 cm².

So $3x^2 + y^2 = 508$ ----------(2)

$12x + 4y = 160$	Divide by 4.
$3x + y = 40$	Rearrange to make y the subject.
$y = 40 - 3x$	Substitute into (2).
$3x^2 + (40 - 3x)^2 = 508$	Expand brackets.
$3x^2 + 1600 - 120x - 120x + 9x^2 = 508$	Simplify.
$12x^2 - 240x + 1092 = 0$	Divide by 12.
$x^2 - 20x + 91 = 0$	Factorise.

7

$$(x - 7)(x - 13) = 0$$

$$x = 7 \text{ or } x = 13$$

Substituting $x = 7$ into equation (1) gives $y = 19$

Substituting $x = 13$ into equation (1) gives $y = 1$

The solutions are: $x = 7, y = 19$ and $x = 13, y = 1$

BUT

As the 3 squares are smaller than the single square, there is a unique solution.

The smaller squares are $7\,\text{cm} \times 7\,\text{cm}$ and the larger square is $19\,\text{cm} \times 19\,\text{cm}$.

EXERCISE 1D

1 Solve the following pairs of simultaneous equations.

    a $y = x + 1, x^2 + y^2 = 25$ b $x + y = 7, x^2 + y^2 = 25$

    c $y = x - 3, y = x^2 - 3x - 8$ d $y = 2 - x, x^2 - y^2 = 8$

    e $2x + y = 5, x^2 + y^2 = 25$ f $y = 1 - x, y^2 - xy = 0$

    g $7y - x = 49, x^2 + y^2 - 2x - 49 = 0$ h $y = 3x - 11, x^2 + 2xy + 3 = 0$

2 The line $y = x - 4$ intersects the curve $y = x^2 + 6x$ at two points.

    Find:

    a   the coordinates of the intersection points

    b   the length of the line joining the intersection points as an exact value

    c   the equation of the perpendicular bisector of the line that joins these points.

3 Find the coordinates of the points of intersection of the given straight lines with the given curves.

    a $y = 2x + 1, y = x^2 - x + 3$ b $y = 3x + 2, x^2 + y^2 = 26$

    c $y = 2x - 2, y = x^2 - 5$ d $x + 2y = 3, x^2 + xy = 2$

    e $3y + 4x = 25, x^2 + y^2 = 25$ f $y + 2x = 3, 2x^2 - 3xy = 14$

    g $y = 2x - 12, x^2 + 4xy - 3y^2 = -27$ h $2x - 5y = 6, 2xy - 4x^2 - 3y = 1$

4 The sum of two numbers is 8 and their product is 9.75.

   a Show that this information can be written as a quadratic equation.

   b What are the two numbers?

5 Find the point where the line $y = 3 - 4x$ meets the curve $y = 4(4x^2 + 5x + 3)$.

6 The straight line $y = x - 1$ meets the curve $y = x^2 - 5x - 8$ at the points A and B.

   The curve $y = p + qx - 2x^2$ also passes through the points A and B. Find the values of p and q.

7 The line $y = 6x + 1$ meets the curve $y = x^2 + 2x + 3$ at two points. Show that the coordinates of one of the points are $(2 - \sqrt{2}, 13 - 6\sqrt{2})$, and find the coordinates of the other point.

8 Solve the equations $xy + x = 0$, $x^2 + y^2 = 4$.

P 9 Curve P has equation $y = x^2 + kx - 3$.

   Line L has equation $y = k - x$.

   Prove that for all real values of k, the line L will intersect the curve P at exactly two points.

10 The figure shows part of the curve with equation $y = -x^2 + 10x + a$ (where a is a constant) and a straight line with equation $y = bx + 25$ (where b is a constant).

   The x-coordinates of A and B are 4 and 8 respectively. Find the values of a and b.

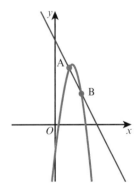

1.5 Solving more complex quadratic equations

WORKED EXAMPLE 1.5

   a Solve the equation $x^{\frac{2}{3}} - 2x^{\frac{1}{3}} - 15 = 0$.

   b Solve the equation $3\sqrt{x} + \dfrac{8}{\sqrt{x}} = 10$.

   c Solve the equation $4y^{-2} + 1 - y^{-4} = 0$ giving your answers to 3 significant figures.

Answer

a   **Method 1:** Substitution method

$$x^{\frac{2}{3}} - 2x^{\frac{1}{3}} - 15 = 0 \qquad \cdots\cdots\cdots\cdots \text{Let } y = x^{\frac{1}{3}}.$$

$$y^2 - 2y - 15 = 0$$

$$(y - 5)(y + 3) = 0$$

$$y = 5 \text{ or } y = -3 \qquad \cdots\cdots\cdots\cdots \text{Substitute } x^{\frac{1}{3}} \text{ for } y.$$

$$x^{\frac{1}{3}} = 5 \text{ or } x^{\frac{1}{3}} = -3$$

$$x = 5^3 \text{ or } (-3)^3$$

$$x = 125 \text{ or } x = -27$$

Method 2: Factorise directly

$$x^{\frac{2}{3}} - 2x^{\frac{1}{3}} - 15 = 0$$

$$\left(x^{\frac{1}{3}} - 5\right)\left(x^{\frac{1}{3}} + 3\right) = 0$$

$$x^{\frac{1}{3}} = 5 \text{ or } x^{\frac{1}{3}} = -3$$

$$x = 125 \text{ or } x = -27$$

b $$3\sqrt{x} + \frac{8}{\sqrt{x}} = 10 \qquad \cdots\cdots\cdots \text{Multiply each term by } \sqrt{x}.$$

$$3x + 8 = 10\sqrt{x} \qquad \cdots\cdots\cdots \text{Rearrange.}$$

$$3x - 10\sqrt{x} + 8 = 0 \qquad \cdots\cdots\cdots \text{Let } y = \sqrt{x}.$$

$$3y^2 - 10y + 8 = 0 \qquad \cdots\cdots\cdots \text{Factorise.}$$

$$(3y - 4)(y - 2) = 0$$

$$y = \frac{4}{3} \text{ or } y = 2 \qquad \cdots\cdots\cdots \text{Substitute } \sqrt{x} \text{ for } y.$$

$$\sqrt{x} = \frac{4}{3} \text{ or } \sqrt{x} = 2$$

$$\therefore x = \frac{16}{9} \text{ or } 4$$

TIP

Remember that

$$x^{\frac{2}{3}} = \left(x^{\frac{1}{3}}\right)^2$$

c $\quad 4y^{-2} + 1 - y^{-4} = 0$ $\quad\cdots\cdots\cdots$ Multiply each term by y^4.

$\quad 4y^2 + y^4 - 1 = 0$ $\quad\cdots\cdots\cdots$ Substitute x for y^2.

$\quad 4x + x^2 - 1 = 0$ $\quad\cdots\cdots\cdots$ Rearrange.

$\quad x^2 + 4x - 1 = 0$ $\quad\cdots\cdots\cdots$ Solve.

$\quad x = \dfrac{-4 \pm \sqrt{4^2 - 4 \times 1 \times (-1)}}{2 \times 1}$

$\quad x = \dfrac{-4 + \sqrt{20}}{2}$ or $x = \dfrac{-4 - \sqrt{20}}{2}$ $\quad$ Evaluate to at least 4 significant figures, if necessary.

$\quad x = 0.2361$ or $x = -4.236$ $\quad\cdots\cdots$ Substitute y^2 for x.

$\quad y^2 = 0.2361$ or $y^2 = -4.236$ $\quad\cdots$ There are no real solutions to $y^2 = -4.236$.

$\quad \therefore y = \pm 0.486$

TIP

If you are asked for your solutions to be to a certain number of significant figures or decimal places, you will need to use the quadratic formula.

EXERCISE 1E

1 Solve the following equations, giving your answers to 3 significant figures where necessary.

a i $\quad a^4 - 10a^2 + 21 = 0$ $\qquad$ ii $\quad x^4 - 7x^2 + 12 = 0$

b i $\quad 2x^6 + 7x^3 = 15$ $\qquad$ ii $\quad a^6 + 7a^3 = 8$

c i $\quad x^2 - 4 = \dfrac{2}{x^2}$ $\qquad$ ii $\quad x^2 + \dfrac{36}{x^2} = 12$

d i $\quad x - 6\sqrt{x} + 8 = 0$ $\qquad$ ii $\quad x - 10\sqrt{x} + 24 = 0$

e i $\quad 3^{2x} - 12 \times 3^x + 27 = 0$ $\qquad$ ii $\quad 2^{2x} - 17 \times 2^x + 16 = 0$

2 Use an appropriate substitution to solve $x^2 + \dfrac{9}{x^2} = 10$.

3 Use a suitable substitution to solve the equation $\dfrac{1}{(3x+1)^2} + 5 = \dfrac{6}{3x+1}$.

4 Use an appropriate substitution to solve $x^3 - 9x^{1.5} + 8 = 0$.

5 Solve the equation $9(1 + 9^{x-1}) = 10 \times 3^x$.

6 Solve the equation $5^x = 6 - 5^{1-x}$.

7 Solve the equation $4^{x+0.5} - 17 \times 2^x + 8 = 0$.

8 Solve $x = \sqrt{x} + 12$.

9 Solve the following equations.

a $x - 8 = 2\sqrt{x}$ **b** $x + 15 = 8\sqrt{x}$

c $t - 5\sqrt{t} - 14 = 0$ **d** $t = 3\sqrt{t} + 10$

e $\sqrt[3]{x^2} - \sqrt[3]{x} - 6 = 0$ **f** $\sqrt[3]{t^2} - 3\sqrt[3]{t} = 4$

1.6 Maximum and minimum values of a quadratic function

WORKED EXAMPLE 1.6

The diagram shows the sketch of the graph of $y = k(x - a)(x - b)$ where k, a and b are constants with $a < b$.

The maximum point on the graph is $(2, 18)$.

a Find the values of the constants a, b and k.

b Find where the graph crosses the y-axis.

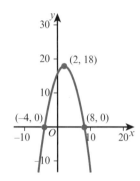

Answer

a $y = k(x - a)(x - b)$ $x = -4$ and $x = 8$ are the x-intercepts.

      $y = k(x + 4)(x - 8)$ Substitute $x = 2$, $y = 18$.

      $18 = k(2 + 4)(2 - 8)$ Simplify.

      $18 = -36k$ Solve.

      $k = -\dfrac{1}{2}$

      $y = -\dfrac{1}{2}(x + 4)(x - 8)$

      $\therefore a = -4, b = 8, k = -\dfrac{1}{2}$

b $y = -\dfrac{1}{2}(x + 4)(x - 8)$ .... $x = 0$ is where the curve meets the y-axis.

$y = -\dfrac{1}{2}(0 + 4)(0 - 8)$ .... Evaluate.

$y = 16$

$\therefore$ The graph crosses the y-axis
at $(0, 16)$

EXERCISE 1F

1   Write down the coordinates of the vertex of these quadratic functions:

   a   i $y = (x - 3)^2 + 4$ ii $y = (x - 5)^2 + 1$

   b   i $y = 2(x - 7)^2 - 1$ ii $y = 3(x - 1)^2 - 5$

   c   i $y = (x + 1)^2 + 3$ ii $y = (x + 7)^2 - 3$

   d   i $y = -5(x + 2)^2 - 4$ ii $y = -(x + 1)^2 + 5$

2   Match each equation with the corresponding graph.

   a   i $y = -x^2 - 3x + 6$ ii $y = 2x^2 - 3x + 3$ iii $y = x^2 - 3x + 6$

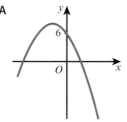 A   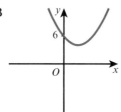 B   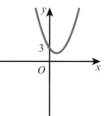 C

   b   i $y = -x^2 + 2x - 3$ ii $y = -x^2 + 2x + 3$ iii $y = x^2 + 2x + 3$

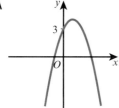 A   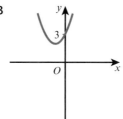 B   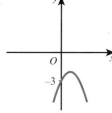 C

3   A parabola passes through the points $(0, 4)$, $(1, 0)$ and $(-2, 0)$.

   Find the equation of the parabola.

13

4 Sketch the following graphs, labelling all axis intercepts.

    a **i** $y = x^2 - 3x - 10$ **ii** $y = 2x^2 + 11x + 12$

    b **i** $y = -3x^2 + 14x - 8$ **ii** $y = 6 - 5x - x^2$

    c **i** $y = 3x^2 + 6x$ **ii** $y = 4x - x^2$

    d **i** $y = -4x^2 - 20x - 25$ **ii** $y = 4x^2 - 4x + 1$

5 Let $f(x) = 3x^2 + 2x + 1$.

    a Complete the square for $f(x)$.

    b Hence explain why the equation $f(x) = 0$ has no real solutions.

    c Write down the equation of the line of symmetry of the graph of $y = f(x)$.

6 Here are the equations of nine parabolas.

    A $y = (x - 3)(x - 8)$ **B** $y = 14 + 5x - x^2$ **C** $y = 6x^2 - x - 70$

    D $y = x(3 - x)$ **E** $y = (x + 2)(x - 7)$ **F** $y = -3(x + 3)(x + 7)$

    G $y = x^2 + 2x + 1$ **H** $y = x^2 + 8x + 12$ **I** $y = x^2 - 25$

    Answer the following questions without drawing the graphs of these parabolas.

    a Which of the parabolas cross the y-axis at a positive value of y?

    b For which of the parabolas is the vertex at the highest point of the graph?

    c For which of the parabolas is the vertex to the left of the y-axis?

    d Which of the parabolas pass through the origin?

    e Which of the parabolas do not cross the x-axis at two separate points?

    f Which of the parabolas have the y-axis as their axis of symmetry?

    g Which two of the parabolas have the same axis of symmetry?

    h Which of the parabolas have the vertex in the fourth quadrant?

7 Express $x^2 + 6x + 4$ in the form $(x + p)^2 + q$. Hence determine the minimum value that $x^2 + 6x + 4$ can take, and the value of x for which this occurs.

8 The quadratic function $y = (x - a)^2 + b$ has a turning point at $(3, 7)$.

    a State whether this turning point is a maximum or a minimum point.

    b State the values of a and b.

9 The diagram represents the graph of the function $f(x) = (x + p)(x - q)$.

    a Write down the values of p and q if they are both positive.

    b The function has a minimum value at the point C. Find the x-coordinate of C.

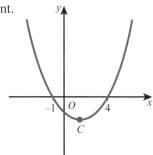

1.7 Solving quadratic inequalities

WORKED EXAMPLE 1.7

a Solve $-x^2 + 6x + 16 < 0$

b **i** Show that $x^2 - 2x + 2 > 0$ for all real x.

   ii Hence solve $\dfrac{x}{x^2 - 2x + 2} > 1$

Answer

a $-x^2 + 6x + 16 < 0$ .... Multiply each term by -1.

   $x^2 - 6x - 16 > 0$ .... Sketch the graph of $y = x^2 - 6x - 16$.

   $y = x^2 - 6x - 16$ .... To find the x-intercepts, set $y = 0$ and factorise.

   $(x + 2)(x - 8) = 0$

   $x = -2$ or $x = 8$

   So the x-axis crossing points are -2 and 8.

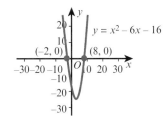

For $x^2 - 6x - 16 > 0$ we need to find the range of values of x for which the curve is positive (above the x-axis).

The solution is $x < -2, x > 8$.

b   **i** $x^2 - 2x + 2 > 0$ ..... Complete the square.

   $(x - 1)^2 - 1^2 + 2 > 0$ .... Simplify.

   $(x - 1)^2 + 1 > 0$

   As $(x - 1)^2 \geqslant 0$ and $1 > 0$

   So $(x - 1)^2 + 1 > 0$

   Hence $x^2 - 2x + 2 > 0$ for all real x.

> **TIP**
>
> Remember to reverse an inequality sign when dividing or multiplying by a negative number.

15

ii $\dfrac{x}{x^2 - 2x + 2} > 1$ We have already shown that $x^2 - 2x + 2 > 0$ for all real x. So:

$x > x^2 - 2x + 2$

$0 > x^2 - 3x + 2$ Rearrange.

$x^2 - 3x + 2 < 0$ Now sketch the graph of $y = x^2 - 3x + 2$.

$y = x^2 - 3x + 2$ To find the x-intercepts, set $y = 0$ and factorise.

$(x - 1)(x - 2) = 0$ Solve.

$x = 1$ or $x = 2$

So the x-axis crossing points are $(1, 0)$ and $(2, 0)$. The graph is a 'U' shape.

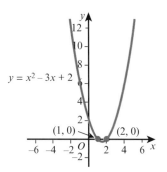

For $x^2 - 3x + 2 < 0$ we need to find the range of values of x for which the curve is negative (below the x-axis).

The solution is $1 < x < 2$.

 TIP

There is just one part of the graph that gives these required values of x so we write one inequality.

16

EXERCISE 1G

1 Solve the following quadratic inequalities:

   a **i** $x^2 \leqslant 8$ **ii** $x^2 < 5$

   b **i** $x^2 > 6$ **ii** $x^2 \geqslant 12$

   c **i** $(x - 4)(x + 1) > 0$ **ii** $(2x - 5)(3x + 2) < 0$

   d **i** $(3 - x)(x + 1) < 0$ **ii** $(4 - x)(x - 2) > 0$

   e **i** $(3 - x)(12 - x) > 0$ **ii** $(2 - x)(-2 - x) < 0$

2 Use an algebraic method to solve the following inequalities. Leave irrational numbers in terms of surds. Some inequalities might be true for all values of x, others for no values of x.

   a $x^2 + 3x - 5 > 0$ **b** $x^2 + 6x + 9 < 0$ **c** $x^2 - 5x + 2 < 0$

   d $x^2 - x + 1 \geqslant 0$ **e** $x^2 - 9 < 0$ **f** $x^2 + 2x + 1 \leqslant 0$

   g $2x^2 - 3x - 1 < 0$ **h** $8 - 3x - x^2 > 0$ **i** $2x^2 + 7x + 1 \geqslant 0$

3 Solve:

   a $\dfrac{x}{x - 2} \leqslant 1$ **b** $\dfrac{x - 1}{(x + 2)(x + 3)} > 0$ **c** $\dfrac{3}{x - 1} < \dfrac{4}{x + 2}$

   d $\dfrac{x^2 + 12}{x} > 7$ **e** $\dfrac{(x - 2)(x + 2)}{(x - 1)(x + 1)} < 0$ **f** $\dfrac{1}{x - 2} \geqslant \dfrac{x}{x + 4}$

4 Solve the inequality $2x^2 > 6 - x$.

5 Find the set of values of x for which $2x^2 + 3x + 1 \leqslant 11 + 4x - x^2$.

6 A ball is thrown upwards and its height h m, at time t s, is given by $h = 7t - 4.9t^2$. How long does the ball spend more than 1.5 m above ground?

7 **a** Solve the following inequalities:

     i $7x - 5 < 3x + 5$ **ii** $2x^2 - 7x < 4x - 5$

   b Hence find the set of values of x for which both $7x - 5 < 3x + 5$ and $2x^2 - 7x < 4x - 5$.

8 Solve simultaneously $x^2 + 6 > 5x$ and $x^2 \geqslant 1$.

9 Find the range of values of x for which both $2x^2 \geqslant 4x$ and $5x^2 - 13x - 6 \leqslant 0$.

PS 10 The cost of producing n items is $\$(950 + 63n)$. The items can be sold for $\$(280 - 5n)$ per item. How many items can be produced and sold in order to make a profit? Give your answer in the form $M \leqslant n \leqslant N$ where M and N are both integers.

1.8 The number of roots of a quadratic equation

WORKED EXAMPLE 1.8

P

    a   Find the values of k for which the equation
       $kx^2 + (4k + 1)x + (3k + 1) = 0$ has one repeated root.

    b   Prove that the equation $(k - 2)x^2 + 2x - k = 0$ has real roots
       whatever the value of k.

Answer

  a   For one repeated root: $b^2 - 4ac = 0$

$$(4k + 1)^2 - 4 \times k \times (3k + 1) = 0$$ Expand brackets.

$$16k^2 + 4k + 4k + 1 - 12k^2 - 4k = 0$$ Simplify.

$$4k^2 + 4k + 1 = 0$$ Factorise.

$$(2k + 1)(2k + 1) = 0$$

$$k = -\frac{1}{2}$$

  b $(k - 2)x^2 + 2x - k = 0$ $a = (k - 2), b = 2,$
                                $c = -k$

$$b^2 - 4ac = 4 - 4(k - 2)(-k)$$ Simplify the right-hand side.

$$4 + 4k^2 - 8k$$ Rearrange.

$$4k^2 - 8k + 4$$ Factorise.

$$4(k - 1)^2$$

$(k - 1)^2$ cannot be negative whatever the value of k.

So, $b^2 - 4ac$ cannot be negative.
Therefore the roots are always real.

TIP

Remember one repeated real root is the same as two equal roots.

TIP

Remember for real roots: $b^2 - 4ac \geqslant 0$

EXERCISE 1H

1 Evaluate the discriminant of the following quadratic equations.

   a i $x^2 + 4x - 5 = 0$ ii $x^2 - 6x - 8 = 0$

   b i $2x^2 + x + 6 = 0$ ii $3x^2 - x + 10 = 0$

   c i $3x^2 - 6x + 3 = 0$ ii $9x^2 - 6x + 1 = 0$

   d i $12 - x - x^2 = 0$ ii $-x^2 - 3x + 10 = 0$

2 State the number of solutions for each equation from question 1.

3 Find the set of values of k for which:

   a i the equation $2x^2 - x + 3k = 0$ has two distinct real roots

      ii the equation $3x^2 + 5x - k = 0$ has two distinct real roots

   b i the equation $5x^2 - 2x + (2k - 1) = 0$ has equal roots

      ii the equation $2x^2 + 3x - (3k + 1) = 0$ has equal roots

   c i the equation $-x^2 + 3x + (k + 1) = 0$ has real roots

      ii the equation $-2x^2 + 3x - (2k + 1) = 0$ has real roots

   d i the equation $3kx^2 - 3x + 2 = 0$ has no real solutions

      ii the equation $-kx^2 + 5x + 3 = 0$ has no real solutions

   e i the quadratic expression $(k - 2)x^2 + 3x + 1$ has a repeated root

      ii the quadratic expression $-4x^2 + 5x + (2k - 5)$ has a repeated root

   f i the graph of $y = x^2 - 4x + (3k + 1)$ is tangent to the x-axis

      ii the graph of $y = -2kx^2 + x - 4$ is tangent to the x-axis

   g i the expression $-3x^2 + 5k$ has no real roots

      ii the expression $2kx^2 - 3$ has no real roots.

4 Find the values of parameter m for which the quadratic equation $mx^2 - 4x + 2m = 0$ has equal roots.

5 Find the exact values of k such that the equation $-3x^2 + (2k + 1)x - 4k = 0$ has a repeated root.

6 Find the range of values of the parameter c such that $2x^2 - 3x + (2c + 1) \geqslant 0$ for all x.

7 Find the set of values of k for which the equation $x^2 - 2kx + 6k = 0$ has no real solutions.

8 Find the range of values of k for which the quadratic equation $kx^2 - (k + 3)x - 1 = 0$ has no real roots.

9 Find the range of values of m for which the equation $mx^2 + mx - 2 = 0$ has one or two real roots.

P 10 Let $q(x) = kx^2 + (k - 2)x - 2$. Show that the equation $q(x) = 0$ has real roots for all values of k.

19

1.9 Intersection of a line and a quadratic curve

WORKED EXAMPLE 1.9

The x-axis is a tangent to the curve whose equation is $y = x^2 - 2x + kx + 4$.

Find the two possible values of the constant k.

Answer

$y = x^2 - 2x + kx + 4$	Curve.
$y = 0$	x-axis.

At the intersection point:

$x^2 - 2x + kx + 4 = 0$	Rearrange.
$x^2 + (k-2)x + 4 = 0$	
$\therefore b^2 - 4ac = 0$	$a = 1, b = k - 2, c = 4$.
$(k-2)^2 - 4(1)(4) = 0$	Expand brackets.
$k^2 - 2k - 2k + 4 - 16 = 0$	Simplify.
$k^2 - 4k - 12 = 0$	Factorise.
$(k - 6)(k + 2) = 0$	
$k = 6$ or $k = -2$	

 TIP

Remember for a line to be a tangent to a curve then $b^2 - 4ac = 0$.

EXERCISE 1I

1. Show that the line with equation $x - y = 6$ is a tangent to the curve with equation $x^2 - 6x + y^2 - 2y + 2 = 0$. *Note: There is another way of finding a tangent to a curve that does not involve the discriminant, which we will study later.*

2. Find the exact values of m for which the line $y = mx + 3$ is a tangent to the curve with equation $y = 3x^2 - x + 5$.

3. Let C be the curve with equation $4x^2 + 9y^2 = 36$. Find the exact values of k for which the line $2x + 3y = k$ is a tangent to C.

4 Find the values of a for which the curve $y = x^2$ never touches the curve $y = a - (x - a)^2$.

P 5 Show algebraically that the line $y = kx + 5$ intersects the parabola $y = x^2 + 2$ twice for all values of k.

6 Find the values of m for which the line $y = mx - 1$ is tangent to the curve $y = x^2$.

7 Find the value or values of m for which the line $y = mx$ is tangent to the curve $x^2 + 2xy + 2x = 1$.

8 Find the values of k for which the line $y = 2x - k$ is tangent to the curve with equation $x^2 + y^2 = 5$.

P 9 a The diagram shows the graphs of $y = x - 1$ and $y = kx^2$, where k is a positive constant. The graphs intersect at two distinct points A and B. Write down the quadratic equation satisfied by the x-coordinates of A and B, and hence show that $k < \dfrac{1}{4}$.

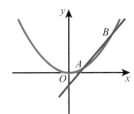

b Describe briefly the relationship between the graphs of $y = x - 1$ and $y = kx^2$ in each of these cases:

  i $k = \dfrac{1}{4}$ ii $k > \dfrac{1}{4}$

c Show, by using a graphical argument or otherwise, that when k is a negative constant, the equation $x - 1 = kx^2$ has two real roots, one of which lies between 0 and 1.

END-OF-CHAPTER REVIEW EXERCISE 1

PS 1 Alexia and Michaela were both trying to solve a quadratic equation of the form $x^2 + bx + c = 0$.

Unfortunately Alexia misread the value of b and found that the solutions were 6 and 1.

Michaela misread the value of c and found that the solutions were 4 and 1. What were the correct solutions?

2 The positive difference between the solutions of the quadratic equation $x^2 + kx + 3 = 0$ is $\sqrt{69}$. Find the possible values of k.

3 The equations $y = (x - 2)(x - 3)^2$ and $y = k$ have one solution for all $k < m$. Find the largest value of m.

4 Solve the equation $x^{\frac{1}{4}} + 2x^{-\frac{1}{4}} = 3$.

5 a Express $6x^2 + 10x + 5$ in the form $a(x + b)^2 + c$, where a, b and c are constants to be found.

b Hence determine the range of values taken by the function $(6x^2 + 10x + 5)^2$ for real values of x.

PS

6 Point O is the intersection of two roads that cross at right angles; one road runs from north to south, the other from east to west. Car A is 100 metres due west of O and travelling east at a speed of $20 \, \mathrm{m \, s^{-1}}$, and Car B is 80 metres due north of O and travelling south at $20 \, \mathrm{m \, s^{-1}}$.

a Show that after t seconds their distance apart, d metres, is given by $d^2 = (100 - 20t)^2 + (80 - 20t)^2$.

b Show that this simplifies to $d^2 = 400((5 - t)^2 + (4 - t)^2)$.

c Show that the minimum distance apart of the two cars is $10\sqrt{2}$ metres.

7 Solve the inequalities.

a $2x^2 - 5x + 2 \leqslant 0$

b $(2x - 3)^2 < 16$

c $\dfrac{1}{3}x - \dfrac{1}{4}(2x - 5) < \dfrac{1}{5}$

P

8 Show that the equation $2^{x+1} + 2^{x-1} = 160$ can be written in the form $2.5 \times 2^x = 160$. Hence find the value of x which satisfies the equation.

9 Solve the simultaneous equations $2x + 3y = 5$ and $x^2 + 3xy = 4$.

10 Use the substitution $y = 3^x$ to find the values of x that satisfy the equation $3^{2x+2} - 10 \times 3^x + 1 = 0$.

Chapter 2
Functions

- Understand the terms function, domain, range, one-one function, inverse function and composition of functions.
- Identify the range of a given function in simple cases, and find the composition of two given functions.
- Determine whether or not a given function is one-one, and find the inverse of a one-one function in simple cases.
- Illustrate in graphical terms the relation between a one-one function and its inverse.
- Understand and use the transformations of the graph $y = f(x)$ given by $y = f(x) + a$, $y = f(x + a)$, $y = af(x)$, $y = f(ax)$ and simple combinations of these.

2.1 Definition of a function

WORKED EXAMPLE 2.1

Determine whether these mappings are one-one, many-one or one-many.

a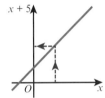

b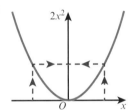

c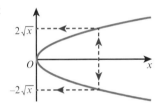

Answer

a   one-one

b   many-one

c   one-many

EXERCISE 2A

1   Determine whether each of these mappings is one-one, many-one or one-many.

a $x \mapsto 2x + 5$ for $x \in \mathbb{R}$

b $x \mapsto 2x^2 - 4$ for $x \in \mathbb{R}$

c $x \mapsto 3x^3 + 1$ for $x \in \mathbb{R}$

d $x \mapsto 2^x + 2$ for $x \in \mathbb{R}$

e $x \mapsto \dfrac{5}{x}$ for $x > 0$

f $x \mapsto x^2 + 3$ for $x \geqslant 0$

g $x \mapsto \dfrac{14}{1 - x}$ for $x \in \mathbb{R}, x \neq 1$

h $x \mapsto \pm x$ for $x \in \mathbb{R}, x \geqslant 6$

2 Look at the following graphs and write down those which represent functions.

a 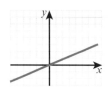 b 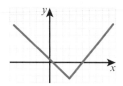 c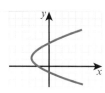

d   e 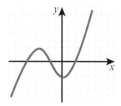 f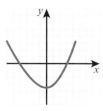

3 Each of the following functions has domain $\mathbb{R}$. Determine which are one-one functions.

a $f: x \mapsto 3x + 4$

b $f: x \mapsto x^2 + 1$

c $f: x \mapsto x^2 - 3x$

d $f: x \mapsto 5 - x$

e $f: x \mapsto \cos x°$

f $f: x \mapsto x^3 - 2$

g $f: x \mapsto \dfrac{1}{2}x - 7$

h $f: x \mapsto \sqrt{x^2}$

i $f: x \mapsto x(x - 4)$

j $f: x \mapsto x^3 - 3x$

k $f: x \mapsto x^9$

l $f: x \mapsto \sqrt{x^2 + 1}$

4 Determine which of the following functions, with the specified domains, are one-one.

a $f: x \mapsto x^2, x > 0$

b $f: x \mapsto \cos x°, -90 \leqslant x \leqslant 90$

c $f: x \mapsto 1 - 2x, x < 0$

d $f: x \mapsto x(x - 2), 0 < x < 2$

e $f: x \mapsto x(x - 2), x > 2$

f $f: x \mapsto x(x - 2), x < 1$

g $f: x \mapsto \sqrt{x}, x > 0$

h $f: x \mapsto x^2 + 6x - 5, x > 0$

i $f: x \mapsto x^2 + 6x - 5, x < 0$

j $f: x \mapsto x^2 + 6x - 5, x > -3$

5 Each of the following functions has domain $x \geqslant k$. In each case, find the smallest possible value of k such that the function is one-one.

a $f: x \mapsto x^2 - 4$

b $f: x \mapsto (x + 1)^2$

c $f: x \mapsto (3x - 2)^2$

d $f: x \mapsto x^2 - 8x + 15$

e $f: x \mapsto x^2 + 10x + 1$

f $f: x \mapsto (x + 4)(x - 2)$

g $f: x \mapsto x^2 - 3x$

h $f: x \mapsto 6 + 2x - x^2$

i $f: x \mapsto (x - 4)^4$

WORKED EXAMPLE 2.2

a $f(x) = 6 - 3x$ for $x \in \mathbb{R}, -4 \leqslant x \leqslant 5$

i Write down the domain of the function f.

ii Sketch the graph of the function f.

iii Write down the range of the function f.

b The function f is defined by $f(x) = 1 - (3 - x)^2$ for $-2 \leqslant x \leqslant 5$.

   i   Write down the domain of the function f.

   ii Sketch the graph of the function f.

   iii Find the range of the function f.

Answer

a **i**   The domain is $-4 \leqslant x \leqslant 5$.

   ii When $x = -4$, $y = 6 - 3(-4) = 18$. · · · · · · · · · The graph of $y = 6 - 3x$ is
          a straight line with gradient
          -3 and y-intercept 6.

          When $x = 5$, $y = 6 - 3(5) = -9$.

   iii The range is $-9 \leqslant f(x) \leqslant 18$.

b **i**   The domain is $-2 \leqslant x \leqslant 5$.

   ii

   iii $f(x) = 1 - (3 - x)^2$ is a negative quadratic
          function so the graph will be of the form:

          $1 - \boxed{(3 - x)^2}$ · · · · · · · · · · · · · · · · · · · The circled part of the
          expression is a square so
          it will always be $\geqslant 0$. The
          smallest value it can be is 0.
          This occurs when $x = 3$.

          The maximum value of the expression is $1 - 0 = 1$
          and this maximum occurs when $x = 3$.

          So the function $f(x) = 1 - (3 - x)^2$ will have a
          maximum point at the point $(3, 1)$.

          When $x = -2$, $y = 1 - (3 - (-2))^2 = -24$.

          When $x = 5$, $y = 1 - (3 - 5)^2 = -3$.

          The range is $-24 \leqslant f(x) \leqslant 1$.

EXERCISE 2B

1 Determine which of these mappings are functions.

   a $x \mapsto 3x - 1$ for $x \in \mathbb{R}$ b $x \mapsto 2x^2 + 2$ for $x \in \mathbb{R}$

   c $x \mapsto 2 - x^3$ for $x \in \mathbb{R}$ d $x \mapsto 3^x$ for $x \in \mathbb{R}$

   e $x \mapsto \dfrac{-4}{x}$ for $x \in \mathbb{R}, x > 0$ f $x \mapsto \sqrt{3x}$ for $x \in \mathbb{R}, x \geqslant 0$

2 Find the range for each of these functions.

   a $f(x) = (2x - 3)^2 + 1$ for $x \in \mathbb{R}$

   b $f(x) = (3x + 1)^2 - 2$ for $x \in \mathbb{R}$

   c $f: x \mapsto 8 - (x - 5)^2$ for $1 \leqslant x \leqslant 5$

   d $f(x) = 1 + \sqrt{2x - 1}$ for $x \geqslant 0.5$

3 Express each function in the form $a(x + b)^2 + c$, where a, b and c are constants and hence state the range of each function.

   a $f(x) = x^2 + 4x - 1$ for $x \in \mathbb{R}$

   b $f(x) = 2x^2 - 4x + 3$ for $x \in \mathbb{R}$

4 Express each function in the form $a - b(x + c)^2$, where a, b and c are constants and hence state the range of each function.

   a $f(x) = 3 - 2x - x^2$ for $x \in \mathbb{R}$

   b $f(x) = 1 - 6x - x^2$ for $x \in \mathbb{R}$

5 The function $g: x \mapsto 6 + 3ax - 3x^2$, where a is a constant is defined for $x \in \mathbb{R}$. Find the range of g in terms of a.

6 $f(x) = x^2 - 4$ for $x \in \mathbb{R}, -a \leqslant x \leqslant a$

  If the range of the function f is $-4 \leqslant f(x) \leqslant 5$, find the value of a.

7 $f(x) = 4x^2 - 8x + 2$ for $x \in \mathbb{R}, 0 \leqslant x \leqslant k$

   a Express f(x) in the form $a(x + b)^2 + c$.

   b State the value of k for which the graph of $y = f(x)$ has a line of symmetry.

   c For your value of k from part **b**, find the range of f.

 8 Find the largest possible domain for each function and state the corresponding range.

   a $f(x) = 2x - 3$ b $f(x) = 3x^2 + 1$

   c $f(x) = 3^{-x}$ d $f(x) = \dfrac{4}{x}$

   e $f(x) = \dfrac{2}{x - 3}$ f $f(x) = \sqrt{2x + 1} - 1$

9 Find the domain and range of each of the following functions.

   a $f: x \mapsto 3x + 2$ b $f: x \mapsto \dfrac{1}{x}$

   c $f: x \mapsto \dfrac{1}{3x + 2}$ d $f: x \mapsto \dfrac{1}{(x - 3)^2}$

> **TIP**
>
> If we draw all possible vertical lines on the graph of a mapping, the mapping is:
>
> - a function if each line cuts the graph no more than once
>
> - not a function if one line cuts the graph more than once.

10 Find the domain and range of each of the following functions.

a $f: x \mapsto x^2$ **b** $f: x \mapsto \cos x°$ **c** $f: x \mapsto \sqrt{x - 3}$

d $f: x \mapsto x^2 + 5$ **e** $f: x \mapsto \dfrac{1}{\sqrt{x}}$ **f** $f: x \mapsto x(4 - x)$

g $f: x \mapsto \sqrt{x(4 - x)}$ **h** $f: x \mapsto x^2 + 4x + 10$ **i** $f: x \mapsto (1 - \sqrt{x - 3})^2$

2.2 Composite functions

WORKED EXAMPLE 2.3

a $f: x \mapsto 1 - x^2$ for $x \in \mathbb{R}$ $g(x) = \dfrac{2}{x - 1}$ for $x \in \mathbb{R}, x \neq 1$

Find:

  i $fg(x)$ **ii** $gf(x)$

b $f(x) = 1 - x^2$ for $x \in \mathbb{R}$ $g(x) = 2x - 1$ for $x \in \mathbb{R}$

Find the values of x (in exact form) that solve the equation $fg(x) = gf(x)$.

Answer

a   **i** $fg(x) = f\left(\dfrac{2}{x - 1}\right)$ g acts on x first and $g(x) = \dfrac{2}{x - 1}$.

              $= 1 - \left(\dfrac{2}{x - 1}\right)^2$ Note: f is the function 'square and then take away from 1'.

           $fg(x) = \dfrac{x^2 - 2x - 3}{(x - 1)^2}$ or $1 - \left(\dfrac{2}{x - 1}\right)^2$ or $\dfrac{(x - 3)(x + 1)}{(x - 1)^2}$.

   ii $gf(x) = g(1 - x^2)$

           $= \dfrac{2}{1 - x^2 - 1}$

       $gf(x) = -\dfrac{2}{x^2}$

b $fg(x) = 1 - (2x - 1)^2$ Expand brackets and simplify.

        $= 4x - 4x^2$

     When $gf(x) = 2(1 - x^2) - 1$ Rearrange and simplify.

              $= 1 - 2x^2$

       $fg(x) = gf(x)$

     $4x - 4x^2 = 1 - 2x^2$ Rearrange.

     $2x^2 - 4x + 1 = 0$ Use the quadratic formula to solve.

27

$$x = \frac{-(-4) \pm \sqrt{(-4)^2 - 4(2)(1)}}{2(2)}$$

$$x = 1 \pm \frac{1}{\sqrt{2}}$$

EXERCISE 2C

1 Given that $f: x \mapsto 5 - x$ and $g: x \mapsto \frac{4}{x}$, where $x \in \mathbb{R}$ and $x \neq 0$ or 5, find the values of the following.

a ff(7)

b ff(−19)

c gg(1)

d $gg\left(\frac{1}{2}\right)$

e $gg\,gg\left(\frac{1}{2}\right)$

f fffff(6)

g fg fg(2)

h fg gf(2)

> **TIP**
>
> To form a composite function, the domain of f must be chosen so that the whole of the range of f is included in the domain of g.

2 Given that $f: x \mapsto 2x + 5$, $g: x \mapsto x^2$ and $h: x \mapsto \frac{1}{x}$, where $x \in \mathbb{R}$ and $x \neq 0$ or $-\frac{5}{2}$, find the following composite functions.

a fg

b gf

c fh

d hf

e ff

f hh

g gfh

h hgf

3 Given that $f: x \mapsto \sin x°$, $g: x \mapsto x^3$ and $h: x \mapsto x - 3$, where $x \in \mathbb{R}$, find the following functions.

a hf

b fh

c fhg

d fg

e hhh

f gf

4 Given that $f: x \mapsto x + 4$, $g: x \mapsto 3x$ and $h: x \mapsto x^2$, where $x \in \mathbb{R}$, express each of the following in terms of f, g, h as appropriate.

a $x \mapsto x^2 + 4$

b $x \mapsto 3x + 4$

c $x \mapsto x^4$

d $x \mapsto 9x^2$

e $x \mapsto 3x + 12$

f $x \mapsto 3(x^2 + 8)$

g $x \mapsto 9x + 16$

h $x \mapsto x^2 + 8x + 16$

i $x \mapsto 9x^2 + 48x + 64$

5 In each of the following, find the domain and the range of the function gf.

a $f: x \mapsto \sqrt{x}$, $g: x \mapsto x - 5$

b $f: x \mapsto x + 3$, $g: x \mapsto \sqrt{x}$

c $f: x \mapsto x - 2$, $g: x \mapsto \frac{1}{x}$

d $f: x \mapsto \sin x°$, $g: x \mapsto \sqrt{x^2}$

e $f: x \mapsto \sqrt{(x-3)^2}$, $g: x \mapsto \sqrt{x}$

f $f: x \mapsto 16 - x^2$, $g: x \mapsto \sqrt[4]{x}$

g $f: x \mapsto x^2 - x - 6$, $g: x \mapsto \sqrt{x}$

h $f: x \mapsto x + 2$, $g: x \mapsto \frac{1}{\sqrt{-x}}$

6 Given that $f: x \mapsto x^2$ and $g: x \mapsto 3x - 2$, where $x \in \mathbb{R}$, find a, b and c such that:

a $fg(a) = 100$

b $gg(b) = 55$

c $fg(c) = gf(c)$

7 For $f: x \mapsto ax + b$, $f(2) = 19$ and $ff(0) = 55$. Find the possible values of a and b.

8 If $f(x) = \cos x°$ and $g(x) = \dfrac{1}{x}$ calculate:

   a $gf(60)$ **b** $gf(0)$

PS 9 Functions f and g are defined for all real numbers.

$g(x) = x^2 + 7$ and $gf(x) = 9x^2 + 6x + 8$

Find possible expressions for $f(x)$.

PS 10 Functions f, g and h are defined as

$f(x) = \dfrac{3}{x+1}$, $g(x) = \dfrac{p}{x^2}$, $h(x) = \dfrac{3x^2}{x^2+2}$

Given that $fg(x) = h(x)$, find the value of the constant p.

2.3 Inverse functions

WORKED EXAMPLE 2.4

$f(x) = 3 - \sqrt{x-1}$ for $x \in \mathbb{R}, x \geqslant 1$

a Find an expression for $f^{-1}(x)$.

b Solve the equation $f^{-1}(x) = f(2)$.

Answer

a $\quad f(x) = 3 - \sqrt{x-1}$ Write the function as $y =$

$\quad y = 3 - \sqrt{x-1}$ Interchange the x and y variables.

$\quad x = 3 - \sqrt{y-1}$ Rearrange to make y the subject.

$\sqrt{y-1} = 3 - x$

$y - 1 = (3-x)^2$

$y = (3-x)^2 + 1$

$f^{-1}(x) = (3-x)^2 + 1$

b $\quad f^{-1}(x) = (3-x)^2 + 1$

$(3-x)^2 + 1 = 3 - \sqrt{2-1}$

$(3-x)^2 + 1 = 2$

$(3-x)^2 = 1$

$3 - x = \pm 1$

$x = 2$ or 4

The range of f is $f(x) \leqslant 3$ so the domain of f^{-1} is $x \leqslant 3$.

Hence the solution of $f^{-1}(x) = f(2)$ is $x = 2$.

> **TIP**
>
> - Only one-to-one functions have inverses that are also functions.
> - Before writing final answers, think about any restrictions on range/domain.

EXERCISE 2D

1 Find the inverse of each of the following functions.

    a $f: x \mapsto 6x + 5, x \in \mathbb{R}$ **b** $f: x \mapsto \dfrac{x + 4}{5}, x \in \mathbb{R}$

    c $f: x \mapsto 4 - 2x, x \in \mathbb{R}$ **d** $f: x \mapsto \dfrac{2x + 7}{3}, x \in \mathbb{R}$

    e $f: x \mapsto 2x^3 + 5, x \in \mathbb{R}$ **f** $f: x \mapsto \dfrac{1}{x} + 4, x \in \mathbb{R}$ and $x \neq 0$

    g $f: x \mapsto \dfrac{5}{x - 1}, x \in \mathbb{R}$ and $x \neq 1$ **h** $f: x \mapsto (x + 2)^2 + 7, x \in \mathbb{R}$ and $x \geqslant -2$

    i $f: x \mapsto (2x - 3)^2 - 5, x \in \mathbb{R}$ and $x \geqslant \dfrac{3}{2}$ **j** $f: x \mapsto x^2 - 6x, x \in \mathbb{R}$ and $x \geqslant 3$

2 A function is called *self-inverse* if $f(x) = f^{-1}(x)$ for all x in the domain. Show that the following functions are self-inverse.

    a $f: x \mapsto 5 - x, x \in \mathbb{R}$ **b** $f: x \mapsto -x, x \in \mathbb{R}$

    c $f: x \mapsto \dfrac{4}{x}, x \in \mathbb{R}$ and $x \neq 0$ **d** $f: x \mapsto \dfrac{6}{5x}, x \in \mathbb{R}$ and $x \neq 0$

    e $f: x \mapsto \dfrac{x + 5}{x - 1}, x \in \mathbb{R}$ and $x \neq 1$ **f** $f: x \mapsto \dfrac{3x - 1}{2x - 3}, x \in \mathbb{R}$ and $x \neq \dfrac{3}{2}$

3 Find the inverse of each of the following functions.

    a $f: x \mapsto \dfrac{x}{x - 2}, x \in \mathbb{R}$ and $x \neq 2$ **b** $f: x \mapsto \dfrac{2x + 1}{x - 4}, x \in \mathbb{R}$ and $x \neq 4$

    c $f: x \mapsto \dfrac{x + 2}{x - 5}, x \in \mathbb{R}$ and $x \neq 5$ **d** $f: x \mapsto \dfrac{3x - 11}{4x - 3}, x \in \mathbb{R}$ and $x \neq \dfrac{3}{4}$

4 The function $f: x \mapsto px + q, x \in \mathbb{R}$, is such that $f^{-1}(6) = 3$ and $f^{-1}(-29) = -2$. Find $f^{-1}(27)$.

5 The function $f: x \mapsto x^2 + x + 6$ has domain $x \in \mathbb{R}$ and $x > 0$. Find the inverse function and state its domain and range.

6 The function $f: x \mapsto -2x^2 + 4x - 7$ has domain $x \in \mathbb{R}$ and $x < 1$. Find the inverse function and state its domain and range.

7 Given that $y = \cos x, 0° \leqslant x \leqslant 180°$. Find the solutions (in degrees) to the following:

    a $\cos^{-1}(0.5)$ **b** $\cos^{-1}(-1)$ **c** $\cos^{-1}\left(\dfrac{\sqrt{3}}{2}\right)$

 8 Given that $f(x) = \dfrac{p}{x} + q, x \in \mathbb{R}$ and $x \neq 0, x \neq q, x \neq \dfrac{-p}{q}$ and $ff(x) = f^{-1}(x)$, prove that the constants p and q satisfy the equation $p + q^2 = 0$.

9 In the following situations, find the value of k that gives the largest possible domain such that the inverse function exists. For this domain, find the inverse function.

a $y = x^2, x \leqslant k$

b $y = (x + 1)^2 + 2, x > k$

c $y = 5 + 2x - x^2, x \leqslant k$

d $y = x^2 + 4x + 3, x > k$

10 Find the value of the constant k so that $g(x) = \dfrac{3x - 5}{x + k}$ is a self-inverse function.

2.4 The graph of a function and its inverse

WORKED EXAMPLE 2.5

a Find the value of the constant k such that $f: x \mapsto \dfrac{2x - 4}{x + k}$ is a self-inverse function.

b What is the graphical relationship between $f(x)$ and $f^{-1}(x)$?

Answer

a $f: x \mapsto \dfrac{2x - 4}{x + k}$ Write function as $y =$.

$y = \dfrac{2x - 4}{x + k}$ Interchange the x and y variables.

$x = \dfrac{2y - 4}{y + k}$ Rearrange to make y the subject.

$x(y + k) = 2y - 4$

$xy + xk = 2y - 4$

$xy - 2y = -4 - xk$

$y(x - 2) = -4 - xk$

$y = \dfrac{-4 - xk}{x - 2}$

Hence $f^{-1}(x) = \dfrac{-4 - xk}{x - 2}$.

The function f is self-inverse so $f^{-1}(x) = f(x)$.

Comparing the denominators of $f^{-1}(x)$ and $f(x)$ gives $k = -2$.

b If drawn on the same axes, the graphs of $y = f(x)$ and $f^{-1}(x)$ are symmetrical about the line $y = x$.

TIP

A self-inverse function is one for which $f(x) = f^{-1}(x)$ for all values of x in the domain.

31

1 For each of the following, find the inverse function $y = f^{-1}(x)$.

  a $f: x \mapsto 4x, x \in \mathbb{R}$

  b $f: x \mapsto x + 3, x \in \mathbb{R}$

  c $f: x \mapsto \sqrt{x}, x \in \mathbb{R}$ and $x \geq 0$

  d $f: x \mapsto 2x + 1, x \in \mathbb{R}$

  e $f: x \mapsto (x - 2)^2, x \in \mathbb{R}$ and $x \geq 2$

  f $f: x \mapsto 1 - 3x, x \in \mathbb{R}$

  g $f: x \mapsto \dfrac{3}{x}, x \in \mathbb{R}$ and $x \neq 0$

  h $f: x \mapsto 7 - x, x \in \mathbb{R}$

2 The function $f: x \mapsto \sqrt{x - 2} + 3$ has domain $x \in \mathbb{R}$ and $x > 2$.

  a Determine the range of f.

  b Find the inverse function f^{-1} and state its domain and range.

  c Sketch the graphs of $y = f(x)$ and $y = f^{-1}(x)$.

> **TIP**
>
> The reflection in the line $y = x$ swaps the domain and range of a function.

3 The function $f: x \mapsto x^2 + 2x + 6$ has domain $x \in \mathbb{R}$ and $x \leq k$. Given that f is one-one, determine the greatest possible value of k. When k has this value:

  a determine the range of f

  b find the inverse function f^{-1} and state its domain and range

  c sketch the graphs of $y = f(x)$ and $y = f^{-1}(x)$.

4 For each of the following functions, sketch the graph of $y = f^{-1}(x)$.

  a $f: x \mapsto \sin x°, x \in \mathbb{R}$ and $-90 < x < 90$

  b $f: x \mapsto \cos x°, x \in \mathbb{R}$ and $0 < x < 180$

  c $f: x \mapsto \tan x°, x \in \mathbb{R}$ and $-90 < x < 90$

5 The inverse of the function $f: x \mapsto ax + b, x \in \mathbb{R}$, is $f^{-1}: x \mapsto 8x - 3$. Find a and b.

6 Given the function $f(x) = \dfrac{4}{x + 3}, x \geq 0, x \neq -3$:

  a sketch the graph of $f(x)$ and state its range

  b find $f^{-1}(x)$

  c calculate the value of x for which $f(x) = f^{-1}(x)$.

7 a Given the function $f(x) = 2x^2 - 3, x \in \mathbb{R}, x \geq 0$:

    i state the range of f and sketch its graph

    ii explain why the inverse $f^{-1}(x)$ exists and sketch its graph.

  b Given also that $g(x) = \sqrt{5x + 2}, x \in \mathbb{R}, x \geq -\dfrac{2}{5}$, solve the inequality $fg(x) \geq x$.

8   Sketch the inverses of the following functions.

a

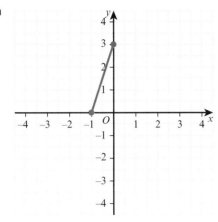

b

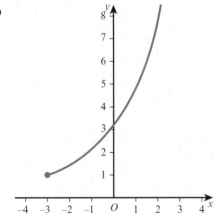

c

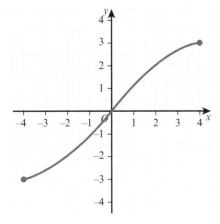

d

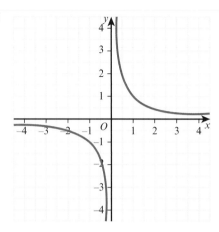

P **9** Let f and g be two functions such that fg(x) is defined, and suppose that f^{-1} and g^{-1} both exist.

Let $h(x) = fg(x)$. Prove that $h^{-1}(x) = g^{-1} f^{-1}(x)$.

10 The diagram shows the graph of $y = f(x)$. The lines $y = -9$ and $y = 9$ are the asymptotes of the graph.

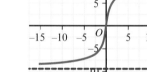

a On the same axes, sketch the graph of $y = f^{-1}(x)$.

b State the domain and range of f^{-1}.

c Solve the equation $f(x) = f^{-1}(x)$.

2.5 Transformations of functions

Translations

WORKED EXAMPLE 2.6

The graph of $y = x^2 + 3x + 1$ is translated by the vector $\begin{pmatrix} 2 \\ -3 \end{pmatrix}$. Find the equation of the resulting graph. Give your answer in the form $y = ax^2 + bx + c$.

Answer

$y = x^2 + 3x + 1$ — Replace all occurrences of x with $x - 2$ and subtract 3.

$y = (x - 2)^2 + 3(x - 2) + 1 - 3$ — Expand and simplify.

$y = x^2 - x - 4$

TIP

Remember the graph of $y = f(x - a) - b$ is the graph of $y = f(x)$ translated by the vector $\begin{pmatrix} a \\ -b \end{pmatrix}$.

EXERCISE 2F

1 The graph of $y = f(x)$ is shown. Sketch the graph of the following functions, including the position of the minimum and maximum points.

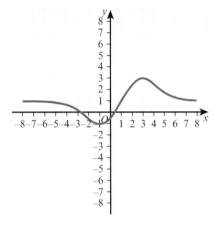

a i $y = f(x) + 3$
  ii $y = f(x) + 5$

b i $y = f(x) - 7$
  ii $y = f(x) - 0.5$

c i $y = f(x + 2)$
  ii $y = f(x + 4)$

d i $y = f(x - 1.5)$
  ii $y = f(x - 2)$

2 Find the equation of each of these graphs after the given transformation is applied:

a i $y = 3x^2$ after a translation of 3 units vertically up
  ii $y = 9x^3$ after a translation of 7 units vertically down

b i $y = 7x^3 - 3x + 6$ after a translation of 2 units down
  ii $y = 8x^2 - 7x + 1$ after a translation of 5 units up

c i $y = 4x^2$ after a translation of 5 units to the right
  ii $y = 7x^2$ after a translation of 3 units to the left

d i $y = 3x^3 - 5x^2 + 4$ after a translation of 4 units to the left
  ii $y = x^3 - 6x + 2$ after a translation of 3 units to the right

3 Find the required translations:

a i transforming the graph $y = x^2 + 3x + 7$ to the graph $y = x^2 + 3x + 2$
  ii transforming the graph $y = x^3 - 5x$ to the graph $y = x^3 - 5x - 4$

b i transforming the graph $y = x^2 + 2x + 7$ to the graph $y = (x + 1)^2 + 2(x + 1) + 7$
  ii transforming the graph $y = x^2 + 5x - 2$ to the graph $y = (x + 5)^2 + 5(x + 5) - 2$

c i transforming the graph $y = \sqrt{2x}$ to the graph $y = \sqrt{2x + 6}$
  ii transforming the graph $y = \sqrt{2x + 1}$ to the graph $y = \sqrt{2x - 3}$

2.6 Reflections

WORKED EXAMPLE 2.7

a Given the function $y = x^2 + 2x - 1$, find the equation of the resulting function if:

i $y = -f(x)$

ii $y = f(-x)$

b Describe the transformation that maps the graph:

i $y = x^2 + 2x + 3$ onto the graph $y = -x^2 - 2x - 3$

ii $y = x^2 - 3x + 1$ onto the graph $y = x^2 + 3x + 1$

iii $y = 6x - x^3$ onto the graph $y = x^3 - 6x$

iv $y = 2x - 5x^2$ onto the graph $y = 5x^2 - 2x$

v $y = x^3 + 2x^2 - 3x + 1$ onto the graph $y = -x^3 - 2x^2 + 3x - 1$

vi $y = \sqrt{3x - 1}$ onto the graph $y = \sqrt{-1 - 3x}$

Answer

a i $y = -f(x)$ is a reflection of $y = f(x)$ in the x-axis.

The resulting equation is $y = -(x^2 + 2x - 1)$ or $y = -x^2 - 2x + 1$.

ii $y = f(-x)$ is a reflection of $y = f(x)$ in the y-axis.

The resulting equation is $y = (-x)^2 + 2(-x) - 1$ or $y = x^2 - 2x - 1$.

b i $y = x^2 + 2x + 3 \longrightarrow y = -(x^2 + 2x + 3)$ is reflection in the x-axis.

ii $y = x^2 - 3x + 1 \longrightarrow y = (-x)^2 - 3(-x) + 1$ is reflection in the y-axis.

iii $y = 6x - x^3 \longrightarrow y = 6(-x) - (-x)^3$ is reflection in the x- or y-axis.

iv $y = 2x - 5x^2 \longrightarrow y = -(2x - 5x^2)$ is reflection in the x-axis.

v $y = x^3 + 2x^2 - 3x + 1 \longrightarrow y = -(x^3 + 2x^2 - 3x + 1)$ is reflection in the x-axis.

vi $y = \sqrt{3x - 1} \longrightarrow y = \sqrt{3(-x) - 1}$ is reflection in the y-axis.

TIP

The graph of $y = f(-x)$ is the same as the graph of $y = f(x)$ reflected in the y-axis.
The graph of $y = -f(x)$ is the same as the graph of $y = f(x)$ reflected in the x-axis.

1 Find the equation of the graph after the given transformation is applied.

   a **i** $y = 3x^2$ after reflection in the x-axis
      ii $y = 9x^3$ after reflection in the x-axis

   b **i** $y = 7x^3 - 3x + 6$ after reflection in the x-axis
      ii $y = 8x^2 - 7x + 1$ after reflection in the x-axis

   c **i** $y = 4x^2$ after reflection in the y-axis
      ii $y = 7x^3$ after reflection in the y-axis

   d **i** $y = 3x^3 - 5x^2 + 4$ after reflection in the y-axis.
      ii $y = x^3 - 6x + 2$ after reflection in the y-axis.

2 The graph of $y = f(x)$ is shown. Sketch the graph of the following functions, including the position of the minimum and maximum points.

   a $y = -f(x)$ **b** $y = f(-x)$

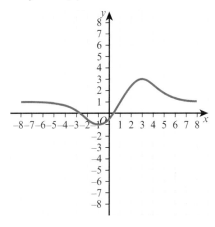

3 Describe the following transformations:

   a **i** transforming the graph $y = x^2 + 3x + 7$ to the graph $y = -x^2 - 3x - 7$
      ii transforming the graph $y = x^3 - 5x$ to the graph $y = 5x - x^3$

   b **i** transforming the graph $y = x^2 + 2x + 7$ to the graph $y = x^2 - 2x + 7$
      ii transforming the graph $y = x^2 - 5x - 2$ to the graph $y = x^2 + 5x - 2$

   c **i** transforming the graph $y = \sqrt{4x}$ to the graph $y = \sqrt{-4x}$
      ii transforming the graph $y = \sqrt{2x - 1}$ to the graph $y = \sqrt{-1 - 2x}$

4 Find the equation of each graph after the given transformation.

   a $y = 6x^2$ after reflection in the x-axis

   b $y = 3x^3$ after reflection in the y-axis

   c $y = 3x^2 - 4x + 2$ after reflection in the y-axis

   d $y = 5 + x - 2x^2$ after reflection in the x-axis

5 Describe the transformation that maps the graph:

a $y = x^2 + 6x - 3$ onto the graph $y = -x^2 - 6x + 3$

b $y = x^2 - 2x + 1$ onto the graph $y = x^2 + 2x + 1$

c $y = 3x - 4x^2$ onto the graph $y = 4x^2 - 3x$

d $y = x^3 + x^2 - 4x + 2$ onto the graph $y = -x^3 - x^2 + 4x - 2$

2.7 Stretches

WORKED EXAMPLE 2.8

a Find the equation of the graph after the given transformation is applied.

i $y = 2x^2$ after a stretch parallel to the y-axis with stretch factor 3

ii $y = 2x^3 - 5$ after a stretch parallel to the y-axis with stretch factor $\dfrac{1}{3}$

iii $y = x^2 + 3x - 1$ after a stretch parallel to the x-axis with stretch factor 3

iv $y = x^3 - 2x$ after a stretch parallel to the x-axis with stretch factor $\dfrac{1}{2}$

b Describe the stretches that transform the graph of:

i $y = 6x^2 + 2$ to $y = 3x^2 + 1$

ii $y = x^2 + x - 2$ to $y = (3x)^2 + (3x) - 2$

iii $y = 2x^3 - 4x$ to $y = 3x^3 - 6x$

iv $y = 2x^2 + 4x$ to $y = 2\left(\dfrac{1}{2}x\right)^2 + 4\left(\dfrac{1}{2}x\right)$ or $y = \dfrac{1}{2}x^2 + 2x$

Answer

a i $\quad f(x) = 2x^2$

$\qquad 3f(x) = 3(2x^2)$

$\qquad\quad y = 6x^2$

ii $\quad f(x) = 2x^3 - 5$

$\qquad \dfrac{1}{3}f(x) = \dfrac{1}{3}(2x^3 - 5)$

$\qquad\quad y = \dfrac{1}{3}(2x^3 - 5)$

iii $\quad f(x) = x^2 + 3x - 1$

$\qquad f\left(\dfrac{1}{3}x\right) = \left(\dfrac{1}{3}x\right)^2 + 3\left(\dfrac{1}{3}x\right) - 1$

$\qquad\quad y = \dfrac{1}{9}x^2 + x - 1$

iv $\quad f(x) = x^3 - 2x$

$\quad f(2x) = (2x)^3 - 2(2x)$

$\qquad y = 8x^3 - 4x$

b i A stretch parallel to the y-axis with stretch factor $\dfrac{1}{2}$.

ii A stretch parallel to the x-axis with stretch factor $\dfrac{1}{3}$.

iii A stretch parallel to the y-axis with stretch factor 1.5.

iv A stretch parallel to the x-axis with stretch factor 2.

EXERCISE 2H

1 The graph of $y = f(x)$ is shown. Sketch the graph of the following functions, including the position of the minimum and maximum points.

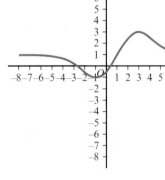

  a i $y = 3f(x)$ ii $y = 5f(x)$

  b i $y = \dfrac{f(x)}{4}$ ii $y = \dfrac{f(x)}{2}$

  c i $y = f(2x)$ ii $y = f(6x)$

  d i $y = f\left(\dfrac{2x}{3}\right)$ ii $y = f\left(\dfrac{5x}{6}\right)$

2 Find the equation of the graph after the given transformation is applied.

  a i $y = 3x^2$ after a vertical stretch factor 7 relative to the x-axis

      ii $y = 9x^3$ after a vertical stretch factor 2 relative to the x-axis

  b i $y = 7x^3 - 3x + 6$ after a vertical stretch factor $\dfrac{1}{3}$ relative to the x-axis

      ii $y = 8x^2 - 7x + 1$ after a vertical stretch factor $\dfrac{4}{5}$ relative to the x-axis

  c i $y = 4x^2$ after a horizontal stretch factor 2 relative to the y-axis

      ii $y = 7x^2$ after a horizontal stretch factor 5 relative to the y-axis

  d i $y = 3x^3 - 5x^2 + 4$ after a horizontal stretch factor $\dfrac{1}{2}$ relative to the y-axis

      ii $y = x^3 + 6x + 2$ after a horizontal stretch factor $\dfrac{2}{3}$ relative to the y-axis

39

3 Describe the following stretches.

    a **i** transforming the graph $y = x^2 + 3x + 7$ to the graph $y = 4x^2 + 12x + 28$

        ii transforming the graph $y = x^3 - 5x$ to the graph $y = 6x^3 - 30x$

    b **i** transforming the graph $y = x^2 + 2x + 7$ to the graph $y = (3x)^2 + 2(3x) + 7$

        ii transforming the graph $y = x^2 + 5x - 2$ to the graph $y = (4x)^2 + 5(4x) - 2$

    c **i** transforming the graph $y = \sqrt{4x}$ to the graph $y = \sqrt{12x}$

        ii transforming the graph $y = \sqrt{2x + 1}$ to the graph $y = \sqrt{x + 1}$

4 Find the equation of each graph after the given transformation.

    a $y = 3x^2$ after a stretch parallel to the y-axis with stretch factor 3

    b $y = x^3 - 1$ after a stretch parallel to the y-axis with stretch factor 2

    c $y = 3^x + 6$ after a stretch parallel to the y-axis with stretch factor $\dfrac{1}{3}$

    d $y = 6x^2 - 6x + 1$ after a stretch parallel to the x-axis with stretch factor 2

    e $y = 2x^3 - 6x$ after a stretch parallel to the x-axis with stretch factor $\dfrac{1}{2}$

5 Describe the transformation that maps the graph:

    a $y = 2x^2 - 4x - 5$ onto the graph $y = 8x^2 - 8x - 5$

    b $y = 2x^2 - 2x + 3$ onto the graph $y = 6x^2 - 6x + 9$

    c $y = 2^x + 1$ onto the graph $y = 2^{x+2} + 4$

    d $y = \sqrt{3x - 1}$ onto the graph $y = \sqrt{9x - 1}$

2.8 Combined transformations

Combining two vertical transformations

WORKED EXAMPLE 2.9

Sketch the graph of $y = x^2 - 1$. On the same diagram, sketch and label the graph after:

    a **i** a translation $\begin{pmatrix} 0 \\ 3 \end{pmatrix}$ then stretch vertically with factor 2

        ii a stretch vertically with factor 2 then translation $\begin{pmatrix} 0 \\ 3 \end{pmatrix}$.

    b Given $y = f(x)$, write the result of each set of transformations **i** and **ii** above in function form.

Answer

    a i $y = x^2 - 1$ Translation $\begin{pmatrix} 0 \\ 3 \end{pmatrix}$.

            $y = x^2 - 1 + 3$ Vertical stretch factor 2.

$y = 2(x^2 - 1 + 3)$ .... Simplify.

$y = 2x^2 + 4$

b   i $y = f(x)$ .... Translation $\begin{pmatrix} 0 \\ 3 \end{pmatrix}$.

$y = f(x) + 3$ .... Vertical stretch factor 2.

$y = 2(f(x) + 3)$ .... Simplify.

$y = 2f(x) + 6$

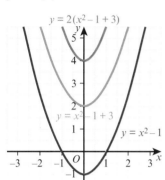

a   ii

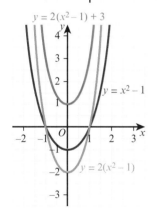

$y = x^2 - 1$ .... Vertical stretch factor 2.

$y = 2(x^2 - 1)$ .... Translation $\begin{pmatrix} 0 \\ 3 \end{pmatrix}$.

$y = 2(x^2 - 1) + 3$ .... Simplify.

$y = 2x^2 + 1$

b   ii $y = f(x)$ .... Vertical stretch factor 2.

$y = 2f(x)$ .... Translation $\begin{pmatrix} 0 \\ 3 \end{pmatrix}$.

$y = 2f(x) + 3$

> **TIP**
>
> Vertical transformations follow the 'normal' order of operations as used in arithmetic.
>
> Horizontal transformations follow the **opposite** order to the 'normal' order of operations as used in arithmetic.

Combining two horizontal transformations

WORKED EXAMPLE 2.10

Sketch the graph of $y = \sin x$, $0° \leqslant x \leqslant 360°$. On the same diagram, sketch and label the graph after:

a i a translation $\begin{pmatrix} 3 \\ 0 \end{pmatrix}$ then stretch horizontally with factor 2

    ii a stretch horizontally with factor 2 then translation $\begin{pmatrix} 3 \\ 0 \end{pmatrix}$.

b Given $y = f(x)$, write the result of each set of transformations **i** and **ii** above in function form.

Answer

a i

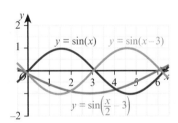

$y = \sin(x)$ ⋯⋯⋯⋯⋯⋯⋯⋯⋯⋯ Translation $\begin{pmatrix} 3 \\ 0 \end{pmatrix}$.

$y = \sin(x - 3)$ ⋯⋯⋯⋯⋯⋯⋯⋯⋯ Horizontal stretch factor 2.

$y = \sin\left(\dfrac{x}{2} - 3\right)$

b i $y = f(x)$ ⋯⋯⋯⋯⋯⋯⋯⋯⋯⋯ Translation $\begin{pmatrix} 3 \\ 0 \end{pmatrix}$.

$y = f(x - 3)$ ⋯⋯⋯⋯⋯⋯⋯⋯⋯ Horizontal stretch factor 2.

$y = f\left(\dfrac{x}{2} - 3\right)$

a ii

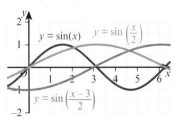

$y = \sin(x)$ .... Horizontal stretch factor 2.

$y = \sin\left(\dfrac{x}{2}\right)$ .... Translation $\begin{pmatrix} 3 \\ 0 \end{pmatrix}$.

$y = \sin\dfrac{(x-3)}{2}$

b   ii $y = f(x)$ .... Horizontal stretch factor 2.

$y = f\left(\dfrac{x}{2}\right)$ .... Translation $\begin{pmatrix} 3 \\ 0 \end{pmatrix}$.

$y = f\left(\dfrac{x-3}{2}\right)$

Combining one horizontal and one vertical transformation

WORKED EXAMPLE 2.11

Sketch the graph of $y = x^2$. On the same diagram, sketch and label the graph after:

a   **i**   a translation $\begin{pmatrix} 0 \\ 3 \end{pmatrix}$ then a stretch horizontally with factor 2

     ii   a stretch horizontally with factor 2 then a translation $\begin{pmatrix} 0 \\ 3 \end{pmatrix}$.

b   Given $y = f(x)$, write the result of each set of transformations **i** and **ii** above in function form.

Answer

a   i

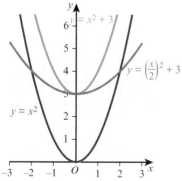

$y = x^2$ .... Translation $\begin{pmatrix} 0 \\ 3 \end{pmatrix}$.

$y = x^2 + 3$ .... Horizontal stretch factor 2.

$y = \left(\dfrac{x}{2}\right)^2 + 3$

43

b   i $y = f(x)$ .... Translation $\begin{pmatrix} 0 \\ 3 \end{pmatrix}$.

$y = f(x) + 3$ .... Horizontal stretch factor 2.

$y = f\left(\dfrac{x}{2}\right) + 3$

a   ii

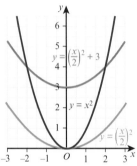

$y = x^2$ .... Horizontal stretch factor 2.

$y = \left(\dfrac{x}{2}\right)^2$ .... Translation $\begin{pmatrix} 0 \\ 3 \end{pmatrix}$.

$y = \left(\dfrac{x}{2}\right)^2 + 3$

b   ii $y = f(x)$ .... Horizontal stretch factor 2.

$y = f\left(\dfrac{x}{2}\right)$ .... Translation $\begin{pmatrix} 0 \\ 3 \end{pmatrix}$.

$y = f\left(\dfrac{x}{2}\right) + 3$

44

EXERCISE 2I

1   Below are the graphs of $y = f(x)$ and $y = g(x)$.

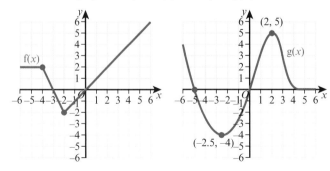

Sketch the graphs of:

a i $2f(x) - 1$ **ii** $\dfrac{1}{2}g(x) + 3$

b i $4 - f(x)$ **ii** $2 - 2g(x)$

c i $3(f(x) - 2)$ **ii** $\dfrac{1 - g(x)}{2}$

d i $f\left(\dfrac{x}{2} - 1\right)$ **ii** $g(2x + 3)$

e i $f\left(\dfrac{4 - x}{5}\right)$ **ii** $g\left(\dfrac{x - 3}{2}\right)$

2 The vertex of a parabolic curve $y = g(x)$ has the coordinates $(2, -4)$. Write down the coordinates of the vertex of the curve with equation:

a $y = g(x - 3)$ **b** $y = g(x) - 5$ **c** $y = -g(x)$

d $y = g(2x)$ **e** $y = 2g(x)$

PS 3 Given the functions $f(x) = -x^2$, $x \in \mathbb{R}$ and $g(x) = x^2 + 2x + 8$, $x \in \mathbb{R}$:

a write $g(x)$ in the form $(x + a)^2 + b$, where a and b are constants

b describe two transformations (and the order in which they should be applied) such that the graph of $g(x)$ can be obtained from the graph of $f(x)$.

4 Given that $f(x) = 2x^2 - 4$, give the function $g(x)$ which represents the graph of $f(x)$ after the following transformations.

a i Translation $\begin{pmatrix} 0 \\ 2 \end{pmatrix}$, followed by a vertical stretch of scale factor 3

ii Translation $\begin{pmatrix} 0 \\ 6 \end{pmatrix}$, followed by a vertical stretch of scale factor $\dfrac{1}{2}$

b i Vertical stretch of scale factor $\dfrac{1}{2}$, followed by a translation $\begin{pmatrix} 0 \\ 6 \end{pmatrix}$

ii Vertical stretch of scale factor $\dfrac{7}{2}$, followed by a translation $\begin{pmatrix} 0 \\ 10 \end{pmatrix}$

c i Reflection through the horizontal axis followed by a translation $\begin{pmatrix} 0 \\ -1 \end{pmatrix}$

ii Reflection through the horizontal axis followed by a translation $\begin{pmatrix} 0 \\ 2 \end{pmatrix}$

TIP

When two vertical or two horizontal transformations are combined, the order in which they are applied **affects** the outcome.

When one horizontal and one vertical transformation are combined, the order in which they are applied **does not affect** the outcome.

45

d i Reflection through the horizontal axis followed by a vertical stretch of scale factor $\dfrac{1}{2}$, followed by a translation $\begin{pmatrix} 0 \\ 3 \end{pmatrix}$

ii Reflection through the horizontal axis followed by a translation $\begin{pmatrix} 0 \\ -6 \end{pmatrix}$ followed by a vertical stretch of scale factor $\dfrac{3}{2}$

5 Given that $f(x) = x^2$, express each of the following functions as $f(ax + b)$ and hence describe the transformation mapping $f(x)$ to the given function.

a i $g(x) = x^2 + 2x + 1$ **ii** $g(x) = x^2 - 6x + 9$

b i $k(x) = 4x^2 + 8x + 4$ **ii** $k(x) = 9x^2 - 6x + 1$

6 Find the resulting equation after the graph of $y = \sin(x)$ is transformed using each sequence of the following transformations.

a A vertical translation c units up, then a vertical stretch with scale factor p relative to the x-axis.

b A vertical stretch with scale factor p, followed by a vertical translation c units up.

c A horizontal stretch with scale factor q, then horizontal translation d units to the left.

d A horizontal translation d units to the left followed by a horizontal stretch with scale factor q.

7 The diagram shows the graph of $y = f(x)$. On separate axes sketch the graphs of:

a $y = f(2x) - 3$

b $y = 1 - 3f(x)$

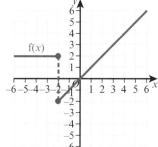

8 The graph of $y = x^2 - 3x$ is translated 2 units to the right and then reflected in the x-axis. Find the equation of the resulting graph, in the form $y = ax^2 + bx + c$.

PS 9 The graph of function $f(x) = ax + b$ is transformed by the following sequence:

- translation by $\begin{pmatrix} 1 \\ 2 \end{pmatrix}$

- reflection through $y = 0$

- horizontal stretch with scale factor $\dfrac{1}{3}$.

The resultant function is $g(x) = 4 - 15x$. Find the values of a and b.

PS 10 The graph of function $f(x) = ax^2 + bx + c$ is transformed by the following sequence:

- reflection through $x = 0$

- translation by $\begin{pmatrix} -1 \\ 3 \end{pmatrix}$

- horizontal stretch with scale factor 2.

The resultant function is $g(x) = 4x^2 + ax - 6$. Find the values of a, b and c.

END-OF-CHAPTER REVIEW EXERCISE 2

1 Find the domain and corresponding range of each of the following functions.

    a $f : x \mapsto 4 - x^2$ **b** $f : x \mapsto (x + 3)^2 - 7$ **c** $f : x \mapsto \sqrt{x + 2}$

    d $f : x \mapsto 5x + 6$ **e** $f : x \mapsto (2x + 3)^2$ **f** $f : x \mapsto 2 - \sqrt{x}$

2 The functions f and g are defined by $f : x \mapsto x^3, x \in \mathbb{R}, g : x \mapsto 1 - 2x, x \in \mathbb{R}$. Find the functions:

    a fg   **b** gf   **c** gff

    d gg   **e** g^{-1}

3 The function f is defined by $f : x \mapsto 2x^3 - 6, x \in \mathbb{R}$. Find the values of the following.

    a $f(3)$ **b** $f^{-1}(48)$ **c** $f^{-1}(-8)$

    d $f^{-1}f(4)$ **e** $ff^{-1}(4)$

4 The functions f, g and h are defined by:

    $f : x \mapsto 2x + 1, x \in \mathbb{R}$ $g : x \mapsto x^5, x \in \mathbb{R}$ $h : x \mapsto \dfrac{1}{x}, x \in \mathbb{R}$ and $x \neq 0$.

Express each of the following in terms of f, g, h as appropriate.

    a $x \mapsto (2x + 1)^5$ **b** $x \mapsto 4x + 3$ **c** $x \mapsto x^{\frac{1}{5}}$

    d $x \mapsto 2x^{-5} + 1$ **e** $x \mapsto \dfrac{1}{2x^5 + 1}$ **f** $x \mapsto \dfrac{x - 1}{2}$

    g $x \mapsto \sqrt[5]{\dfrac{2}{x^5} + 1}$ **h** $x \mapsto \dfrac{2}{x - 1}$

5 Functions f and g are defined by:

$f: x \mapsto x^2 + 2x + 3, x \in \mathbb{R}, g: x \mapsto ax + b, x \in \mathbb{R}$

Given that $fg(x) = 4x^2 - 48x + 146$ for all x, find the possible values of a and b.

6 Functions f and g are defined by $f: x \mapsto 2x + 7, x \in \mathbb{R}$ and $g: x \mapsto x^3 - 1, x \in \mathbb{R}$. Find:

a f^{-1} b g^{-1} c $g^{-1}f^{-1}$

d $f^{-1}g^{-1}$ e fg   f gf

g $(fg)^{-1}$ h $(gf)^{-1}$

7 Given the function $f: x \mapsto 10 - x, x \in \mathbb{R}$, evaluate:

a $f(7)$ b $f^2(7)$

c $f^{15}(7)$ d $f^{100}(7)$

(The notation f^2 represents the composite function ff, f^3 represents fff, and so on.)

8 The functions f and g are defined by:

$f: x \mapsto \dfrac{1}{x} \qquad 0 < x \leqslant 3$

$g: x \mapsto 2x - 1 \qquad x \in \mathbb{R}$

a Using a graphical method, or otherwise, find the range of f.

b Calculate gf(2).

c Find an expression in terms of x for $g^{-1}(x)$.

d Sketch, in a single diagram, the graphs of $y = g(x)$ and $y = g^{-1}(x)$, and state a geometrical relationship between these graphs.

 9 The function f is defined for the domain $x \geqslant 0$ by $f: x \mapsto 4 - x^2$.

a Sketch the graph of f and state the range of f.

b Describe a simple transformation whereby the graph of $y = f(x)$ may be obtained from the graph of $y = x^2$ for $x \geqslant 0$.

c The inverse of f is denoted by f^{-1}. Find an expression for $f^{-1}(x)$ and state the domain of f^{-1}.

d Show, by reference to a sketch, or otherwise, that the solution to the equation $f(x) = f^{-1}(x)$ can be obtained from the quadratic equation $x^2 + x - 4 = 0$.

Determine the solution of $f(x) = f^{-1}(x)$, giving your value to 2 decimal places.

Coordinate geometry

- Find the equation of a straight line given sufficient information.
- Interpret and use any of the forms $y = mx + c$, $y - y_1 = m(x - x_1)$, $ax + by + c = 0$ in solving problems.
- Understand that the equation $(x - a)^2 + (y - b)^2 = r^2$ represents the circle with centre (a, b) and radius r.
- Use algebraic methods to solve problems involving lines and circles.
- Understand the relationship between a graph and its associated algebraic equation, and use the relationship between points of intersection of graphs and solutions of equations.

3.1 Length of a line segment and midpoint

WORKED EXAMPLE 3.1

a The three points D, E and F have coordinates $(2, 2)$, $(7, e)$ and $(9, 3)$ respectively.

If DE and DF are of equal length, find the two possible values of e.

b $L(5, 1)$ is the midpoint of the straight line joining point $C(p, -3)$ to point $D(7, q)$.
Find p and q.

Answer

a

$$D = (2, 2) \qquad E = (7, e)$$
$$\quad\uparrow\uparrow \qquad\qquad \uparrow\uparrow$$
$$(x_1, y_1) \qquad\quad (x_2, y_2)$$

Decide which values to use for x_1, y_1, x_2, y_2.

$$DE = \sqrt{(x_2 - x_1)^2 + (y_2 - y_1)^2}$$
$$DE = \sqrt{(7 - 2)^2 + (e - 2)^2}$$

$$D = (2, 2) \qquad F = (9, 3)$$
$$\quad\uparrow\uparrow \qquad\qquad \uparrow\uparrow$$
$$(x_1, y_1) \qquad\quad (x_2, y_2)$$

Decide which values to use for x_1, y_1, x_2, y_2.

$$DF = \sqrt{(x_2 - x_1)^2 + (y_2 - y_1)^2}$$
$$DF = \sqrt{(9 - 2)^2 + (3 - 2)^2}$$

$$DE = DF$$

$$\sqrt{(7 - 2)^2 + (e - 2)^2} = \sqrt{(9 - 2)^2 + (3 - 2)^2}$$

Square both sides.

$$(7 - 2)^2 + (e - 2)^2 = (9 - 2)^2 + (3 - 2)^2$$

Expand brackets and simplify.

$$25 + e^2 - 4e + 4 = 49 + 1$$

Collect terms on one side.

$$e^2 - 4e - 21 = 0$$

Factorise.

$(e - 7)(e + 3) = 0$ .... Solve.

$e - 7 = 0$ or $e + 3 = 0$

$\therefore e = 7$ or $e = -3$

b $C = (p, -3)$ $\qquad$ $D = (7, q)$ .... Decide which values to use for x_1, y_1, x_2, y_2.

$\uparrow \uparrow \qquad\qquad \uparrow \uparrow$

$(x_1, y_1) \qquad\qquad (x_2, y_2)$

Using $\left(\dfrac{x_1 + x_2}{2}, \dfrac{y_1 + y_2}{2}\right)$ and midpoint $= (5, 1)$

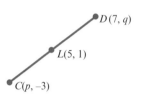

$\left(\dfrac{p + 7}{2}, \dfrac{-3 + q}{2}\right) = (5, 1)$

$\dfrac{p + 7}{2} = 5$ .... Equating the x-coordinates.

$p + 7 = 10$

$p = 3$

$\dfrac{-3 + q}{2} = 1$ .... Equating the y-coordinates.

$-3 + q = 2$

$q = 5$

$\therefore p = 3$ and $q = 5$

EXERCISE 3A

1 Find the exact distance between the points.

$\quad$ **a** $\;$ **i** $\;$ $(0, 0)$ and $(5, 12)$ $\qquad\qquad$ **b** $\;$ **i** $\;$ $(1, 4)$ and $(2, 6)$

$\qquad\quad$ **ii** $\;$ $(3, 4)$ and $(0, 0)$ $\qquad\qquad\qquad$ **ii** $\;$ $(2, 2)$ and $(3, 5)$

$\quad$ **c** $\;$ **i** $\;$ $(-1, 4)$ and $(3, 2)$ $\qquad\qquad$ **d** $\;$ **i** $\;$ $(-2, -3)$ and $(-3, 0)$

$\qquad\quad$ **ii** $\;$ $(-1, 3)$ and $(-3, 1)$ $\qquad\qquad\;$ **ii** $\;$ $(-1, -5)$ and $(-2, -1)$

2 Find the coordinates of the midpoints of the line segments joining these pairs of points.

$\quad$ **a** $\;$ $(2, 11), (6, 15)$ $\qquad\qquad\qquad$ **b** $\;$ $(5, 7), (-3, 9)$

$\quad$ **c** $\;$ $(-2, -3), (1, -6)$ $\qquad\qquad\;$ **d** $\;$ $(-3, 4), (-8, 5)$

$\quad$ **e** $\;$ $(p + 2, 3p - 1), (3p + 4, p - 5)$ $\qquad$ **f** $\;$ $(p + 3, q - 7), (p + 5, 3 - q)$

$\quad$ **g** $\;$ $(p + 2q, 2p + 13q), (5p - 2q, -2p - 7q)$ $\qquad$ **h** $\;$ $(a + 3, b - 5), (a + 3, b + 7)$

3 Find in terms of a the exact distance between the points $(a, 2a)$ and $(-2a, 8a)$ where $a > 0$.

4 Show that the points $(1, -2)$, $(6, -1)$, $(9, 3)$ and $(4, 2)$ are vertices of a parallelogram.

P **5 a** The point A has coordinates $(0, 1)$, the point B has coordinates $(4, 4)$ and the point C has coordinates $(7, 8)$. Show that the distance AB equals the distance BC.

b Explain why this does not mean that B is the midpoint of AC.

6 The point $(a, 2a)$ is 3 units away from the point $(3, 1)$. Find the possible values of a.

P **7** Point A has coordinates (x_1, y_1), point B has coordinates (x_2, y_2) and point M has coordinates $\left(\dfrac{x_1 + x_2}{2}, \dfrac{y_1 + y_2}{2}\right)$.

Prove that $AM = \dfrac{1}{2}AB$.

P **8** The points A and B have coordinates $(-2, 4)$ and $(4a, 2a)$. M is the midpoint of A and B.

a Find and simplify in terms of a:

i the distance AB

ii the midpoint of A and B.

b If O is the origin, show that the ratio $AB:OM$ is independent of a.

PS **9** A spider starts at one corner of a cuboidal room with dimensions 5 m by 5 m by 5 m. It can crawl freely across the surface of the wall.

What is the shortest distance it needs to travel to get to the opposite corner of the room?

3.2 Parallel and perpendicular lines

WORKED EXAMPLE 3.2

a Show that the points $A(-4, 3)$, $B(-1, 5)$ and $C(8, 11)$ are collinear.

b Triangle $P(-4, 3)$, $Q(-1, 5)$ and $R(0, -3)$ is right-angled. Find which side is the hypotenuse.

Answer

a If A, B and C are collinear then they lie on the same line.

Gradient of AB = Gradient of BC

$$\frac{5-3}{-1-(-4)} = \frac{11-5}{8-(-1)}$$ Simplify.

$$\frac{2}{3} = \frac{6}{9}$$

∴ The gradients are the same.

Point B is a common point to the lines AB and BC.

The points A, B and C are collinear.

b   Gradient of PQ Gradient of QR Gradient of PR

$= \dfrac{5-3}{-1-(-4)}$ $= \dfrac{-3-5}{0-(-1)}$ $= \dfrac{-3-3}{0-(-4)}$

$= \dfrac{2}{3}$ $= \dfrac{-8}{1}$ $= \dfrac{-6}{4}$

$= \dfrac{2}{3}$ $= -8$ $= \dfrac{-3}{2}$

Gradient $PQ \times$ gradient $PR = \dfrac{2}{3} \times \dfrac{-3}{2} = -1$

$\therefore PQ$ is perpendicular to PR.

$\therefore$ Angle $QPR = 90°$.

$\therefore QR$ is the hypotenuse.

EXERCISE 3B

1   Points A and B have coordinates $A(-2, 3)$ and $B(1, 5)$. O is the origin. Show that the triangle ABO is right-angled, and find its area.

2   Point P has coordinates $(0, 7)$ and point R has coordinates $(12, 4)$. Point Q lies on the x-axis and PQR is a right angle. Find the possible coordinates of Q, giving your answers in surd form.

3   The line joining the point $A(a, 3)$ to the point $B(2, -3)$ is perpendicular to the line joining point $C(10, 1)$ to point B. Find the value of a.

4   The points $A(0, 2)$, $B(8, 0)$ and $C(5, c)$ form a triangle ABC right-angled at C. Using the gradients of AC and BC find the two possible values of c.

 TIP

You may need to review the properties of special quadrilaterals when attempting these questions.

5   The vertices of a quadrilateral $PQRS$ are $P(1, 2)$, $Q(7, 0)$, $R(6, -4)$ and $S(-3, -1)$.

   a   Find the gradient of each side of the quadrilateral.

   b   What type of quadrilateral is $PQRS$?

6   The vertices of a quadrilateral $DEFG$ are $D(3, -2)$, $E(0, -3)$, $F(-2, 3)$ and $G(4, 1)$.

   a   Find the length of each side of the quadrilateral.

   b   What type of quadrilateral is $DEFG$?

7   The points $A(2, 1)$, $B(6, 10)$ and $C(10, 1)$ form an isosceles triangle
    with AB and BC of equal length. The point G is $(6, 4)$.

    a   Write down the coordinates of M, the midpoint of AC.

    b   Show that $BG = 2GM$ and that BGM is a straight line.

    c   Write down the coordinates of N, the midpoint of BC.

    d   Show that AGN is a straight line and that $AG = 2GN$.

PS   8   Point M has coordinates $(3, 5)$. Points A and B lie on the coordinate
    axes and have coordinates $(0, p)$ and $(q, 0)$, so that angle AMB is a
    right angle.

    a   Show that $5p + 3q = 34$.

    b   Given that $p = 4$, find the value of q and the exact area of the
    quadrilateral $AOMB$ (where O is the origin).

PS   9   Four points have coordinates $A(k, 2)$, $B(k + 1, k + 2)$,
    $C(k - 3, k + 4)$ and $D(k - 4, 4)$.

    a   Show that $ABCD$ is a parallelogram for all values of k.

    b   Find the value of k for which $ABCD$ is a rectangle.

P   10   Prove that the triangle with vertices $(-2, 8)$, $(3, 20)$ and $(11, 8)$ is
    isosceles. Find its area.

3.3 Equations of straight lines

WORKED EXAMPLE 3.3

    a   Find the equation of the straight line passing through the points $A(2, -3)$ and $B(6, 5)$.

    b   Find the equation of the perpendicular bisector of the line joining the points $A(2, -3)$
    and $B(6, 5)$. Write your answer in the form $ax + by + c = 0$.

Answer

    a $A(2, -3)$ $B(6, 5)$ Decide which values to use for
            ↑ ↑   ↑ ↑ x_1, y_1, x_2, y_2.
          (x_1, y_1) (x_2, y_2)

       Gradient $= m = \dfrac{y_2 - y_1}{x_2 - x_1} = \dfrac{5 - (-3)}{6 - 2} = \dfrac{8}{4} = 2$

       Using $y - y_1 = m(x - x_1)$ with $m = 2$,
       $x_1 = 2$ and $y_1 = -3$.

       $y - (-3) = 2(x - 2)$

         $y + 3 = 2x - 4$

           $y = 2x - 7$

b We have already found the gradient of line $AB = 2$.

Therefore, gradient of a line perpendicular to AB

has gradient $-\dfrac{1}{2}$.

Midpoint of $AB = \left(\dfrac{2+6}{2}, \dfrac{-3+5}{2}\right) = (4, 1)$. .... Using $\left(\dfrac{x_1 + x_2}{2}, \dfrac{y_1 + y_2}{2}\right)$.

$\therefore$ the perpendicular bisector is the line with

gradient $-\dfrac{1}{2}$ passing through the point $(4, 1)$

Using $y - y_1 = m(x - x_1)$ with $x_1 = 4, y_1 = 1$

and $m = -\dfrac{1}{2}$:

$\qquad y - 1 = -\dfrac{1}{2}(x - 4)$ .... Expand brackets and simplify.

$\qquad y - 1 = -\dfrac{1}{2}x + 2$ .... Multiply both sides by 2.

$\qquad 2y - 2 = -x + 4$

$x + 2y - 6 = 0$

EXERCISE 3C

1 Determine whether each pair of lines is parallel, perpendicular or neither.

a i $y = 3 - 4x$ and $y = \dfrac{1}{4}x - 5$

ii $y = 3 - x$ and $y = 5 - x$

b i $3x - y + 7 = 0$ and $y - 3x + 5 = 0$

ii $5x - 2y + 3 = 0$ and $2y - 5x + 3 = 0$

c i $7x + 2y - 3 = 0$ and $2x - 7y + 4 = 0$

ii $2x + 4y - 4 = 0$ and $4x + 2y + 1 = 0$

d i $5x + 3y - 1 = 0$ and $3y - 5x + 2 = 0$

ii $2y - 7x = 3$ and $7x + 2y = 7$

2 a Show that the point $P(1, 4)$ lies on the line l_1 with equation $5x - 2y + 3 = 0$.

b Line l_2 passes through P and is perpendicular to l_1. Find the equation of l_2 in the form $ax + by + c = 0$ where a, b and c are integers.

3 a Find the coordinates of the midpoint of the line segment connecting points $A(5, 2)$ and $B(-1, 7)$.

b Hence find the equation of the perpendicular bisector of AB, giving your answer in the form $y = mx + c$.

4   a   Find the equation of the line that is parallel to the line with equation $2x + 3y = 6$ and passes through the point $(-4, 1)$.

    b   The two lines cross the x-axis at points P and Q. Find the distance PQ.

PS 5   Line l has equation $x - 2y + 3 = 0$ and point P has coordinates $(-1, 6)$.

    a   Find the equation of the line through P that is perpendicular to l.

    b   Hence find the shortest distance from P to l.

6   Find the equations of the lines joining the following pairs of points. Leave your final answer without fractions and in one of the forms $y = mx + c$ or $ax + by + c = 0$.

    a (p, q) and $(p + 3, q - 1)$ b $(p, -q)$ and (p, q)

    c (p, q) and $(p + 2, q + 2)$ d $(p, 0)$ and $(0, q)$

7   Find the equation of the line through $(1, 7)$ parallel to the x-axis.

8   Find the equation of the line through $(d, 0)$ parallel to $y = mx + c$.

P 9   Let P, with coordinates (p, q), be a fixed point on the 'curve' with equation $y = mx + c$ and let Q, with coordinates (r, s), be any other point on $y = mx + c$. Use the fact that the coordinates of P and Q satisfy the equation $y = mx + c$ to show that the gradient of PQ is m for all positions of Q.

PS 10   There are some values of a, b and c for which the equation $ax + by + c = 0$ does not represent a straight line. Give an example of such values.

3.4 The equation of a circle

> **TIP**
>
> The equation of a circle in the **standard** form is
>
> $(x - a)^2 + (y - b)^2 = r^2$
>
> The equation of a circle in the **general** form is
>
> $x^2 + y^2 + 2gx + 2fy + c = 0$

WORKED EXAMPLE 3.4

A circle passes through the points $P(4, 6)$, $Q(6, 2)$ and $R(5, -1)$.

Find the equation of the circle in the form:

$x^2 + y^2 + 2gx + 2fy + c = 0$

Answer

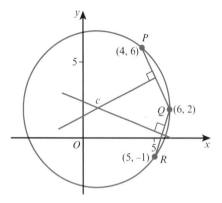

The centre of the circle lies on the perpendicular bisector of PQ and on the perpendicular bisector of QR.

Midpoint of $PQ = \left(\dfrac{4+6}{2}, \dfrac{6+2}{2} \right) = (5, 4)$

Gradient of $PQ = \dfrac{2-6}{6-4} = -2$

Gradient of perpendicular bisector of $PQ = \dfrac{1}{2}$

Equation of perpendicular bisector of PQ is

$(y - 4) = \dfrac{1}{2}(x - 5)$

$\qquad y = \dfrac{1}{2}x + \dfrac{3}{2}$ -------------- (1)

Midpoint of $QR = \left(\dfrac{6+5}{2}, \dfrac{2-1}{2} \right) = \left(\dfrac{11}{2}, \dfrac{1}{2} \right)$

Gradient of $QR = \dfrac{-1-2}{5-6} = 3$

Gradient of perpendicular bisector of $QR = -\dfrac{1}{3}$

Equation of perpendicular bisector of QR is

$\left(y - \dfrac{1}{2} \right) = -\dfrac{1}{3}\left(x - \dfrac{11}{2} \right)$

$\qquad y = -\dfrac{1}{3}x + \dfrac{7}{3}$ -----------(2)

Solving equations (1) and (2) gives

$x = 1, y = 2$

Centre of circle $= (1, 2)$

Radius $= CP = \sqrt{(4-1)^2 + (6-2)^2} = \sqrt{25}$

Hence, the equation of the circle is $(x-1)^2 + (y-2)^2 = 25$

Expanding brackets and rearranging to the general form gives:

$x^2 + y^2 - 2x - 4y - 20 = 0$

EXERCISE 3D

1 Find the equation of the circle with the given centre and radius.

    a i centre $(3, 7)$, radius 4   **ii** centre $(5, 1)$, radius 6

    b i centre $(3, -1)$, radius $\sqrt{7}$ **ii** centre $(-4, 2)$, radius $\sqrt{5}$

2 Write down the centre and radius of the following circles:

    a i $(x-2)^2 + (y+3)^2 = \dfrac{9}{4}$ **ii** $(x+1)^2 + (y+5)^2 = \dfrac{4}{25}$

    b i $(x-3)^2 + \left(y-\dfrac{1}{2}\right)^2 = 6$ **ii** $\left(x+\dfrac{3}{4}\right)^2 + \left(y-\dfrac{1}{5}\right)^2 = 3$

3 Find the centre and radius of the following circles:

    a i $x^2 + 4x + y^2 - 6y + 4 = 0$ **ii** $x^2 - 8x + y^2 + 2y + 8 = 0$

    b i $x^2 - 2x + y^2 + 6y + 1 = 0$ **ii** $x^2 - 10x + y^2 + 4y - 1 = 0$

    c i $x^2 + 5x + y^2 - y + 2 = 0$ **ii** $x^2 - 3x + y^2 + 7y - 3 = 0$

    d i $x^2 + y^2 - 5y = 12$ **ii** $x^2 + y^2 + 3x = 10$

4 Determine whether each point lies on, inside or outside the given circle.

    a i point $(1, 7)$, circle centre $(-2, 3)$, radius 5

      ii point $(2, -1)$, circle centre $(-3, 3)$, radius $\sqrt{41}$

    b i point $(-1, 1)$, circle centre $(3, 6)$, radius 5

      ii point $(2, 1)$, circle centre $(5, -1)$, radius 7

5 **a** Write down the equation of the circle with centre $(-6, 3)$ and radius $\sqrt{117}$.

    b Find the coordinates of the points where the circle cuts the y-axis.

6 **a** Find the centre and the radius of the circle with equation $x^2 - 5x + y^2 + y = 3$.

    b Determine whether the point $A(-1, 3)$ lies inside or outside the circle.

7   A circle with centre $(3, -5)$ and radius 7 crosses the x-axis at points P and Q. Find the exact distance PQ.

8   Points A, B and C have coordinates $A(-7, 3)$, $B(3, 9)$ and $C(12, -6)$.

   a   Show that ABC is a right angle.

   b   Find the distance AC.

   c   Hence find the equation of the circle passing through the points A, B and C.

PS   9   The circle with equation $(x - p)^2 + (y + 3)^2 = 26$ where p is a positive constant passes through the origin.

   a   Find the value of p.

   b   Determine whether the point $(3, 2)$ lies inside or outside the circle.

P   10   A diameter of a circle has endpoints $P(a, b)$ and $Q(c, d)$. Let $Z(x, y)$ be any other point on the circle.

   a   Write down the size of the angle PZQ.

   b   Hence prove that the equation of the circle can be written as

   $$(x - a)(x - c) + (y - b)(y - d) = 0.$$

58

3.5 Problems involving intersections of lines and circles

WORKED EXAMPLE 3.5

For what value of the constant k does the line $y = 3x + k$ intersect the circle $x^2 + y^2 = 25$ at two distinct points?

Answer

$y = 3x + k$ ⁻⁻⁻⁻⁻⁻⁻⁻⁻⁻⁻⁻⁻(1)	
$x^2 + y^2 = 25$ ⁻⁻⁻⁻⁻⁻⁻⁻⁻⁻⁻⁻(2)	Substitute $3x + k$ for y.
$x^2 + (3x + k)^2 = 25$	Expand and simplify.
$10x^2 + 6kx + (k^2 - 25) = 0$	For two distinct solutions $b^2 - 4ac > 0$.
$(6k)^2 - 4(10)(k^2 - 25) > 0$	Expand and simplify.
$1000 - 4k^2 > 0$	

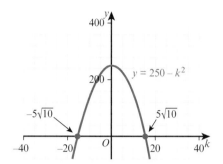

$250 - k^2 > 0$ . . . . Sketch the graph of $y = 250 - k^2$.

$250 - k^2 = y$ . . . . $y = 0$ on the x-axis. Now factorise.

$(\sqrt{250} + k)(\sqrt{250} - k) = 0$ . . . . $\sqrt{250} = \pm 5\sqrt{10}$

$k = 5\sqrt{10}$ and $k = -5\sqrt{10}$

So the line intersects the circle at two distinct points provided $-5\sqrt{10} < k < 5\sqrt{10}$

1 Find the equations of the following:

a **i** tangent to the circle $x^2 - 2x + y^2 = 15$ at the point $(1, 4)$

ii tangent to the circle $x^2 + y^2 + 6y = 25$ at the point $(-3, 2)$

b **i** normal to the circle $x^2 + 4x + y^2 - 6y = 0$ at the point $(1, 1)$

ii normal to the circle $x^2 - 4x + y^2 = 9$ at the point $(5, 2)$

c **i** tangent to the circle with centre $(1, 2)$ and radius $\sqrt{5}$ at the point $(3, 3)$

ii tangent to the circle with centre $(-3, 1)$ and radius $\sqrt{32}$ at the point $(1, 5)$

2 Determine whether the two circles intersect, are disjointed or tangent to each other, or whether one circle is completely inside the other one.

a **i** $(x - 3)^2 + (y - 5)^2 = 16$ and $(x + 1)^2 + (y - 2)^2 = 25$

ii $(x + 2)^2 + (y - 1)^2 = 64$ and $(x - 1)^2 + (y + 2)^2 = 64$

b **i** $(x - 4)^2 + (y + 1)^2 = 20$ and $(x + 3)^2 + (y - 5)^2 = 17$

ii $x^2 + (y - 2)^2 = 10$ and $(x - 3)^2 + (y + 3)^2 = 12$

c **i** $x^2 + y^2 = 30$ and $(x + 1)^2 + (y - 1)^2 = 6$

ii $(x + 3)^2 + (y - 2)^2 = 9$ and $(x + 7)^2 + (y + 1)^2 = 4$

3   A circle with centre $C(2, 5)$ passes through the origin.

   a   Find the equation of the circle.

   b   Show that the point $A(0, 10)$ lies on the circle.

   B is another point on the circle such that the chord AB is perpendicular to the radius OC (extended).

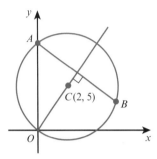

   c   Find the length of AB correct to 3 significant figures.

4   Circle C_1 has centre $(-2, 5)$ and radius 7. Circle C_2 has centre $(12, 5)$.

   a   Given that the two circles are tangent to each other, find the two possible values for the radius of C_2.

   b   Given instead that the radius of C_2 is 16, find the coordinates of the intersection points of C_1 and C_2.

5   A circle with centre at the origin passes through the point $(2, 6)$. The tangent to the circle at $(2, 6)$ cuts the coordinate axes at points P and Q. Find the area of the triangle OPQ.

6   Find the values of k for which the line $y = kx$ is tangent to the circle with centre $(3, 6)$ and radius 2.

7   The line $3x - y = 3$ is tangent to the circle with centre $(5, -1)$ and radius r. Find the value of r.

8   The circle with centre at the origin and radius 5 cuts the negative y-axis at point B. Point $A(4, 3)$ lies on the circle. Let M be the midpoint of the chord AB. The line through O and M cuts the circle at the point P, as shown in the diagram.

   a   Find the coordinates of M.

   b   Show that the quadrilateral $OAPB$ is not a rhombus.

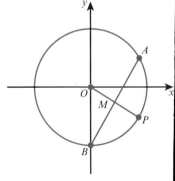

9   A circle has equation $x^2 + y^2 - 10x - 10y + 25 = 0$.

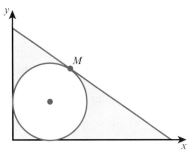

    a   Show that the circle is tangent to both coordinate axes.

    b   Show that the point $M(8, 9)$ lies on the circle.

    The diagram shows the circle and the tangent at M.

    c   Find the exact value of the shaded area.

 10 Find a condition of a and b so that the curve $x^2 + y^2 = 1$ touches the curve $(x - a)^2 + (y - b)^2 = r^2$ at exactly one point.

END-OF-CHAPTER REVIEW EXERCISE 3

1   The point P is the foot of the perpendicular from the point $A(0, 3)$ to the line $y = 3x$.

    a   Find the equation of the line AP.

    b   Find the coordinates of the point P.

    c   Find the perpendicular distance of A from the line $y = 3x$.

2   The points $A(-3, -4)$ and $C(5, 4)$ are the ends of the diagonal of a rhombus $ABCD$.

    a   Find the equation of the diagonal BD.

    b   Given that the side BC has gradient $\dfrac{5}{3}$, find the coordinates of B and hence of D.

3   Line l_1 has equation $3x - 2y + 7 = 0$.

    a   Point $A(2k, 2k + 1)$ lies on l_1. Find the value of k.

    b   Point B has coordinates $(-2, p)$. Find the value of p so that AB is perpendicular to l_1.

    c   Line l_2 is parallel to l_1 and passes through B. Find the equation of l_2 in the form $ax + by + c = 0$ where a, b and c are integers.

    d l_2 crosses the x-axis at the point C. Find the coordinates of C.

4   Circle C has equation $x^2 - 2x + y^2 - 10y - 19 = 0$.

    a   Find the coordinates of the centre, P, of the circle.

    b   Show that point $A(7, 2)$ lies on the circle.

    Point M has coordinates $(1, -1)$. Line l is perpendicular to PA and passes through M. It cuts PA at the point S.

    c   Find the coordinates of S.

61

5 $y = -3x + 5$ is tangent to the circle C at the point $(4, -7)$. The centre of C is at the point $(k - 4, k + 3)$. Find the value of k.

6 Consider the points $A(4, 3)$, $B(3, -2)$ and $C(9, 2)$.

a Show that BAC is a right angle.

b Hence find the equation of the circle through A, B and C.

c Find the equation of the tangent to the circle at B. Give your answer in the form $ax + by + c = 0$ where a, b and c are integers.

7 A circle has centre $(3, 0)$ and radius 5. The line $y = 2x + k$ intersects the circle at two points. Find the set of possible values of k, giving your answers in surd form.

8 A circle has centre $C(7, 12)$ and passes through the point $D(4, 10)$. The tangent to the circle at D cuts the coordinate axes at points A and B. Find the area of these triangles:

a AOB b ABC

9 Find the condition that m and c satisfy, if the line $y = mx + c$ touches the circle $x^2 + y^2 - 2ax = 0$.

10 Find the range of values for r for which two circles: $C_1{:}(x - 1)^2 + (y - 3)^2 = r^2$ and $C_2{:}(x - 4)^2 + (y + 1)^2 = 9$ intersect at two points.

Chapter 4
Circular measure

- Understand the definition of a radian, and use the relationship between radians and degrees.
- Use the formulae $s = r\theta$ and $A = \dfrac{1}{2}r^2\theta$ in solving problems concerning the arc length and sector area of a circle.

4.1 Radians

a Change 60° to radians, giving your answer in terms of π.

b Change $\dfrac{3\pi}{4}$ radians to degrees.

Answer

a **Method 1**

$180° = \pi \text{ radians}$

$\left(\dfrac{180}{3}\right)° = \dfrac{\pi}{3} \text{ radians}$

$60° = \dfrac{\pi}{3} \text{ radians}$

Method 2

$60° = \left(60 \times \dfrac{\pi}{180}\right) \text{ radians}$

$60° = \dfrac{\pi}{3} \text{ radians}$

b **Method 1**

$\pi \text{ radians} = 180°$

$\dfrac{\pi}{4} \text{ radians} = 45°$

$\dfrac{3\pi}{4} \text{ radians} = 135°$

Method 2

$\dfrac{3\pi}{4} \text{ radians} = \left(\dfrac{3\pi}{4} \times \dfrac{180}{\pi}\right)°$

$\dfrac{3\pi}{4} \text{ radians} = 135°$

1 Write each of the following angles in radians, leaving your answer as a multiple of π.

a 90°	**b** 135°	**c** 45°	**d** 30°
e 72°	**f** 18°	**g** 120°	**h** $22\frac{1}{2}°$
i 720°	**j** 600°	**k** 270°	**l** 1°

TIP

You do not need to change the angle to degrees. You should set the angle mode on your calculator to radians.

2 Each of the following is an angle in radians. Without using a calculator, change these to degrees.

a $\dfrac{1}{3}\pi$ b $\dfrac{1}{20}\pi$ c $\dfrac{1}{5}\pi$ d $\dfrac{1}{8}\pi$

e $\dfrac{1}{9}\pi$ f $\dfrac{2}{3}\pi$ g $\dfrac{5}{8}\pi$ h $\dfrac{3}{5}\pi$

i $\dfrac{1}{45}\pi$ j 6π k $-\dfrac{1}{2}\pi$ l $\dfrac{5}{18}\pi$

3 Without the use of a calculator, write down the exact values of the following.

a $\sin\dfrac{1}{3}\pi$ b $\cos\dfrac{1}{4}\pi$ c $\tan\dfrac{1}{6}\pi$ d $\cos\dfrac{3}{2}\pi$

e $\sin\dfrac{7}{4}\pi$ f $\cos\dfrac{7}{6}\pi$ g $\tan\dfrac{5}{3}\pi$ h $\sin^2\dfrac{2}{3}\pi$

4 Express the following angles in radians, correct to 3 significant figures.

a i 320°   ii 20°

b i 270°   ii 90°

c i 65°   ii 145°

d i 100°   ii 83°

5 Express the following angles in degrees. Give answers to 3 significant figures if not exact.

a i $\dfrac{\pi}{3}$ ii $\dfrac{\pi}{4}$

b i $\dfrac{5\pi}{6}$ ii $\dfrac{2\pi}{3}$

c i $\dfrac{3\pi}{2}$ ii $\dfrac{5\pi}{3}$

d i 1.22   ii 4.63

6 Write each of these angles in degrees correct to 3 significant figures.

a 1.5 rad   b 2.2 rad   c 1.06 rad   d 1.93 rad

e 0.68 rad

7 Use your calculator to find the following to 3 significant figures:

a $\sin 1.2$ rad   b $\cos 0.8$ rad   c $\tan 1.2$ rad   d $\sin\dfrac{\pi}{3}$

e $\cos\dfrac{\pi}{5}$ f $\tan\dfrac{3\pi}{4}$

64

8 The triangle shown has sides marked
7 units, 10 units and a units and an angle
marked $\dfrac{5\pi}{13}$ radians. Find the length a
giving your answer to 3 significant figures.

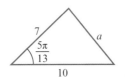

PS 9 The diagram shows a ladder (of
length 6 m) leaning against a vertical
wall. The ladder stands on horizontal
ground and its bottom is 2.25 m from
the base of the wall.

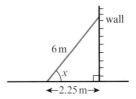

A ladder is safe to use when the angle
marked x is no less than 1.2 radians.

Find the value of x in radians. Is the ladder safe to use?

4.2 Length of an arc

WORKED EXAMPLE 4.2

a A sector AOB of angle $\dfrac{5\pi}{6}$ is cut from a circle of radius 8 cm.
Calculate the perimeter of the sector remaining. Give your answer
to 3 significant figures.

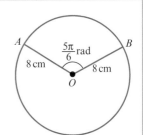

b An arc of length 6 cm, subtends an angle of θ radians at the centre
of a circle with radius 4 cm. Find θ in terms of π.

Answer

a Arc length $= r\theta$ $\cdots\cdots\cdots$ $r = 8$, angle of remaining sector $2\pi - \dfrac{5\pi}{6} = \dfrac{7\pi}{6}$.

$= 8 \times \dfrac{7\pi}{6}$

$= \dfrac{28}{3}\pi$ cm

Perimeter of remaining sector

$= 8 + 8 + \dfrac{28}{3}\pi$ cm

$= 45.3$ cm (to 3 significant figures)

b Arc length $= r\theta$
$6 = 4 \times \theta$

$\theta = 1.5$ radians

In this exercise, give answers to three significant figures where appropriate.

1 In the diagram below, the radius of the circle is 8 cm and the length of the minor arc AB is 7.5 cm. Calculate the size of the angle AOB:

    a in radians   **b** in degrees.

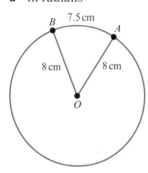

2 Points P and Q lie on the circumference of the circle with centre O. The length of the minor arc PQ is 12 cm and angle $POQ = 1.6$ radians. Find the radius of the circle.

3 Find, in terms of π, the arc length of a sector of:

    a radius 4 cm and angle $\dfrac{\pi}{2}$ **b** radius 3 cm and angle $\dfrac{3\pi}{4}$

    c radius 10 cm and angle $\dfrac{3\pi}{5}$ **d** radius 12 cm and angle $\dfrac{5\pi}{6}$

4 Find the arc length of a sector of:

    a radius 12 cm and angle 1.2 radians   **b** radius 4.5 cm and angle 0.55 radians.

5 Find, in radians, the angle of a sector of:

    a radius 20 cm and arc length 5 cm   **b** radius 9.36 cm and arc length 5.2 cm.

6 An arc PQ of a circle centre O and radius r, subtends an angle θ radians at O.

The length of the arc PQ is L.

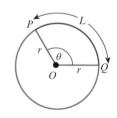

Find:

    a L when $r = 9$ and $\theta = \dfrac{3\pi}{5}$ radians

    b r when $L = 14.9$ and $\theta = 2.98$ radians

    c θ when $L = \dfrac{49\pi}{9}$ and $r = 7$.

7 The sector of a circle of radius 15 cm subtends an angle of θ radians. Given that the perimeter of the sector is 50 cm, find the value of θ.

8   The diagram shows the sector OAB of a circle centre O in which angle AOB is 2.3 radians. Given that the perimeter of the sector is 30 cm, find the length of OA.

9   Find the perimeter of the segment cut off by a chord of length 14 cm from a circle radius 25 cm.

4.3 Area of a sector

a   Find the area of a sector of a circle with radius 9 cm and angle $\dfrac{\pi}{6}$ radians. Give your answer in terms of π.

b   The circle has radius r cm and centre O. AB is a chord and angle $AOB = 1.9$ radians. The shaded area is 50 cm^2.

Find:

   i   the area of sector AOB in terms of r

   ii   the area of triangle AOB in terms of r

   iii   the radius of the circle.

Answer

a   Area of sector
$$= \frac{1}{2}r^2\theta$$
$$= \frac{1}{2} \times 9^2 \times \frac{\pi}{6}$$
$$= \frac{27\pi}{4} \text{ cm}^2$$

b   i   Area of sector AOB
$$= \frac{1}{2}r^2\theta$$
$$= \frac{1}{2} \times r^2 \times 1.9$$
$$= 0.95r^2 \text{ cm}^2$$

   ii   Area of triangle AOB
$$= \frac{1}{2}ab\sin C$$
$$= \frac{1}{2} \times r \times r \times \sin 1.9$$
$$= 0.4731\ldots r^2 \text{ cm}^2$$
$$= 0.473r^2 \text{ cm}^2 \text{ (to 3 significant figures)}$$

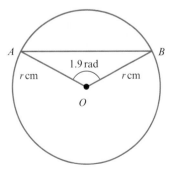

Make sure your calculator is in radians here.

67

iii   Area of shaded segment

$= $ area of sector AOB $-$ area of triangle AOB

$50 = 0.95r^2 - 0.4731...r^2$

$50 = 0.4768...r^2 \text{ cm}^2$

$r^2 = 104.85...$

$r = 10.2 \text{ cm (3 significant figures)}$

EXERCISE 4C

1   A sector of a circle with angle 1.2 radians has area 54 cm². Find the radius of the circle.

2   The perimeter of the sector shown in the diagram is 28 cm. Find its area.

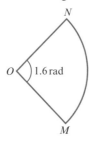

3   A sector of a circle with angle 162° has area 180 cm². Find the radius of the circle.

4   Find the area of the shaded region.

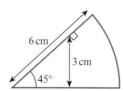

5   Points P and Q lie on the circumference of the circle with centre O and radius 5 cm. The difference between the areas of the major sector POQ and the minor sector POQ is 15 cm². Find the size of the angle POQ.

6   Find the area of the segment cut off by a chord of length 10 cm from a circle radius 13 cm.

P   7   A chord of a circle that subtends an angle of θ at the centre cuts off a segment equal in area to $\frac{1}{4}$ of the area of the whole circle.

a   Show that $\theta - \sin\theta = \frac{1}{2}\pi$.

b   Verify that $\theta = 2.31$, correct to 3 significant figures.

8   *ABC* is a sector of a circle centre *A* and radius 10 cm. Angle
    BAC is θ radians. The area of the semicircle (with diameter
    AC) is twice the area of the sector *ABC*.

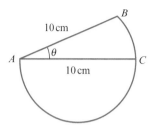

Find:

a θ in terms of π

b   the perimeter of the complete figure in terms of π.

9   A coin is made by starting with an equilateral triangle *ABC* of
    side 2 cm. With centre *A*, an arc of a circle is drawn joining *B* to *C*.
    Similar arcs join *C* to *A* and *A* to *B*.
    Find, exactly, the perimeter of the coin and the area of one of
    its faces.

10 A circle with centre *O* has radius *r* cm. A sector of the circle, which has an angle of θ radians
    at *O*, has perimeter 6 cm.

a   Show that $\theta = \dfrac{6}{r} - 2$, and express the area *A* cm^2 of the sector in terms of *r*.

b   Show that *A* is a maximum, and not a minimum, when $r = \dfrac{3}{2}$, and calculate the
    corresponding value of θ.

END-OF-CHAPTER REVIEW EXERCISE 4

1   The following questions refer to the diagram, where
    r = radius of circle (in cm), *s* = arc length (in cm),
    A = area of sector (in cm^2),
    θ = angle subtended at centre (in radians).

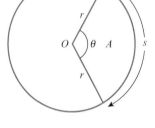

a   *r* = 7, θ = 1.2. Find *s* and *A*.   b   *r* = 3.5, θ = 2.1. Find *s* and *A*.

c   *s* = 12, *r* = 8. Find θ and *A*.   d   *s* = 14, θ = 0.7. Find *r* and *A*.

e   *A* = 30, *r* = 5. Find θ and *s*.   f   *A* = 64, *s* = 16. Find *r* and θ.

g   *A* = 24, *r* = 6. Find *s*.   h   *A* = 30, *s* = 10. Find θ.

2   A sector of a circle has perimeter *p* = 12 cm and angle at the centre θ = 0.4 radians. Find
    the radius of the circle.

3   A sector of a circle has perimeter 7 cm and area 3 cm^2. Find the possible values of the radius
    of the circle.

4   A circle has centre *O* and radius 5 cm. Chord *PQ* subtends angle θ at the centre of the circle.
    Given that the area of the minor segment is 15 cm^2, show that $\sin \theta = \theta - 1.2$.

5 Two circles, with centres A and B, intersect at P and Q.
   The radii of the circles are 6 cm and 4 cm, and $PAQ = 45°$.

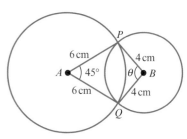

   a Show that $PQ = 6\sqrt{2 - \sqrt{2}}$.

   b Find the size of angle PBQ.

   c Find the area of the shaded region.

6 The diagram shows a sector PQR of a circle with centre
   P and radius 15 cm. The angle QPR is 0.7 radians. The
   length PS is 7 cm.

   a Find the area of QSR.

   b Find the perimeter of QSR.

7 The diagram shows PQC, a sector of a circle of radius 5 cm with centre P.
   Angle QPC is 0.8 radians.

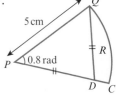

   Calculate (giving your answers to 3 significant figures where necessary):

   a the length of the arc QC

   b the area of sector PQC

   c the length PD

   d the area of R.

8 $ABCD$ is a sector of a circle, centre B, radius 6 cm. AC is $6\sqrt{3}$ cm.

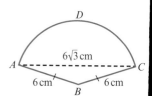

   Find:

   a the exact size of angle ABC

   b the exact area of $ABCD$

   c the exact area of triangle ABC

   d the area of segment ACD (to 3 significant figures)

   e the perimeter of $ABCD$ (to 3 significant figures).

9 The diagram shows two intersecting circles of radius 6 cm
   and 4 cm with centres 7 cm apart. Find the perimeter and
   area of the shaded region common to both circles. (Give
   answers to 3 significant figures.)

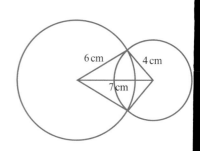

Chapter 5
Trigonometry

- Sketch and use graphs of the sine, cosine and tangent functions (for angles of any size, and using either degrees or radians).
- Use the exact values of the sine, cosine and tangent of $30°, 45°, 60°$ and related angles.
- Use the notations $\sin^{-1} x$, $\cos^{-1} x$, $\tan^{-1} x$ to denote the principal values of the inverse trigonometric relations.
- Use the identities $\dfrac{\sin\theta}{\cos\theta} \equiv \tan\theta$ and $\sin^2\theta + \cos^2\theta \equiv 1$.
- Find all the solutions of simple trigonometrical equations lying in a specified interval (general forms of solution are not included).

5.1 Angles between 0° and 90°

WORKED EXAMPLE 5.1

Given $\cos\theta = \dfrac{\sqrt{5}}{5}$ where $0° \leqslant \theta \leqslant 90°$, find the exact values of:

a $\sin\theta$

b $\sin^2\theta$

c $\dfrac{2\sin\theta}{1 - \sin\theta}$, giving your answers in their simplest forms.

Answer

The right-angled triangle to represent θ is:

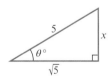

Using Pythagoras' theorem,

$$x = \sqrt{5^2 - \left(\sqrt{5}\right)^2} = \sqrt{20} = 2\sqrt{5}$$

a $\sin\theta = \dfrac{2\sqrt{5}}{5}$

b $\sin^2\theta = \left(\dfrac{2\sqrt{5}}{5}\right)^2 = \dfrac{4}{5}$

c $\dfrac{2\sin\theta}{1-\sin\theta}$

$=\dfrac{2\left(\dfrac{2\sqrt{5}}{5}\right)}{1-\dfrac{2\sqrt{5}}{5}}$

$=\dfrac{4\sqrt{5}}{5-2\sqrt{5}}$ ·········· Rationalise denominator.

$=\dfrac{4\sqrt{5}\left(5+2\sqrt{5}\right)}{\left(5-2\sqrt{5}\right)\left(5+2\sqrt{5}\right)}$

$=\dfrac{20\sqrt{5}+40}{5}$

$=4\sqrt{5}+8$

EXERCISE 5A

1   For each triangle sketched below:

   i   use Pythagoras' theorem to find the length of the third side in an exact form

   ii write down the exact value of $\sin\theta°$, $\cos\theta°$ and $\tan\theta°$.

2   Given that $\cos\theta = \dfrac{3}{5}$ and that θ is acute, find the exact value of:

   a $\sin\theta$
         b $\tan\theta$
         c $3\sin\theta\cos\theta$

   d $\dfrac{3}{\tan^2\theta}$
     e $\dfrac{\cos^2\theta}{\sin\theta}$
     f $\dfrac{1-\sin\theta}{1+\sin\theta}$

3   Given that $\tan\theta = \dfrac{\sqrt{5}}{2}$ and that θ is acute, find the exact value of:

   a $\sin\theta$
         b $\cos\theta$
         c $\sin^2\theta+\cos^2\theta$

   d $\dfrac{2\cos\theta}{\tan\theta}$
     e $\dfrac{2}{\sin^2\theta+\cos^2\theta}$
     f $\dfrac{5\sin\theta}{1-\cos\theta}$

> **TIP**
>
> $\sin^2 30°$ means
> $(\sin 30°)^2$

4 Find the exact value of each of the following.

   a $\sin 60°\cos 60°$ b $\sin^2 60°$ c $\sin 30° + \cos 30°$

   d $\dfrac{\sin 30°}{\sin 60°}$ e $\dfrac{\tan^2 45°}{2 + \tan 30°}$ f $\dfrac{\sin^2 30° + \cos^2 30°}{\sin 30°\cos 30°}$

5 Evaluate the following, simplifying as far as possible.

   a $1 - \sin^2 30°$ b $1 + \tan^2 30°$

   c $\sin 45° + \sin 60°$ d $\cos 60° - \cos 30°$

P 6 Show that:

   a $\sin 60°\cos 30° + \cos 60°\sin 30° = \sin 90°$

   b $\sin^2 45° + \cos^2 45° = 1$

   c $\cos^2 30° - \sin^2 30° = \cos 60°$

   d $(1 + \tan 60°)^2 = 4 + 2\sqrt{3}$

P 7 Show that $\sin 60° + \tan 30° = \dfrac{5\sqrt{3}}{6}$.

P 8 Show that $\dfrac{\sin 30° + \sin 45°}{\cos 30° + \cos 45°} = \sqrt{6} + \sqrt{3} - \sqrt{a} + b$, where a and b are constants to be found.

5.2 The general definition of an angle

WORKED EXAMPLE 5.2

Draw a diagram showing the quadrant in which the rotating line OP lies for each of the following angles. In each case find the acute angle that the line OP makes with the x-axis.

   a $130°$ b $\dfrac{7\pi}{3}$ c $\dfrac{7\pi}{9}$ d $-130°$

Answer

a

$130°$ is an anticlockwise rotation.

acute angle made with x-axis $= 50°$

b

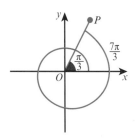

$\dfrac{7\pi}{3}$ is an anticlockwise rotation.

acute angle made with x-axis $= \dfrac{\pi}{3}$

c

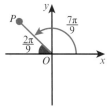

$\dfrac{7\pi}{9}$ is an anticlockwise rotation.

acute angle made with x-axis $= \dfrac{2\pi}{9}$

d

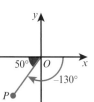

$-130°$ is a clockwise rotation.

acute angle made with x-axis $= 50°$

EXERCISE 5B

1 For each of the following diagrams, find the basic angle of θ.

a

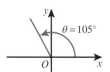

b

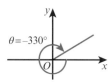

c

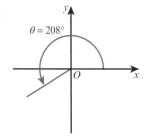

d

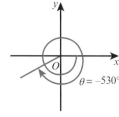

2 State the quadrant that OP lies in when the angle that OP makes with the positive x-axis is:

    a $145°$ **b** $340°$ **c** $-100°$ **d** $185°$

    e $-380°$ **f** $\dfrac{2\pi}{5}$ **g** $-\dfrac{12\pi}{5}$

3 In each part question you are given the basic angle, b, the quadrant in which θ lies and the range in which θ lies. Find the value of θ.

    a $b = 75°$, second quadrant, $0° < \theta < 360°$ **b** $b = 30°$, third quadrant, $-180° < \theta < 0°$

    c $b = 54°$, fourth quadrant, $360° < \theta < 720°$ **d** $b = \dfrac{\pi}{3}$, third quadrant, $0 < \theta < 2\pi$

    e $b = \dfrac{\pi}{4}$, second quadrant, $2\pi < \theta < 4\pi$ **f** $b = \dfrac{\pi}{5}$, fourth quadrant, $-4\pi < \theta < -2\pi$

5.3 Trigonometric ratios of general angles

> **TIP**
>
> This diagram reminds you which trigonometric functions are positive in each quadrant.
>
>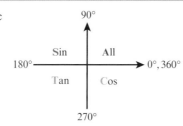

WORKED EXAMPLE 5.3

Given that $\cos\theta = -\dfrac{4}{5}$ and that $180° \leqslant \theta \leqslant 270°$, find the value of $\sin\theta$.

Answer

$y^2 + (-4)^2 = 5^2$ θ is in the third quadrant.

$y^2 = 25 - 16 = 9$ sin is negative in this quadrant.

Since $y < 0$, $y = -3$

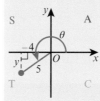

$\sin\theta = -\dfrac{3}{5} = -\dfrac{3}{5}$

1 $\cos\theta = \dfrac{2}{3}$ and $270° < \theta < 360°$. Find the exact value of:

    a $\sin\theta$ **b** $\tan\theta$

2 If $\tan\theta = 3$ find, in exact form, the possible values of $\sin\theta$.

3 If $s = \sin x$ and $90° < x < 180°$, express $\cos x$ in terms of s.

4 Given that $\sin\theta = \dfrac{12}{13}$ and that θ is obtuse, find the value of:

    a $\cos\theta$ **b** $\tan\theta$

5 Given that $\tan P = \dfrac{3}{4}$, and $\sin Q = -\dfrac{\sqrt{3}}{2}$, where P and Q are in the same quadrant, find the value of:

    a $\sin P$ **b** $\cos P$

    c $\cos Q$ **d** $\tan Q$

6 Find the exact values of:

    a **i** $\cos\dfrac{3\pi}{4}$ **ii** $\cos\dfrac{5\pi}{4}$

    b **i** $\sin\left(-\dfrac{\pi}{6}\right)$ **ii** $\sin\left(-\dfrac{\pi}{3}\right)$

    c **i** $\tan\dfrac{3\pi}{4}$ **ii** $\tan\left(-\dfrac{\pi}{4}\right)$

7 Evaluate the following, simplifying as far as possible.

    a $1 - \sin^2\left(\dfrac{\pi}{6}\right)$ **b** $\sin\left(\dfrac{\pi}{4}\right) + \sin\left(\dfrac{\pi}{3}\right)$ **c** $\cos\dfrac{\pi}{3} - \cos\dfrac{\pi}{6}$

 8 Show that $\cos^2\left(\dfrac{\pi}{6}\right) - \sin^2\left(\dfrac{\pi}{6}\right) \equiv \cos\left(\dfrac{\pi}{3}\right)$.

 9 Show that $\left(1 + \tan\dfrac{\pi}{3}\right)^2 \equiv 4 + 2\sqrt{3}$.

5.4 Graphs of trigonometric functions

💡 **TIP**

Before you start Section 5.4, make sure you understand what is meant by the following terms: period, amplitude, asymptote, radian, domain, range, function.

WORKED EXAMPLE 5.4

a $f(x) = 2\cos(3x) + 1$ for $0° \leqslant x \leqslant 360°$

   i Write down the period and amplitude of f.

   ii Write down the coordinates of the maximum and minimum points on the curve $y = f(x)$.

   iii Sketch the graph of $y = f(x)$.

b On the same grid, sketch the graph of $g(x) = \sin(2x + 90°)$ for $0° \leqslant x \leqslant 360°$.

   i Write down the period and amplitude of g.

   ii Write down the coordinates of the maximum and minimum points on the curve $y = g(x)$.

c State the number of roots of the equation $2\cos(3x) + 1 = \sin(2x + 1)$ for $0° \leqslant x \leqslant 360°$.

Answer

a i $y = 2\cos(3x) + 1$ has period $120°$ and amplitude 2.

   ii $y = \cos x$ has max and min points at: $(0°, 1), (180°, -1),$ $(360°, 1)\ldots(1080°, 1)$

      $y = 2\cos(3x) + 1$ has max and min points at: $(0°, 3), (60°, -1),$ $(120°, 3), (180°, -1), (240°, 3),$ $(300°, -1), (360°, 3)$

   iii

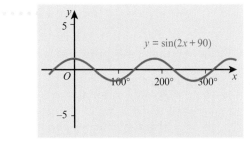

b i $y = \sin(2x + 90°)$ has period $180°$ and amplitude 1.

   ii $y = \sin x$ has max and min points at: $(90°, 1), (270°, -1), (450°, 1),$ $(630°, -1), (810°, 1)\ldots$ $y = \sin(2x + 90°)$ has max and min points at: $(0°, 1), (90°, -1),$ $(180°, 1), (270°, -1), (360°, 1)$

77

c   The curves intersect at 6 points, therefore there are 6 roots to the equation
$2\cos(3x) + 1 = \sin(2x + 1)$ for $0° \leqslant x \leqslant 360°$.

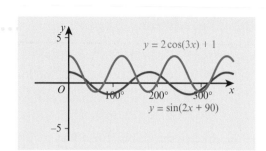

> **TIP**
>
> Translations and vertical stretches do not affect the period.
>
> Translations and horizontal stretches do not affect the amplitude.

EXERCISE 5D

1   State the amplitude and the period of the following functions, where x is in radians.

    a $f(x) = 3\sin 4x$ **b** $f(x) = \cos\left(\dfrac{x}{2}\right)$

    c $f(x) = \cos 3x$ **d** $f(x) = 2\sin \pi x$

> **TIP**
>
> The graph of $y = \cos x$ is obtained from the graph of $y = \sin x$ by translating it $90°$ to the left and vice versa.

2   Sketch the following graphs, giving coordinates of maximum and minimum points.

    a **i** $y = 2\cos\left(x - \dfrac{\pi}{3}\right)$ for $0 \leqslant x \leqslant 2\pi$

         ii $y = 3\sin\left(x + \dfrac{\pi}{2}\right)$ for $0 \leqslant x \leqslant 2\pi$

    b **i** $y = \sin 2x$ for $-\pi \leqslant x \leqslant \pi$

         ii $y = \cos 3x$ for $0 \leqslant x \leqslant \pi$

    c **i** $y = \tan\left(x - \dfrac{\pi}{2}\right)$ for $0 \leqslant x \leqslant \pi$

         ii $y = \tan\left(x + \dfrac{\pi}{3}\right)$ for $0 \leqslant x \leqslant \pi$

    d **i** $y = 3\cos x - 2$ for $0 \leqslant x \leqslant 4\pi$

         ii $y = 2\sin x + 1$ for $-\pi \leqslant x \leqslant \pi$

M 3 The depth of water in a harbour varies during the day and is given by the equation $d = 16 + 7\sin\left(\dfrac{\pi}{12}t\right)$, where d is measured in metres and t in hours after midnight.

 a Find the depth of the water at low and high tide.

 b At what time does high tide occur?

M 4 A small ball is attached to one end of an elastic spring, and the other end is fixed to the ceiling. The ball is pulled down and released, and starts to oscillate vertically. The graph shows how the length of the spring, x cm, varies with time. The equation of the graph is $x = L + A\cos(5\pi t)$.

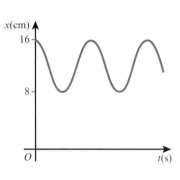

 a Write down the amplitude of the oscillations.

 b How long does it take for the ball to perform five complete oscillations?

M 5 The graph shown below has equation $y = p\sin(qx)$ for $0 \leqslant x \leqslant 2\pi$. Find the values of p and q.

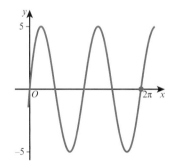

> **TIP**
>
> $\cos 2x$ is not the same as $2\cos x$.

> **TIP**
>
> Given $y = \cos(bx + c)$ or $y = \sin(bx + c)$ the period is $\dfrac{2\pi}{b}$.

M 6 The graph shown below has equation $y = a\cos(x - b)$ for $0° \leqslant x \leqslant 720°$. Find the values of a and b.

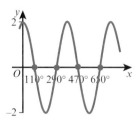

7 a On the same set of axes, sketch the graphs of $y = 1 + \sin 2x$ and $y = 2\cos x$ for $0 \leqslant x \leqslant 2\pi$.

 b Hence state the number of solutions of the equation $1 + \sin 2x = 2\cos x$ for $0 \leqslant x \leqslant 2\pi$.

 c Write down the number of solutions of the equation $1 + \sin 2x = 2\cos x$ for $-2\pi \leqslant x \leqslant 6\pi$.

M **8** The graph shows the height of water below the level of a walkway as a function of time. The equation of the graph is of the form $y = a\cos(bt) + m$. Find the values of a, b and m.

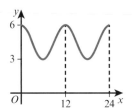

M **9** A Ferris wheel has radius 12 m and the centre of the wheel is 14 m above ground. The wheel takes four minutes to complete a full rotation.

Seats are attached to the circumference of the wheel. Let θ radians be the angle the radius connecting a seat to the centre of the wheel makes with the downward vertical, and h be the height of the seat above ground.

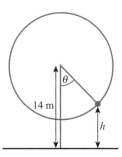

   a Find an expression for h in terms of θ.

   b Initially the seat is at the lowest point on the wheel. Assuming that the wheel rotates at constant speed, find an expression for θ in terms of t, where t is the time measured in minutes.

   c Write down an expression for h in terms of t. For how long is the seat more than 20 m above ground?

10 For each of the following functions, determine the maximum and minimum values of y and the least positive values of x at which these occur.

   a $y = 1 + \cos 2x°$

   b $y = 5 - 4\sin(x + 30)°$

   c $y = 29 - 20\sin(3x - 45)°$

   d $y = 8 - 3\cos^2 x°$

   e $y = \dfrac{12}{3 + \cos x°}$

   f $y = \dfrac{60}{1 + \sin^2(2x - 15)°}$

5.5 Inverse trigonometric functions

WORKED EXAMPLE 5.5

The function $f(x) = 2\sin\left(\dfrac{x}{3}\right) + 1$ is defined for the domain $-\dfrac{3}{2}\pi \leqslant x \leqslant \dfrac{3}{2}\pi$.

   a Sketch the graph of $y = f(x)$ and explain why f has an inverse function.

   b Find the range of f.

   c Find $f^{-1}(x)$ and state its range.

Answer

a

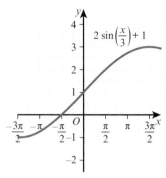

f has an inverse function because f is
a one-to-one function.

b Range is $-1 \leqslant f(x) \leqslant 3$

c $f(x) = 2 \sin\left(\dfrac{x}{3}\right) + 1$ Write the function as $y =$.

$\quad y = 2 \sin\left(\dfrac{x}{3}\right) + 1$ Interchange the x and y variables.

$\quad x = 2 \sin\left(\dfrac{y}{3}\right) + 1$ Rearrange to make y the subject.

$\quad \dfrac{x-1}{2} = \sin\left(\dfrac{y}{3}\right)$

$\quad \dfrac{y}{3} = \sin^{-1}\left(\dfrac{x-1}{2}\right)$

$\quad y = 3 \sin^{-1}\left(\dfrac{x-1}{2}\right)$

The inverse function is $f^{-1}(x) = 3 \sin^{-1}\left(\dfrac{x-1}{2}\right)$ for $-\dfrac{3\pi}{2} \leqslant f^{-1}(x) \leqslant \dfrac{3\pi}{2}$.

81

EXERCISE 5E

1 Without using a calculator, write down, in degrees, the principal value of:

a $\cos^{-1}\dfrac{1}{2}\sqrt{3}$

b $\tan^{-1} 1$

c $\cos^{-1} 0$

d $\sin^{-1}\dfrac{1}{2}\sqrt{3}$

e $\tan^{-1}(-\sqrt{3})$

f $\sin^{-1}(-1)$

g $\tan^{-1}(-1)$

h $\cos^{-1}(-1)$

TIP

$\sin^{-1} x$ has domain
$-1 \leqslant x \leqslant 1$ and range
$-\dfrac{\pi}{2} \leqslant \sin^{-1} x \leqslant \dfrac{\pi}{2}$

$\cos^{-1} x$ has domain
$-1 \leqslant x \leqslant 1$ and range
$0 \leqslant \cos^{-1} x \leqslant \pi$

$\tan^{-1} x$ has domain
$\mathbb{R}$ and range
$-\dfrac{\pi}{2} \leqslant \tan^{-1} x \leqslant \dfrac{\pi}{2}$

2 Without using a calculator, write down in terms of π, the principal value of:

a $\cos^{-1}\dfrac{1}{\sqrt{2}}$

b $\sin^{-1}(-0.5)$

c $\cos^{-1}(-0.5)$

d $\tan^{-1}(3x)$

3 Find:

a $\sin(\sin^{-1}0.5)$

b $\cos(\cos^{-1}(-1))$

c $\tan(\tan^{-1}\sqrt{3})$

d $\cos(\cos^{-1}0)$

4 Find:

a $\cos^{-1}\left(\cos\dfrac{3}{2}\pi\right)$

b $\sin^{-1}\left(\sin\dfrac{13}{6}\pi\right)$

c $\tan^{-1}\left(\tan\dfrac{1}{6}\pi\right)$

d $\cos^{-1}(\cos 2\pi)$

5 Find:

a $\sin\left(\cos^{-1}\dfrac{1}{2}\sqrt{3}\right)$

b $\dfrac{1}{\tan(\tan^{-1}2)}$

c $\cos(\sin^{-1}(0.5))$

d $\tan\left(\cos^{-1}\dfrac{1}{2}\sqrt{2}\right)$

6 Identify the domain and range of each. Then sketch the graph.

a $y = \tan^{-1}(3x)$

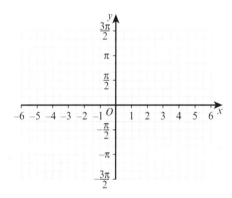

b $y = \cos^{-1}(x) - 2$

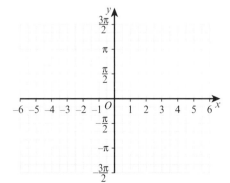

7 The function $f(x) = 2\sin x + 3$ is defined for the domain $-\dfrac{\pi}{2} \leqslant x \leqslant \dfrac{\pi}{2}$.

    a Find the range of f.   **b** Find $f^{-1}(x)$.

8 The function $f(x) = 4 - 3\cos x$ is defined for the domain $0 \leqslant x \leqslant \pi$. Find the range of f.

9 The function $f(x) = 5 - 2\sin x$ is defined for the domain $\dfrac{\pi}{2} \leqslant x \leqslant p$.

    a Find the largest value of p for which f has an inverse.

    b For this value of p, find $f^{-1}(x)$ and state the domain of f^{-1}.

5.6 Trigonometric equations

WORKED EXAMPLE 5.6

    a Solve $\sin x = 0.5$ for $-2\pi \leqslant x \leqslant 2\pi$. Give your answers as exact values.

    b Solve $\tan(2x - 45°) = -3$ for $0° \leqslant x \leqslant 180°$.

    c Solve $2\sin^2 x - \sin x \cos x = 0$ for $-2\pi \leqslant x \leqslant 2\pi$. Give your answers to 3 significant figures.

Answer

    a $\sin x = 0.5$ Use your calculator (in radian mode) to find $\sin^{-1}(0.5)$.

        $x = \dfrac{\pi}{6}$

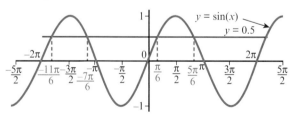

                                       The sketch graph shows there are four values of x, between -2π and 2π, for which $\sin x = 0.5$.

    Using the symmetry of the curve, the other values are:

$$\left(\frac{\pi}{6} - 2\pi\right) = -\frac{11\pi}{6}, \left(\pi - \frac{\pi}{6}\right) = \frac{5\pi}{6}, \left(\frac{5\pi}{6} - 2\pi\right) = -\frac{7\pi}{6}$$

    Hence the solutions of $\sin x = 0.5$ for $-2\pi \leqslant x \leqslant 2\pi$ are:

$$x = -\frac{11\pi}{6}, -\frac{7\pi}{6}, \frac{\pi}{6}, \frac{5\pi}{6}$$

    b $\tan(2A - 45°) = -3$ Let $2A - 45° = x$.

        $\tan x = -3$ Use a calculator to find $\tan^{-1}(-3)$.

$x = -71.57°$

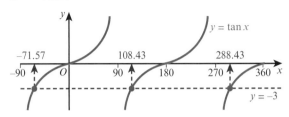

$x = -71.57$	$x = (-71.57 + 180)$	$x = (108.43 + 180)$	Using the symmetry of the
	$= 108.43$	$= 288.43$	curve.

$2A = -71.57 + 45$	$2A = 108.43 + 45°$	$2A = 288.43 + 45°$	Using $2A - 45 = x$.
$A = -13.29$	$A = 76.72$	$A = 166.72$	

Hence the solution of $\tan(2A - 45°) = -3$
for $0° \leqslant x \leqslant 180°$ is $A = 76.7°$ or $167°$
(correct to 3 significant figures)

c $2\sin^2 x - \sin x \cos x = 0$ ·   Factorise.

$\sin x(2\sin x - \cos x) = 0$

$\therefore \ \sin x = 0 \qquad$ or $\qquad 2\sin x - \cos x = 0$

If $\sin x = 0 \quad$ then $\quad x = -2\pi, -\pi, 0, \pi, 2\pi$

$x = -6.28, -3.14, 0, 3.14, 6.28$ radians (3 significant figures)

If $2\sin x - \cos x = 0$ ·   Rearrange.

$2\sin x = \cos x$ ·   Divide both sides by
$\cos x$.

$\tan x = \dfrac{1}{2}$

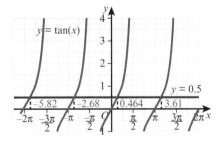

$x = 0.4636$ or $0.4636 - \pi$

or $0.4636 - 2\pi$ or $0.4636 + \pi$

$x = -5.82, -2.68, 0.464, 3.61$ radians (3 significant figures)

Solution:
$x = -6.28, -5.82, -3.14, -2.68, 0, 0.464, 3.14,$
$3.61, 6.28$ radians (3 significant figures)

EXERCISE 5F

1 Solve the following equations.

    a **i** $2\sin\theta + 1 = 1.2$ for $0° < \theta < 360°$

       ii $4\sin x + 3 = 2$ for $-90° < \theta < 270°$

    b **i** $3\cos x - 1 = \dfrac{1}{3}$ for $0° < \theta < 360°$

       ii $5\cos x + 2 = 4.7$ for $0° < \theta < 360°$

    c **i** $3\tan t - 1 = 4$ for $-180° < t < 180°$

       ii $5\tan t - 3 = 8$ for $0° < t < 360°$

2 Solve $(\tan x + 1)(5\sin x - 2) = 0$ for $0° \leqslant x \leqslant 360°$.

3 Find the values of θ in the interval $-360° < \theta < 360°$ for which
$3\sin\left(\dfrac{\theta}{2}\right) = -2$.

4 Solve $2\tan\left(\dfrac{\theta}{3}\right) = 5$ for $0° < \theta < 540°$.

5 Find the values of x in the interval $-360° < x < 360°$ for which
$2\sin(2x + 30°) + \sqrt{3} = 0$.

6 Solve $2\cos(3x - 50°) - \sqrt{2} = 0$ for $-90° < x < 90°$.

7 Find the values of x in the interval $-\sqrt{180°} < x < \sqrt{180°}$ for
which $\sin(x^2) = \dfrac{1}{2}$.

8 Solve the following equations in the interval $0° \leqslant x \leqslant 360°$
giving your answers to 3 significant figures.

    a **i** $3\sin^2\theta = 2$ **ii** $3\tan^2\theta = 5$

    b **i** $\tan^2 x - \tan x - 6 = 0$ **ii** $3\cos^2 x + \cos x - 2 = 0$

    c **i** $4\cos^2 x - 11\cos x + 6 = 0$ **ii** $5\sin^2 x + 6\sin x - 8 = 0$

    d **i** $3\sin^2 x + \sin x = 0$ **ii** $4\tan^2 x + 5\tan x = 0$

9 Solve the following equations in the interval $-180° \leqslant \theta \leqslant 180°$
giving your answers to 3 significant figures.

    a **i** $2\sin\theta - 5\sin\theta\cos\theta = 0$

       ii $4\cos\theta + 5\sin\theta\cos\theta = 0$

    b **i** $4\sin\theta\cos\theta = \cos\theta$

       ii $3\sin\theta = 5\sin\theta\cos\theta$

10 Find the values of θ in the interval $0° < \theta < 360°$ for which
$2\sin 2\theta = \sqrt{3}\sin 2\theta\cos 2\theta$.

TIP

Watch out for
disguised quadratics
in this exercise (first
seen in Section 1.5).

TIP

Remember $\pm$ when
taking the square
root.

TIP

$\sin^2 x$ means $(\sin x)^2$

85

5.7 Trigonometric identities

WORKED EXAMPLE 5.7

Prove the identity $\dfrac{\tan x \sin x}{1 - \cos x} \equiv 1 + \dfrac{1}{\cos x}$.

Answer

$\text{LHS} \equiv \dfrac{\tan x \sin x}{1 - \cos x}$ Multiply top and bottom by $1 + \cos x$.

$\equiv \dfrac{\tan x \sin x (1 + \cos x)}{(1 - \cos x)(1 + \cos x)}$ Expand denominator.

$\equiv \dfrac{\tan x \sin x (1 + \cos x)}{1 - \cos^2 x}$ Use $\sin^2 x + \cos^2 x \equiv 1$.

$\equiv \dfrac{\tan x \sin x (1 + \cos x)}{\sin^2 x}$ Cancel $\sin x$.

$\equiv \dfrac{\tan x (1 + \cos x)}{\sin x}$ Expand brackets and split into 2 fractions.

$\equiv \dfrac{\tan x}{\sin x} + \dfrac{\tan x \cos x}{\sin x}$ Use $\tan x \equiv \dfrac{\sin x}{\cos x}$.

$\equiv \dfrac{\frac{\sin x}{\cos x}}{\sin x} + \dfrac{\frac{\sin x}{\cos x}(\cos x)}{\sin x}$ Simplify.

$\equiv \dfrac{1}{\cos x} + 1$

$\equiv 1 + \dfrac{1}{\cos x}$

$\equiv \text{RHS. Proven}$

EXERCISE 5G

1 Find the exact value of:

    a $3\sin^2 x + 3\cos^2 x$ **b** $\sin^2 5x + \cos^2 5x$

    c $-2\cos^2 2x - 2\sin^2 2x$ **d** $\dfrac{3}{2\sin^2 4x} - \dfrac{3}{2\tan^2 4x}$

2   **a**   Express $3\sin^2 x + 4\cos^2 x$ in terms of $\sin x$ only.

    b   Express $\cos^2 x - \sin^2 x$ in terms of $\cos x$ only.

 TIP

These identities are also true:

$\tan 2x \equiv \dfrac{\sin 2x}{\cos 2x}$

$\sin^2 2x + \cos^2 2x \equiv 1$

$2\sin^2 x + 2\cos^2 x \equiv 2$

P **3** Prove the following identities:

    a   **i** $(\sin x + \cos x)^2 + (\sin x - \cos x)^2 \equiv 2$

       ii $(2\sin x - \cos x)^2 + (\sin x + 2\cos x)^2 \equiv 5$

    b   **i** $\sin\theta\tan\theta + \cos\theta \equiv \dfrac{1}{\cos\theta}$

       ii $\dfrac{\cos^2\theta}{\sin\theta} \equiv \dfrac{1}{\sin\theta} - \sin\theta$

4 Express the following in terms of $\cos x$ only:

    a $3 - 2\tan^2 x$ **b** $\dfrac{1}{1 + \tan^2 x}$

5 Simplify fully the expression $\left(\dfrac{1}{\sin x} - \dfrac{1}{\tan x}\right)\left(\dfrac{1}{\sin x} + \dfrac{1}{\tan x}\right)$.

P **6** Show that for all x, $2\tan^2 2x - \dfrac{2}{\cos^2 2x} = k$, stating the value of the constant k.

7 If $t = \tan x$ express the following in terms of t:

    a $\cos^2 x$ **b** $\sin^2 x$

    c $\cos^2 x - \sin^2 x$ **d** $\dfrac{2}{\sin^2 x} + 1$

P **8** Prove the identity $\dfrac{1}{\cos\theta} - \cos\theta \equiv \sin\theta\tan\theta$.

P **9** Use $\tan\theta° \equiv \dfrac{\sin\theta°}{\cos\theta°}$, $\cos^2\theta° \neq 0$ and $\cos^2\theta° + \sin^2\theta° \equiv 1$ to establish the following.

    a $\dfrac{1}{\sin\theta°} - \dfrac{1}{\tan\theta°} \equiv \dfrac{1 - \cos\theta°}{\sin\theta°}$

    b $\dfrac{\sin^2\theta°}{1 - \cos\theta°} \equiv 1 + \cos\theta°$

    c $\dfrac{1}{\cos\theta°} + \tan\theta° \equiv \dfrac{\cos\theta°}{1 - \sin\theta°}$

    d $\dfrac{\tan\theta°\sin\theta°}{1 - \cos\theta°} \equiv 1 + \dfrac{1}{\cos\theta°}$

10 Solve the following equations for θ, giving all the roots in the interval $0° \leqslant \theta \leqslant 360°$ correct to the nearest 0.1.

    a $4\sin^2\theta° - 1 = 0$

    b $\sin^2\theta° + 2\cos^2\theta° = 2$

    c $10\sin^2\theta° \quad 5\cos^2\theta° + 2 = 4\sin\theta°$

    d $4\sin^2\theta°\cos\theta° = \tan^2\theta°$

5.8 Further trigonometric equations

WORKED EXAMPLE 5.8

a Prove the identity $\dfrac{\cos\theta}{1+\sin\theta} + \dfrac{1+\sin\theta}{\cos\theta} \equiv \dfrac{2}{\cos\theta}$.

b Hence solve the equation $\dfrac{\cos\theta}{1+\sin\theta} + \dfrac{1+\sin\theta}{\cos\theta} = 4$ for $-2\pi < \theta < 2\pi$.

Give your answers as exact values.

Answer

a $\text{LHS} \equiv \dfrac{\cos\theta}{1+\sin\theta} + \dfrac{1+\sin\theta}{\cos\theta}$ Make denominators the same.

$\equiv \dfrac{\cos^2\theta}{\cos\theta(1+\sin\theta)} + \dfrac{(1+\sin\theta)(1+\sin\theta)}{\cos\theta(1+\sin\theta)}$ Add fractions.

$\equiv \dfrac{\cos^2\theta + (1+\sin\theta)(1+\sin\theta)}{\cos\theta(1+\sin\theta)}$ Expand numerator.

$\equiv \dfrac{\cos^2\theta + 1 + 2\sin\theta + \sin^2\theta}{\cos\theta(1+\sin\theta)}$ Use $\sin^2\theta + \cos^2\theta \equiv 1$.

$\equiv \dfrac{2 + 2\sin\theta}{\cos\theta(1+\sin\theta)}$ Factorise numerator.

$\equiv \dfrac{2(1+\sin\theta)}{\cos\theta(1+\sin\theta)}$ Simplify.

$\equiv \dfrac{2}{\cos\theta}$

$\equiv \text{RHS. Proven}$

b $\dfrac{\cos\theta}{1+\sin\theta} + \dfrac{1+\sin\theta}{\cos\theta} = 4$ Use the result from **part a**.

$\dfrac{2}{\cos\theta} = 4$ Rearrange.

$\cos\theta = \dfrac{1}{2}$

$\theta = \cos^{-1}\left(\dfrac{1}{2}\right)$

$\theta = \dfrac{\pi}{3}$ or $2\pi - \dfrac{\pi}{3} = \dfrac{5\pi}{3}$

or $\dfrac{\pi}{3} - 2\pi = -\dfrac{5\pi}{3}$ or $\dfrac{5\pi}{3} - 2\pi = -\dfrac{\pi}{3}$

Solution is $\theta = -\dfrac{5\pi}{3}, -\dfrac{\pi}{3}, \dfrac{\pi}{3}, \dfrac{5\pi}{3}$

EXERCISE 5H

1 By using the identity $\tan x \equiv \dfrac{\sin x}{\cos x}$ solve the following equations for $0° \leqslant x \leqslant 180°$.

  a i $3\sin x = 2\cos x$ ii $3\sin x = 5\cos x$

  b i $7\cos x - 3\sin x = 0$ ii $\sin x - 5\cos x = 0$

2 Use the identity $\sin^2 x + \cos^2 x \equiv 1$ to solve the equations for x in the interval $0° \leqslant x \leqslant 360°$.

  a i $7\sin^2 x + 3\cos^2 x = 5$ ii $\sin^2 x + 4\cos^2 x = 2$

  b i $3\sin^2 x - \cos^2 x = 1$ ii $\cos^2 x - \sin^2 x = 1$

3 Find the values of x in the interval $0° < x < 360°$ for which $\sin 2x + \cos 2x = 0$.

4 Solve $\sin x + \dfrac{\sin^2 x}{\cos x} = 0$ for $0° \leqslant x \leqslant 360°$.

5 Solve the equation $\sin x \tan x = \sin^2 x$ for $-180° \leqslant x \leqslant 180°$.

6 Solve the equation $5\sin^2 \theta = 4\cos^2 \theta$ for $-180° \leqslant x \leqslant 180°$. Give your answer to the nearest $0.1°$.

7 Solve the equation $2\cos^2 t - \sin t - 1 = 0$ for $0° \leqslant t \leqslant 360°$.

8 Find the values of x in the interval $-180° \leqslant x \leqslant 180°$ that satisfy $4\cos^2 x - 5\sin x - 5 = 0$.

9 a Given that $6\sin^2 x + \cos x = 4$, find the exact values of $\cos x$.

  b Hence solve the equation $6\sin^2 x + \cos x = 4$ for $0° \leqslant x \leqslant 360°$ giving your answers to 3 significant figures.

 10 a Show that the equation $2\sin^2 x - 3\sin x \cos x + \cos^2 x = 0$ can be written in the form $2\tan^2 x - 3\tan x + 1 = 0$.

  b Hence solve the equation $2\sin^2 x - 3\sin x \cos x + \cos^2 x = 0$ giving all solutions in the interval $-180° < x < 180°$.

END-OF-CHAPTER REVIEW EXERCISE 5

1 a Given the angle A is obtuse and $\sin A° = \dfrac{5}{14}\sqrt{3}$, find the exact value of $\cos A°$.

  b Given that $180° < B < 360°$ and that $\tan B° = -\dfrac{21}{20}$, find the exact value of $\cos B°$.

  c Find all possible values of $\sin C°$ for which $\cos C° = \dfrac{1}{2}$.

  d Find the values of D for which $-180° < D < 180°$ and $\tan D° = 5\sin D°$.

2 Solve the following equations for θ, giving solutions in the interval $0° \leqslant \theta \leqslant 360°$.

  a $\sin \theta° = \tan \theta°$ b $2 - 2\cos^2 \theta° = \sin \theta°$

  c $\tan^2 \theta° - 2\tan \theta° = 1$ d $\sin 2\theta° - \sqrt{3}\cos 2\theta° = 0$

3   Find the values of x in the interval $0° < x < 720°$ for which $2\cos\left(\dfrac{1}{2}x + 45°\right) = \sqrt{3}$.

4   How many solutions are there to the equation $\sin^2 2x = \dfrac{1}{4}$ in the interval $-180° < x < 180°$?

5   The diagram shows the graph of the function $f(x) = a\sin(bx)$. Find the values of a and b.

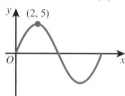

P 6   Prove the identity $\dfrac{2}{\cos^2 x} - \tan^2 x \equiv 2 + \tan^2 x$.

7   Find all values of x in the interval $-90° < x < 90°$ that satisfy $6\cos^2 2x = \sin 2x + 4$.

8   a   Find the values of k for which the equation $4x^2 - kx + 1 = 0$ has a repeated root.

    b   Show that the equation $4\sin^2\theta = 5 - k\cos\theta$ can be written as $4\cos^2\theta - k\cos\theta + 1 = 0$.

    c   Let $f_k(\theta) = 4\cos^2\theta - k\cos\theta + 1$.

        i   State the number of values of $\cos\theta$ that satisfy the equation $f_4(\theta) = 0$.

        ii   Find all the values in the interval $-360° \leqslant \theta \leqslant 360°$ that satisfy the equation $f_4(\theta) = 0$.

        iii Find the value of k for which $x = 1$ is a solution of the equation $4x^2 - kx + 1 = 0$.

        iv   For this value of k, find the number of solutions of the equation $f_k(\theta) = 0$ for interval $-360° \leqslant \theta \leqslant 360°$.

9   In each of the following cases find the smallest positive value of α for which:

    a $\cos(\alpha - \theta)° = \sin\theta°$ b $\sin(\alpha - \theta)° = \cos(\alpha + \theta)°$

    c $\tan\theta° = \tan(\theta + \alpha)°$ d $\sin(\theta + 2\alpha)° = \cos(\alpha - \theta)°$

    e $\cos(2\alpha - \theta)° = \cos(\theta - \alpha)°$ f $\sin(5\alpha + \theta)° = \cos(\theta - 3\alpha)°$

M 10 One end of a piece of elastic is attached to a point at the top of a door frame and the other end hangs freely. A small ball is attached to the free end of the elastic. When the ball is hanging freely it is pulled down a small distance and then released, so that the ball oscillates up and down on the elastic. The depth d centimeters of the ball from the top of the door frame after t seconds is given by $d = 100 + 10\cos 500t°$.

    Find:

    a   the greatest and least depths of the ball

    b   the time at which the ball first reaches its highest position

    c   the time taken for a complete oscillation

    d   the proportion of the time during a complete oscillation for which the depth of the ball is less than 99 cm.

Chapter 6
Series

- Use the expansion of $(a + b)^n$, where n is a positive integer.
- Recognise arithmetic and geometric progressions.
- Use the formulae for the nth term and for the sum of the first n terms to solve problems involving arithmetic or geometric progressions.
- Use the condition for the convergence of a geometric progression, and the formula for the sum to infinity of a convergent geometric progression.

6.1 Binomial expansion of $(a + b)^n$

WORKED EXAMPLE 6.1

Use Pascal's triangle to find the expansion of:

a $(2x - 1)^3$

b $(2 - 3x)^4$

c   i   Use Pascal's triangle to expand $(1 - 3x)^5$.

    ii   Find the coefficient of x^3 in the expansion of $(1 - 5x)(1 - 3x)^5$.

Answer

a $(2x - 1)^3$

    $(2x - 1)^3 = 1(2x)^3 + 3(2x)^2(-1) + 3(2x)(-1)^2 + 1(-1)^3$

    $8x^3 - 12x^2 + 6x - 1$

> The index is 3 so use the row for $n = 3$ in Pascal's triangle: $(1, 3, 3, 1)$

b $(2 - 3x)^4$

    $(2 - 3x)^4 = 1(2)^4 + 4(2)^3(-3x)$
               $+ 6(2)^2(-3x)^2 + 4(2)(-3x)^3 + 1(-3x)^4$

        $= 16 - 96x + 216x^2 - 216x^3 + 81x^4$

> The index is 4 so use the row for $n = 4$ in Pascal's triangle: $(1, 4, 6, 4, 1)$

c   i $(1 - 3x)^5$

       $(1 - 3x)^5 = 1(1)^5 + 5(1)^4(-3x) + 10(1)^3(-3x)^2$
                  $+ 10(1)^2(-3x)^3 + 5(1)(-3x)^4 + 1(-3x)^5$

        $= 1 - 15x + 90x^2 - 270x^3 + 405x^4 - 243x^5$

> The index is 5 so use the row for $n = 5$ in Pascal's triangle: $(1, 5, 10, 10, 5, 1)$

   ii $(1 - 5x)(1 - 3x)^5 = (1 - 5x)(1 - 15x + 90x^2 - 270x^3$
                              $+ 405x^4 - 243x^5)$

The term in x^3 comes from the products:

$(1 - 5x)(1 - 15x + 90x^2 - 270x^3 + 405x^4 - 243x^5)$

$1 \times (-270x^3) = -270x^3$ and $(-5x) \times 90x^2 = -450x^3$

Coefficient of $x^3 = -270 - 450 = -720$

EXERCISE 6A

1 Expand and simplify the following.

    a   **i** $(2 - x)^5$ **ii** $(3 + x)^6$

    b   **i** $(2 - 3x)^4$ **ii** $(2x - 7)^3$

    c   **i** $(3x + y)^5$ (first 3 terms only)   **ii** $(2c - d)^4$ (first 3 terms only)

    d   **i** $(2x^2 - 3x)^3$ **ii** $(2x^{-1} + 5y)^3$

    e   **i** $\left(2x + \dfrac{1}{x}\right)^3$ **ii** $\left(x - \dfrac{3}{x}\right)^4$

2   **a**   Find the coefficient of xy^3 in the expansion of $(x + y)^4$.

    b   Find the coefficient of x^3y^4 in the expansion of $(x + y)^7$.

    c   Find the coefficient of ab^6 in the expansion of $(a + b)^7$.

    d   Find the coefficient of a^5b^3 in the expansion of $(a + b)^8$.

3   Determine which term in the expansion of $(1 - 2y)^5$ has the given coefficient:

    a   80   **b** -80

4   Find the first four terms in the expansion of $(y + 3y^2)^6$ in ascending powers of y.

5   The expansion of $(x + ay)^n$ contains the term $60x^4y^2$.

    a   Write down the value of n.   **b**   Find the value of a.

6   The expansion of $\left(3x^2y + \dfrac{5x}{y}\right)^n$ begins with $27x^6y^3 + 135x^5y$.

    a   Write down the value of n.

    b   Complete and simplify the expansion.

7   Find the constant term in the expansion of $(x - 2x^{-2})^9$.

8   Find the term in x^5 in $\left(x^2 - \dfrac{3}{x}\right)^7$.

9   Find the term that is independent of x in the expansion of $\left(2x - \dfrac{5}{x^2}\right)^{12}$.

6.2 Binomial coefficients

 TIP

To find $\begin{pmatrix} 5 \\ 0 \end{pmatrix}$, key in 5 ^nC_r 0.

WORKED EXAMPLE 6.2

Find, in ascending powers of x, the first four terms in the expansion of:

   a $(1 + x)^{12}$ **b** $(3 - 2x)^8$

Answer

a $(1 + x)^{12} = \binom{12}{0} + \binom{12}{1}x + \binom{12}{2}x^2 + \binom{12}{3}x^3 + \ldots$

                $= 1 + 12x + 66x^2 + 220x^3 + \ldots$

b $(3 - 2x)^8 = \binom{8}{0}3^8 + \binom{8}{1}3^7(-2x)^1 + \binom{8}{2}3^6(-2x)^2 + \binom{8}{3}3^5(-2x)^3 + \ldots$

                $= 6561 - 34992x + 81648x^2 - 108864x^3 + \ldots$

EXERCISE 6B

1 Use the formula to evaluate these binomial coefficients:

    a **i** $\binom{8}{1}$ **ii** $\binom{15}{1}$

    b **i** $\binom{15}{0}$ **ii** $\binom{7}{6}$

    c Find the value of n in each equation.

       i $\binom{n}{2} = 45$ **ii** $\binom{n}{2} = 66$

2 If $(1 + 2x)^n = 1 + 20x + ax^2 + \ldots$

    a find the value of n

    b find the value of a.

3 If $\left(1 + \dfrac{x}{2}\right)^n = 1 + ax + \dfrac{33}{2}x^2 + \ldots$

    a find the value of n

    b find the value of a.

4 **a** Find the first four terms, in ascending powers of x, in the expansion of $(2 - 5x)^7$.

    b Hence find the coefficient of x^3 in the expansion of $(1 + 2x)(2 - 5x)^7$.

5 **a** Find the first three terms in the expansion of $(3 - 5x)^4$.

    b Using a suitable value of x, use your answer to find a 5 significant figure approximation for 2.995^4.

TIP

$\dbinom{n}{r} = \dfrac{n!}{r!(n-r)!}$

6 a Find the first three terms in the expansion of $(2 + 3x)^7$.

b Hence find an approximation to:

  i 2.3^7 ii 2.03^7

c Which of your answers in part **b** provides a more accurate approximation? Justify your answer.

7 a Find the first three terms in the expansion of $(4 - x)^7$.

b Hence find the coefficient of x^2 in the expansion of $(2 + 2x - x^2)(4 - x)^7$.

8 a Expand $\left(e + \dfrac{2}{e}\right)^5$.

b Simplify $\left(e + \dfrac{2}{e}\right)^5 + \left(e - \dfrac{2}{e}\right)^5$.

PS 9 This question explores why binomial coefficients appear in Pascal's triangle.

Consider the expansion of $(a + b)^2$ and $(a + b)^3$:

$$(a + b)^2 = 1a^2 + 2ab + 1b^2$$

$$(a + b)^3 = (a + b)(1a^2 + 2ab + 1b^2)$$

$$= 1a^3 + 2a^2b + 1ab^2 + 1a^2b + 2ab^2 + 1b^3$$

In the expansion of $(a + b)^3$, the coefficient a^2b (which is 3) is found by adding $2a^2b$ and $1a^2b$. This exactly corresponds to the way that you get from one row of Pascal's triangle to the next row:

a Multiply out $(a + b)(a + b)^3$ in a similar way to show which two coefficients add up to give the coefficient of a^2b^2 in the expansion of $(a + b)^4$.

b Try some other examples to see how multiplying out successive powers of $(a + b)$ leads to Pascal's triangle.

6.3 Arithmetic progressions

TIP

nth term $= a + (n - 1)d$

$$S_n = \frac{n}{2}(a + l) = \frac{1}{2}n\{2a + (n - 1)d\}$$

WORKED EXAMPLE 6.3

The sum, S_n, of the first n terms of an arithmetic progression is given by $S_n = pn + qn^2$. Given that $S_3 = 6$ and $S_5 = 11$:

   a   find the values of p and q

   b   find the expression for the nth term and the value of the common difference.

Answer

  a $S_n = pn + qn^2$

      $6 = 3p + 9q$ $\cdots\cdots$ (1)

               The sum of the first 3 terms is 6 when $n = 3$.

      $11 = 5p + 25q$ $\cdots$ (2)

      $30 = 15p + 45q$ $\cdots$ (3)

      $33 = 15p + 75q$ $\cdots$ (4)

               The sum of the first 5 terms is 11 when $n = 5$. Multiply (1) by 5 and (2) by 3. This produces the equations (3) and (4).

      $3 = 30q$

               Subtract (3) from (4).

      $q = 0.1$

               Substitute $q = 0.1$ into (1).

      $6 = 3p + 9(0.1)$

      $5.1 = 3p$

      $p = 1.7$

  b $S_n = pn + qn^2$

      $S_{n-1} = p(n-1) + q(n-1)^2$

      nth term $= S_n - S_{n-1}$

              $= pn + qn^2 - [p(n-1) + q(n-1)^2]$

              $= pn + qn^2 - pn + p - qn^2 + 2qn - q$

              $= p + 2qn - q$

              $= 1.7 + 2(0.1)n - 0.1$

      The nth term $= 1.6 + 0.2n$

      The $(n+1)$th term $= 1.6 + 0.2(n+1)$.

      The difference between the $(n+1)$th term and the nth term is d

      $d = 1.6 + 0.2(n+1) - (1.6 + 0.2n)$

         $= 1.6 + 0.2n + 0.2 - 1.6 - 0.2n$

         $= 0.2$

      The common difference is 0.2.

1 How many terms are there in the following sequences?

    a i   1, 3, 5, ..., 65

        ii 18, 13, 8, ..., 1, 3, 5, ..., −122

    b i   First term 8, common difference 9, last term 899

        ii First term 0, ninth term 16, last term 450

PS 2 The height of the rungs in a ladder forms an arithmetic sequence. The third rung is 70 cm above the ground and the tenth rung is 210 cm above the ground. If the top rung is 350 cm above the ground, how many rungs does the ladder have?

PS 3 The first four terms of an arithmetic progression are 2, $a - b$, $2a + b + 7$, and $a - 3b$, where a and b are constants. Find a and b.

P 4 A book starts at page 1 and has a page number on every page.

    a Show that the first eleven page numbers contain thirteen digits in total.

    b The total number of digits used for all the page numbers is 1260. How many pages are in the book?

5 The sum of the first 3 terms of an arithmetic progression is −12, and the sum of the first 12 terms is 114. Find the first term, a, and the common difference, d.

P 6 Prove that the sum of the first n odd numbers is n^2.

7 The sum of the first n terms of an arithmetic sequence is $S_n = 3n^2 - 2n$. Find the nth term u_n.

8 A circular disc is cut into twelve sectors whose areas are in an arithmetic sequence. The angle of the largest sector is twice the angle of the smallest sector. Find the size of the angle of the smallest sector.

9 a Find the sum of all multiples of 7 between 1 and 1000.

    b Hence find the sum of all integers between 1 and 1000 that are not divisible by 7.

10 Find the sum of all three digit numbers that are multiples of 14 but not 21.

6.4 Geometric progressions

TIP

$$S_n = \frac{a(1 - r^n)}{1 - r} \quad \text{or} \quad S_n = \frac{a(r^n - 1)}{r - 1}$$

(These formulae are not defined when $r = 1$.)

WORKED EXAMPLE 6.4

In a geometric progression, the 3rd term is 32 and the 6th term is 4.

Find the first term, the common ratio and the sum of the first 8 terms of the progression.

Answer

$ar^2 = 32$ -------- (1)

$ar^5 = 4$ --------- (2)   Divide (1) by (2).

Gives $\dfrac{ar^5}{ar^2} = \dfrac{4}{32}$

$r^3 = \dfrac{1}{8}$

$r = \dfrac{1}{2}$ Substituting for r in (1).

$a\left(\dfrac{1}{2}\right)^2 = 32$

$a = 128$

$S_n = \dfrac{a(1 - r^n)}{1 - r}$ Substituting $a = 128$, $r = \dfrac{1}{2}$, $n = 8$.

$S_n = \dfrac{128\left(1 - \left(\dfrac{1}{2}\right)^8\right)}{1 - \dfrac{1}{2}}$

$S_n = 255$

The first term is 128, the common ratio is $\dfrac{1}{2}$
and the sum of the first 8 terms is 255.

EXERCISE 6D

1 The second term of a geometric sequence is 6 and the fifth term is 162.
   a Find a formula for the nth term of the sequence.
   b Hence find the tenth term.

2 The third term of a geometric progression is 12 and the fifth term is 48.
   a Find the possible values of the first term and the common ratio.
   b Hence find the two possible values of the eighth term.

3 The first three terms of a geometric sequence are a, $a + 14$, $9a$.
   a Find the possible values of a.
   b In each case, find the tenth term of the sequence.

4 The third term of a geometric sequence is 112 and the sixth term is 7168. Which term takes the value 1 835 008?

5 Find the sums of the following geometric series (there may be more than one possible answer).

   a   i   7, 35, 175, ...(10 terms)

        ii   1152, 576, 288, ...(12 terms)

   b   i   16, 24, 36, ..., 182.25

        ii   1, 1.1, 1.21, ..., 1.771561

   c   i   First term 8, common ratio -3, last term 52 488

        ii   First term -6, common ratio -3, last term 13 122

   d   i   Third term 24, fifth term 6, 12 terms

        ii   Ninth term 50, thirteenth term 0.08, last term 0.0032

6 Find the possible values of the common ratio if:

   a   i   first term is 11, sum of the first two terms is 12.65

        ii   first term is 1, sum of the first two terms is 3.7

   b   i   first term is 12, sum of the first three terms is 16.68

        ii   first term is 10, sum of the first four terms is 1

7 The first term of a geometric sequence is 6 and the sum of the first three terms is 29. Find the common ratio.

8 The sum of the first four terms of a geometric sequence is 520, the sum of the first five terms is 844 and the sum of the first six terms is 1330.

   a   Find the common ratio.

   b   Find the sum of the first two terms.

PS   9 A well-known story concerns the inventor of the game of chess. As a reward for inventing the game it is rumoured that he was asked to choose his own prize. He asked for 1 grain of rice to be placed on the first square of the board, 2 grains on the second square, 4 grains on the third square and so on in geometric progression until all 64 squares had been covered. Calculate the total number of grains of rice he would have received. Give your answer in standard form.

PS   10 If x, y and z are the first three terms of a geometric sequence, show that x^2, y^2 and z^2 form another geometric sequence.

6.5 Infinite geometric series

TIP

$$S_\infty = \frac{a}{1 - r} \text{ provided that } -1 < r < 1$$

WORKED EXAMPLE 6.5

For the following geometric progressions, write down the first 5 terms, find the nth term and the sum to infinity if it exists.

a $\quad a = 2, r = 2$ b $\quad a = -1, r = -1$ c $\quad a = 4, r = \dfrac{1}{4}$

Answer

a The progression is $2, 4, 8, 16, 32, \ldots$.

The nth term is $ar^{n-1} = 2(2)^{n-1} = 2^n$

It is not possible to find the sum to infinity of this series since $r > 1$. (The series diverges.)

b The progression is $-1, +1, -1, +1, \ldots$.

The nth term is $ar^{n-1} = (-1)(-1)^{n-1} = (-1)^n$

It is not possible to find the sum to infinity of this series since $r = -1$. (The series oscillates.)

c The progression is $4, 1, \dfrac{1}{4}, \dfrac{1}{16}, \dfrac{1}{64}, \ldots$.

The nth term is $ar^{n-1} = 4\left(\dfrac{1}{4}\right)^{n-1} = \left(\dfrac{1}{4}\right)^{n-2}$

There is a sum to infinity since $-1 < r < 1$. (The series converges.)

$S_\infty = \dfrac{a}{1 - r} = \dfrac{4}{1 - \frac{1}{4}} = \dfrac{16}{3}$

EXERCISE 6E

1 Find the value of the following infinite geometric series, or state that they are divergent.

a i $\quad 9 + 3 + 1 + \dfrac{1}{3} + \ldots$ ii $\quad 56 + 8 + 1\frac{1}{7} \ldots$

b i $\quad 0.3 + 0.03 + 0.003 \ldots$ ii $\quad 0.78 + 0.0078 + 0.000078 \ldots$

c i $\quad 0.01 + 0.02 + 0.04 \ldots$ ii $\quad \dfrac{19}{10\,000} + \dfrac{19}{1000} + \dfrac{19}{100} \ldots$

d i $\quad 10 - 2 + 0.4 \ldots$ ii $\quad 6 - 4 + \dfrac{8}{3} \ldots$

e i $\quad 10 - 40 + 160 \ldots$ ii $\quad 4.2 - 3.36 + 2.688 \ldots$

2 Find the values of x that allow the following geometric series to converge.

a i $\quad 9 + 9x + 9x^2 \ldots$ ii $\quad -2 - 2x - 2x^2 \ldots$

b i $\quad 1 + 3x + 9x^2 \ldots$ ii $\quad 1 + 10x + 100x^2 \ldots$

c i $\quad -2 - 10x - 50x^2 \ldots$ ii $\quad 8 + 24x + 72x^2 \ldots$

d i $\quad 40 + 10x + 2.5x^2 \ldots$ ii $\quad 144 + 12x + x^2 \ldots$

e **i** $243 - 81x + 27x^2 \ldots$ **ii** $1 - \dfrac{5}{4}x + \dfrac{25}{16}x^2 \ldots$

f **i** $3 - \dfrac{6}{x} + \dfrac{12}{x^2} \ldots$ **ii** $18 - \dfrac{9}{x} + \dfrac{9}{2x^2} \ldots$

g **i** $5 + 5(3 - 2x) + 5(3 - 2x)^2 \ldots$ **ii** $7 + \dfrac{7(2 - x)}{2} + \dfrac{7(2 - x)^2}{4} \ldots$

h **i** $1 + \left(3 - \dfrac{2}{x}\right) + \left(3 - \dfrac{2}{x}\right)^2 \ldots$ **ii** $1 + \dfrac{1 + x}{x} + \dfrac{(1 + x)^2}{x^2} \ldots$

i **i** $7 + 7x^2 + 7x^4 \ldots$ **ii** $12 - 48x^3 + 192x^6 \ldots$

3 The first and fourth terms of a geometric series are 18 and $-\dfrac{2}{3}$ respectively. Find:

     a the sum of the first n terms of the series

     b the sum to infinity of the series.

4 A geometric sequence has all positive terms. The sum of the first two terms is 15 and the sum to infinity is 27. Find the value of:

     a the common ratio

     b the first term.

5 The sum to infinity of a geometric series is 32. The sum of the first four terms is 30 and all the terms are positive. Find the difference between the sum to infinity and the sum of the first eight terms.

6 Consider the infinite geometric series $1 + \left(\dfrac{2x}{3}\right) + \left(\dfrac{2x}{3}\right)^2 \ldots$

     a For what values of x does the series converge?

     b Find the sum of the series if $x = 1.2$.

7 The sum of an infinite geometric progression is 13.5, and the sum of the first three terms is 13. Find the first term.

8 The common ratio of the terms in a geometric series is 2^x.

     a State the set of values of x for which the sum to infinity of the series exists.

     b If the first term of the series is 35, find the value of x for which the sum to infinity is 40.

PS **9** A 'supa-ball' is dropped from a height of 1 metre onto a level table. It always rises to a height equal to 0.9 of the height from which it was dropped. How far does it travel in total before it stops bouncing?

PS **10** A frog sits at one end of a table which is 2 m long. In its first jump the frog goes a distance of 1 m along the table, with its second jump $\dfrac{1}{2}$ m, with its third jump $\dfrac{1}{4}$ m and so on.

     a What is the frog's final position?

     b After how many jumps will the frog be within 1 cm of the far end of the table?

6.6 Further arithmetic and geometric series

WORKED EXAMPLE 6.6

The first three terms of an arithmetic series are $(x-4), (x+2)$ and $(3x+1)$.

a Find the value of x and use it to write down the first 4 terms of the progression.

Given that $(x-4), (x+2)$ and $(3x+1)$ are part of a geometric progression:

b find the two possible values of x and use them to write down the first 4 terms of each of the two geometric progressions

c find the value of the common ratio of each progression and the sum to infinity if possible.

Answer

a Arithmetic series is: $(x-4), (x+2), (3x+1)$ Use common differences.

$(x+2)-(x-4) = (3x+1)-(x+2)$

$6 = 2x - 1$

$x = \dfrac{7}{2}$

The first 4 terms of this arithmetic progression are $-\dfrac{1}{2}, \dfrac{11}{2}, \dfrac{23}{2}, \dfrac{35}{2}$

b Geometric series is: $(x-4), (x+2), (3x+1)$ Use common ratios.

$$\dfrac{x+2}{x-4} = \dfrac{3x+1}{x+2}$$

$(x+2)(x+2) = (3x+1)(x-4)$ Expand and simplify.

$x^2 + 4x + 4 = 3x^2 - 12x + x - 4$ Rearrange.

$2x^2 - 15x - 8 = 0$ Factorise and solve.

$(2x+1)(x-8) = 0$

$x = -\dfrac{1}{2}$ or $x = 8$

First progression $-\dfrac{9}{2}, \dfrac{3}{2}, -\dfrac{1}{2}, \dfrac{1}{6}$

Second progression $4, 10, 25, \dfrac{125}{2}$

c First progression common ratio is $\dfrac{\frac{3}{2}}{-\frac{9}{2}} = -\dfrac{1}{3}$, which satisfies $-1 < r < 1$.

Second progression common ratio is $\dfrac{10}{4} = \dfrac{5}{2}$, which does not satisfy $-1 < r < 1$.

Therefore only the first geometric progression has a sum to infinity.

$S_\infty = \dfrac{a}{1-r}$ .... Use $a = -\dfrac{9}{2}$ and $r = -\dfrac{1}{3}$.

$S_\infty = \dfrac{-\dfrac{9}{2}}{1-\left(-\dfrac{1}{3}\right)} = -\dfrac{27}{8}$

 1 An arithmetic progression has first term a and common difference d.

   a Write down expressions, in terms of a and d, for the second and sixth terms of the progression.

   b The first, second and sixth terms of this arithmetic progression are also the first three terms of a geometric progression. Prove that $d = 3a$.

   c Given that $a = 2$, find the sum of the first 15 terms of each progression.

2 A geometric sequence and an arithmetic sequence both start with a first term of 1. The third term of the arithmetic sequence is the same as the second term of the geometric sequence. The fourth term of the arithmetic sequence is the same as the third term of the geometric sequence. Find the possible values of the common difference of the arithmetic sequence.

3 The first, second and fourth terms of a geometric sequence form consecutive terms of an arithmetic sequence. Given that the sum to infinity of the geometric sequence exists, find the exact value of the common ratio.

4 The first two terms of a geometric progression are 2 and x respectively $(x \neq 2)$.

   a Find the third term in terms of x.

   The first and third terms of an arithmetic progression are 2 and x respectively.

   b Find an expression for the eleventh term in terms of x.

   Given that the third term of the geometric progression and the 11th term of the arithmetic progression have the same value:

   c find the value of x

   d find the sum of the first 50 terms of the arithmetic progression.

5 The second, fourth and eighth terms of an arithmetic progression are in geometrical progression, and the sum of the third and fifth terms is 20.

   Find the first four terms of the arithmetic progression.

6 The second, fifth and eleventh terms of an arithmetical progression are in geometrical progression, and the seventh term is 4.

   a Find the first term and the common difference.

   b What is the common ratio of the geometrical progression?

7   The three terms $a, 1, b$ are in arithmetic progression. The three terms $1, a, b$ are in geometric progression. Find the value of a and b given that $a \neq b$.

(PS)   8   The sum of the first n terms of an arithmetic sequence is given by the formula $S_n = 4n^2 - 2n$. Three terms of this sequence, u_2, u_m and u_{32}, are consecutive terms in a geometric sequence. Find m.

END-OF-CHAPTER REVIEW EXERCISE 6

1   $a = 2 - \sqrt{2}$. Using binomial expansion or otherwise, express a^5 in the form $m + n\sqrt{2}$.

2   The constant term in the expansion of $\left(x^2 + \dfrac{a}{x^4}\right)^9$ is $-\dfrac{28}{9}$. What is the value of a?

3   Find the coefficient of x^6 in the expansion of $(1 - x^2)(1 + x)^5$.

4   Find the coefficient of x^2 in the expansion of $\left(2x + \dfrac{1}{\sqrt{x}}\right)^5$.

5   $(1 + ax)^n = 1 + 10x + 40x^2 + ...$

   Find the values of a and n.

6   The sum of the first 3 terms of a geometric progression is 19. The sum to infinity is 27. Find the common ratio, r.

7   The first three terms of a geometric sequence are $2x + 4, x + 5, x + 1$.
   a   Find the two possible values of x.
   b   Given that it exists, find the sum to infinity of the series.

8   Find the sum of all the integers between 300 and 600 that are divisible by 7.

9   Expand and simplify $(3x + 5)^3 - (3x - 5)^3$.

   Hence solve the equation $(3x + 5)^3 - (3x - 5)^3 = 730$.

(P)   10   An infinite geometric series has first term a and sum to infinity b, where $b \neq 0$.

   Prove that a lies between 0 and $2b$.

103

- Understand that the gradient of a curve at a point is the limit of the gradients of a suitable sequence of chords, and use the notations $f'(x)$, $f''(x)$, $\dfrac{dy}{dx}$ and $\dfrac{d^2y}{dx^2}$ for the first and second derivatives.
- Use the derivative of x^n (for any rational n), together with constant multiples, sums, differences of functions and of composite functions using the chain rule.
- Apply differentiation to gradients, tangents and normals.

7.1 Derivatives and gradient functions

TIP

$$\frac{d}{dx}(x^n) = nx^{n-1}$$

WORKED EXAMPLE 7.1

a Differentiate $\dfrac{1}{x\sqrt{x}}$ with respect to x, writing your answer in the form ax^n.

b Hence find the gradient of the tangent to the curve $\dfrac{1}{x\sqrt{x}}$ at the point where $x = 4$.

Answer

a $\dfrac{d}{dx}\left(\dfrac{1}{x\sqrt{x}}\right) = \dfrac{d}{dx}\left(x^{-\frac{3}{2}}\right)$

$\dfrac{d}{dx} = -\dfrac{3}{2}x^{-\frac{5}{2}}$

b When $x = 4$, $\dfrac{dy}{dx} = \left(-\dfrac{3}{2}(4)^{-\frac{5}{2}}\right)$

$\dfrac{dy}{dx} = -\dfrac{3}{2(4)^{\frac{5}{2}}}$

$\dfrac{dy}{dx} = -\dfrac{3}{64}$

Gradient of curve at $x = 4$ is $-\dfrac{3}{64}$.

EXERCISE 7A

1 Find $\dfrac{dy}{dx}$ for the following.

a i $y = \sqrt[3]{x}$ **ii** $y = \sqrt[5]{x}$

b i $y = 8\sqrt[4]{x}$ **ii** $y = \dfrac{\sqrt{x}}{3}$

c i $y = -\dfrac{1}{x}$ **ii** $y = \dfrac{1}{x^4}$

d i $y = \dfrac{3}{x^2}$ **ii** $y = -\dfrac{2}{5x^{10}}$

e i $y = \dfrac{1}{\sqrt{x}}$ **ii** $y = \dfrac{1}{\sqrt[3]{x}}$

f i $y = \dfrac{10}{\sqrt[5]{x}}$ **ii** $y = \dfrac{8}{3\sqrt[4]{x}}$

2 Find $f'(x)$ for the following.

a i $f(x) = (2x-3)(x+4)$ **ii** $f(x) = 3x(x-5)$

b i $f(x) = \sqrt{x}(4x+3)$ **ii** $f(x) = \sqrt[3]{x}(x-1)$

c i $f(x) = (\sqrt{x}+2x)^2$ **ii** $f(x) = (\sqrt[4]{x}-4)^2$

d i $f(x) = \left(x+\dfrac{1}{x}\right)^2$ **ii** $f(x) = \left(x+\dfrac{2}{x}\right)\left(x-\dfrac{2}{x}\right)$

3 Differentiate the following functions.

a $2\sqrt{x}$ **b** $\left(1+\sqrt{x}\right)^2$ **c** $x - \dfrac{1}{2}\sqrt{x}$

d $x\left(1-\dfrac{1}{\sqrt{x}}\right)^2$ **e** $x-\dfrac{1}{x}$ **f** $\dfrac{x^3+x^2+1}{x}$

g $\dfrac{(x+1)(x+2)}{x}$ **h** $\left(\dfrac{\sqrt{x}+x}{\sqrt{x}}\right)^2$

4 $f(x) = \dfrac{9x^2+3}{2\sqrt[3]{x}}$. Find $f'(x)$.

5 A curve has equation $y = (4x^2-1)(3-x)$. Find $\dfrac{dy}{dx}$.

6 Given that $f(x) = 3\sqrt{x} - \dfrac{2}{\sqrt{x}}$ find:

a $f'(x)$

b the gradient of the graph of $y=f(x)$ at the point where $x=4$.

7 $f(x) = x^2 + bx + c$. If $f(1)=2$ and $f'(2)=12$ find the values of b and c.

8 Find the coordinates of the two points on the curve $y = 2x^3 - 5x^2 + 9x - 1$ at which the gradient of the tangent is 13.

TIP

Use the following in this exercise.

$\dfrac{d}{dx}[kf(x)] = k\dfrac{d}{dx}[f(x)]$

$\dfrac{d}{dx}[f(x) \pm g(x)]$

$= \dfrac{d}{dx}[f(x)] \pm \dfrac{d}{dx}[g(x)]$

TIP

In this exercise, take care when manipulating negative and fractional indices,

e.g. $\dfrac{-1}{\frac{1}{2x^2}} = -\dfrac{1}{2}x^{-\frac{1}{2}}$

7.2 The chain rule

WORKED EXAMPLE 7.2

a Find $\dfrac{dy}{dx}$ if $y = \sqrt{3x - 2}$.

b Find the x-coordinates of the points on the curve $f(x) = \dfrac{1}{x + 4} + x$ where $f'(x) = 0$.

Answer

a $y = \sqrt{3x - 2}$

Let $u = 3x - 2$ (always the expression under the square root). Find $\dfrac{du}{dx}$.

$\dfrac{du}{dx} = 3$

$y = u^{\frac{1}{2}}$

Always use powers instead of roots here. Find $\dfrac{dy}{du}$.

$\dfrac{dy}{du} = \dfrac{1}{2}u^{-\frac{1}{2}}$

$\dfrac{dy}{dx} = \dfrac{dy}{du} \times \dfrac{du}{dx}$

Substitute into the chain rule.

$\dfrac{dy}{dx} = \dfrac{1}{2}u^{-\frac{1}{2}} \times 3$

$\dfrac{dy}{dx} = \dfrac{3}{2}(3x - 2)^{-\frac{1}{2}}$

$\dfrac{dy}{dx} = \dfrac{3}{2(3x - 2)^{\frac{1}{2}}}$ or $\dfrac{dy}{dx} = \dfrac{3}{2\sqrt{3x - 2}}$

b $f(x) = \dfrac{1}{x + 4} + x$

To differentiate $\dfrac{1}{x + 4}$, you need to write it in index form and use the chain rule.

Let $y = (x + 4)^{-1}$

Let $u = x + 4$ (always the part in brackets). Find $\dfrac{du}{dx}$.

$\dfrac{du}{dx} = 1$

$y = u^{-1}$

Find $\dfrac{dy}{du}$.

$\dfrac{dy}{du} = -1u^{-2}$

$$\frac{dy}{dx} = \frac{dy}{du} \times \frac{du}{dx}$$

Substitute into the chain rule.

$$\frac{dy}{dx} = -1u^{-2} \times 1$$

$$\frac{dy}{dx} = -\frac{1}{u^2}$$

$$\frac{dy}{dx} = -\frac{1}{(x+4)^2}$$

As $f(x) = \dfrac{1}{x+4} + x$ then

$$f'(x) = -\frac{1}{(x+4)^2} + 1.$$

If $f'(x) = 0$ then $-\dfrac{1}{(x+4)^2} + 1 = 0.$

$$\frac{1}{(x+4)^2} = 1$$

Rearrange.

$$(x+4)^2 = 1$$

Square root both sides (remembering that $\sqrt{1} = \pm 1$)

$$x + 4 = \pm 1$$

The x-coordinates are $x = -3$ or $x = -5$.

EXERCISE 7B

1 Use the chain rule to differentiate the following expressions with respect to x.

   a i $(3x+4)^5$ ii $(5x+4)^7$

   b i $\sqrt{3x-2}$ ii $\sqrt{x+1}$

   c i $\dfrac{1}{3-x}$ ii $\dfrac{1}{(2x+3)^2}$

2 Differentiate the following with respect to x.

   a $y = (5x+3)^6$ b $y = (5x+3)^{\frac{1}{2}}$ c $y = \dfrac{1}{5x+3}$

3 Differentiate the following with respect to x.

   a $y = (1-4x)^5$ b $y = (1-4x)^{-3}$ c $y = \sqrt{1-4x}$

4 Differentiate the following with respect to x.

   a $y = (1+x^3)^5$ b $y = (1+x^3)^{-4}$ c $y = \sqrt[3]{1+x^3}$

5 Differentiate the following with respect to x.

    a $y = (2x^2 + 3)^6$
        b $y = \dfrac{1}{2x^2 + 3}$
        c $y = \dfrac{1}{\sqrt{2x^2 + 3}}$

6 Given that $f(x) = \dfrac{1}{1 + x^2}$, find:

    a $f'(2)$

    b the value of x such that $f'(x) = 0$.

7 Given that $y = \sqrt[4]{x^3 + 8}$, find the value of $\dfrac{dy}{dx}$ when $x = 2$.

8 Differentiate the following with respect to x.

    a $y = (x^2 + 3x + 1)^6$
        b $y = \dfrac{1}{(x^2 + 5x)^3}$

7.3 Tangents and normals

WORKED EXAMPLE 7.3

    a Prove that the normal to the curve $y = \dfrac{16}{x}$ at the point $(8, 2)$ has equation $y = 4x - 30$.

    b The normal to the curve $y = \dfrac{16}{x}$ at the point $(8, 2)$ is also the tangent to the curve at
        $y = x^2 + k$ at the point $(a, a^2 + k)$. Find the values of a and k.

Answer

    a $y = \dfrac{16}{x}$

        $y = 16x^{-1}$ Differentiate.

        $\dfrac{dy}{dx} = -16x^{-2}$

        $\dfrac{dy}{dx} = -\dfrac{16}{x^2}$ At $x = 8$.

        $\dfrac{dy}{dx} = -\dfrac{16}{64}$

        $\dfrac{dy}{dx} = -\dfrac{1}{4}$ The gradient of the tangent at $x = 8$ is $-\dfrac{1}{4}$.

                                       The gradient of the normal at $x = 8$ is 4.

        $y - y_1 = m(x - x_1)$ Using $m = 4, x = 8, y = 2$.

$y - 2 = 4(x - 8)$ · · · · · · · · · · · · · · · · Expand brackets and rearrange.

$y = 4x - 30$. Proven.

b $y = x^2 + k$ · · · · · · · · · · · · · · · · · Differentiate.

$\dfrac{dy}{dx} = 2x$ · · · · · · · · · · · · · · · · · · · Substitute $x = a$. The gradient of the tangent is $2a$.

$\dfrac{dy}{dx} = 2a$

$y - y_1 = m(x - x_1)$ · · · · · · · · · · · Using $x = a$, $y = a^2 + k$, $m = 2a$.

$y - (a^2 + k) = 2a(x - a)$ · · · · · · · · · Expand brackets.

$y - a^2 - k = 2ax - 2a^2$ · · · · · · · · · Rearrange.

$y = 2ax - (a^2 - k)$ · · · · · · · · · · · · Compare with $y = 4x - 30$.

   $2a = 4$

    $a = 2$

$a^2 - k = 30$

$2^2 - k = 30$

$\therefore k = -26, \quad a = 2$

EXERCISE 7C

1   One of the tangents to the curve with equation $y = 4x - x^3$ is the line with equation $y = x - 2$. Find the equation of the other tangent parallel to $y = x - 2$.

2   Find the equation of the tangent at the point $(4, 2)$ to the curve with equation $y = \sqrt{x}$.

3   Find the equation of the normal at the point $(1, 2)$ to the graph $y = x + \dfrac{1}{x}$.

4   The graphs of $y = x^2 - 2x$ and $y = x^3 - 3x^2 - 2x$ both pass through the origin. Show that they share the same tangent at the origin.

5   Find the equation of the tangent to the curve with the equation $y = x^3 - 3x^2 - 2x - 6$ at the point where it crosses the y-axis.

6   Find the equations of the tangent and the normal to $y = \sqrt[3]{x^2}$ at the point $(8, 4)$.

7   The tangent to the curve with equation $y = \dfrac{1}{x^2}$ at the point $\left(\dfrac{1}{2}, 4\right)$ meets the axes at P and Q. Find the coordinates of P and Q.

8   Find the equation of the tangent to the curve $y = (x^2 - 5)^3$ at the point $(2, -1)$.

9 Find the equation of the tangent to the curve $y = \dfrac{1}{\sqrt{x} - 1}$ at the point $(4, 1)$.

10 Find the equation of the normal to the curve $y = \dfrac{8}{1 - x^3}$ at the point $(-1, 4)$.

7.4 Second derivatives

WORKED EXAMPLE 7.4

Given $f(x) = \dfrac{2}{\sqrt{3x + 7}}$ find $f''(-1)$.

Answer

$f(x) = \dfrac{2}{\sqrt{3x + 7}}$	Rewrite in index form.
$f(x) = 2(3x + 7)^{-\frac{1}{2}}$	Chain rule.
$f'(x) = 2(3)\left(-\dfrac{1}{2}\right)(3x + 7)^{-\frac{3}{2}}$	
$f'(x) = -3(3x + 7)^{-\frac{3}{2}}$	Chain rule.
$f''(x) = -3(3)\left(-\dfrac{3}{2}\right)(3x + 7)^{-\frac{5}{2}}$	Simplify.
$f''(x) = \dfrac{27}{2}(3x + 7)^{-\frac{5}{2}}$	Substitute $x = -1$.
$f''(-1) = \dfrac{27}{2}(4)^{-\frac{5}{2}}$	
$f''(-1) = \dfrac{27}{64}$	

EXERCISE 7D

1 Find $\dfrac{d^2y}{dx^2}$ for each of the following functions.

a $y = 2x^2 + x - 4$

b $y = 3x^4 - 7x^3 - 5$

c $y = 4 - \dfrac{6}{x^3}$

d $y = (3x + 1)^4$

e $y = \sqrt{1 - 2x}$

f $y = \dfrac{5}{\sqrt{x + 1}}$

g $y = \dfrac{3x - 5}{x^2}$

h $y = (2x + 3)(x - 1)$

i $y = \dfrac{4 - 3x}{\sqrt{x}}$

2 Find $f''(x)$ for each of the following functions.

a $f(x) = \dfrac{1 - 4x^2}{3x}$

b $f(x) = \dfrac{(2 - x)(1 + x)}{x^2}$

c $f(x) = \sqrt{1 - 3x^2}$

d $f(x) = \dfrac{1}{x^3} - \dfrac{3}{2x^2}$

e $f(x) = x^3\left(\sqrt{x} - 3\right)$

f $f(x) = (x^2 + 3)(x - 1)$

3 Given that $y = 2x - (3x - 1)^3$, find $\dfrac{dy}{dx}$ and $\dfrac{d^2y}{dx^2}$.

4 Given that $f(x) = x^3 - x^2 - x - 1$, find:

a $f(-1)$

b $f'(-1)$

c $f''(-1)$

5 a i If $y = x^3 - 5x$, find $\dfrac{d^2y}{dx^2}$ when $x = 9$.

ii If $y = 8 + 2x^4$, find $\dfrac{d^2y}{dx^2}$ when $x = 4$.

b i If $S = 3A^2 + \dfrac{1}{A}$, find $\dfrac{d^2S}{dA^2}$ when $A = 1$.

ii If $J = v - \sqrt{v}$, find $\dfrac{d^2J}{dv^2}$ when $v = 9$.

6 a If $y = 3x^3$, find x at the point where $\dfrac{d^2y}{dx^2} = -54$.

b If $y = \dfrac{2}{x}$, find x at the point where $\dfrac{d^2y}{dx^2} = \dfrac{1}{2}$.

7 Find the x-coordinates of the points on the curve $y = x^4 - 12x^2 + 3x - 1$ where $\dfrac{d^2y}{dx^2} = 0$.

P 8 If $y = 4x^3$:

a find:

i $\dfrac{dy}{dx}$

ii $\dfrac{d^2y}{dx^2}$

b show that y satisfies $3y\dfrac{d^2y}{dx^2} - 2\left(\dfrac{dy}{dx}\right)^2 \equiv 0$.

P 9 Given that $y = \dfrac{1}{\sqrt{x}}$, show that $2x\left(\dfrac{d^2y}{dx^2}\right) + 3\left(\dfrac{dy}{dx}\right) \equiv 0$.

10 Given that $y = ax^2 + bx$ and $\dfrac{d^2y}{dx^2} \equiv 4\left(\dfrac{dy}{dx}\right)^2 - 32y$, find the possible values of the constants a and b. $(a \neq 0 \neq b)$

111

END-OF-CHAPTER REVIEW EXERCISE 7

1   Find the gradient of the graph of $y = \dfrac{1}{2\sqrt{x}}$ at the point where the y-coordinate is 3.

2   $f(x) = ax^3 + bx^{-2}$ where a and b are constants. $f'(1) = 18$ and $f''(1) = 18$. Find a and b.

3   $f(x) = \sqrt{x^3} + 15\sqrt{x}$. Find the values of x for which the gradient of $f(x)$ is 9.

4   **a**   **i**   If $y = ax^2 + (1-a)x$ where a is a constant, find $\dfrac{dy}{dx}$.

      ii   If $y = x^3 + b^2$ where b is a constant, find $\dfrac{dy}{dx}$.

   b   **i**   If $Q = \sqrt{ab} + \sqrt{b}$ where b is a constant, find $\dfrac{dQ}{da}$.

      ii   If $D = 3(av)^2$ where a is a constant, find $\dfrac{dD}{dv}$.

5   Find the equation of the normal to $y = x^4 - 4x^3$ at the point for which $x = \dfrac{1}{2}$.

6   Show that the equation of the tangent to $y = \dfrac{1}{x}$ at the point for which $x = p$ is $p^2 y + x = 2p$.
    At what point on the curve is the equation of the tangent $9y + x + 6 = 0$?

7   The tangent to the curve $y = 6\sqrt{x}$ at the point $(4, 12)$ meets the axes at A and B. Show that
    the distance AB may be written in the form $k\sqrt{13}$, and state the value of k.

8   At a particular point of the curve $y = 5x^2 - 12x + 1$ the equation of the normal is
    $x + 18y + c = 0$. Find the value of the constant c.

(PS) 9   The graphs of $y = x^m$ and $y = x^n$ intersect at the point $P(1, 1)$. Find the connection between
    m and n if the tangent at P to each curve is the normal to the other curve.

10 The normals at $x = 2$ to $y = \dfrac{1}{x^2}$ and $y = \dfrac{1}{x^3}$ meet at Q. Find the coordinates of Q.

Chapter 8
Further differentiation

- Apply differentiation to increasing and decreasing functions and rates of change.
- Locate stationary points and determine their nature, and use information about stationary points in sketching graphs.

8.1 Increasing and decreasing functions

WORKED EXAMPLE 8.1

Find the intervals in which the function $f(x) = x^{\frac{2}{3}}(1 - x)$ is increasing and those in which it is decreasing.

Answer

$f(x) = x^{\frac{2}{3}}(1 - x)$ .... Expand brackets.

$f(x) = x^{\frac{2}{3}} - x^{\frac{5}{3}}$ .... Differentiate.

$f'(x) = \frac{2}{3}x^{-\frac{1}{3}} - \frac{5}{3}x^{\frac{2}{3}}$ .... Now factorise.

$f'(x) = \frac{1}{3}x^{-\frac{1}{3}}(2 - 5x)$

The factor $x^{-\frac{1}{3}}$ is positive when $x > 0$ and negative when $x < 0$.

The factor $2 - 5x$ is positive when $x < 0.4$ and negative when $x > 0.4$.

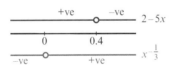

Therefore $f'(x) = \frac{1}{3}x^{-\frac{1}{3}}(2 - 5x)$

is positive for $0 < x < 0.4$ and

negative for $x < 0$ and $x > 0.4$.

The function $f(x) = x^{\frac{2}{3}}(1 - x)$ is increasing for $0 < x < 0.4$ and decreasing for $x < 0$ and $x > 0.4$.

TIP

The common factor of $x^{-\frac{1}{3}}$ and $x^{\frac{2}{3}}$ is $x^{-\frac{1}{3}}$ (look for the smaller index).

113

1 For each of the following functions $f(x)$, find $f'(x)$ and the interval in which $f(x)$ is decreasing.

   a $x^2 + 4x - 9$ b $x^2 - 3x - 5$ c $5 - 3x + x^2$

   d $2x^2 - 8x + 7$ e $4 + 7x - 2x^2$ f $3 - 5x - 7x^2$

2 a i Find the interval in which $x^2 - x$ is an increasing function.

      ii Find the interval in which $x^2 + 2x - 5$ is a decreasing function.

   b i Find the range of values of x for which $x^3 - 3x$ is an increasing function.

      ii Find the range of values of x for which $x^3 + 2x^2 - 5$ is a decreasing function.

   c i Find the interval in which the gradient of $y = x^3 - 3x$ is decreasing.

      ii Find the interval in which the gradient of $y = 2x^3 - x^2$ is increasing.

3 a Find the rate of change of $y = \dfrac{3}{\sqrt{x}}$ at the point where $x = 9$.

   b Is the gradient increasing or decreasing at this point?

4 Show that $y = x^3 + kx + c$ is always increasing if $k > 0$.

5 The function $f(x) = 12x - 2x^2 - \dfrac{1}{3}x^3$ is increasing for $a < x < b$. Find the constants a and b.

6 Find the range of values of x for which the function $f(x) = x^3 - 6x^2 + 9x + 2$ is decreasing but its gradient is increasing.

7 a Find the gradient of the curve $y = 3\sqrt{x} - 2$ at the point where it crosses the x-axis.

   b Is the curve increasing or decreasing at this point? Give a reason for your answer.

8 This graph shows the gradient function, $f'(x)$, of a function $f(x)$.
   Which of the following is definitely true at the point A?

   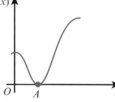

   A $f(x)$ has a minimum

   B $f(x)$ has a maximum

   C $f(x) = 0$

   D $f''(x) = 0$

8.2 Stationary points

WORKED EXAMPLE 8.2

Find the coordinates of the stationary points on the curve $y = (x + 3)^2(2 - x)$ and determine the nature of these points.

Answer

$y = (x + 3)^2(2 - x)$ ···················· Expand.

$y = -x^3 - 4x^2 + 3x + 18$

$\dfrac{dy}{dx} = -3x^2 - 8x + 3$ ···················· Factorise.

$\dfrac{dy}{dx} = (1 - 3x)(x + 3)$

For stationary points: $\dfrac{dy}{dx} = 0$

$1 - 3x = 0$ or $x + 3 = 0$

$x = -3$ or $x = \dfrac{1}{3}$

When $x = -3$, $y = (-3 + 3)^2(2 - -3) = 0$

When $x = \dfrac{1}{3}$, $y = \left(\dfrac{1}{3} + 3\right)^2 \left(2 - \dfrac{1}{3}\right) = \dfrac{500}{27}$

The stationary points are $(-3, 0)$ and $\left(\dfrac{1}{3}, \dfrac{500}{27}\right)$.

To determine the nature of these stationary points, consider two methods:

Method 1

Consider the gradient on either side of the points $(-3, 0)$ and $\left(\dfrac{1}{3}, \dfrac{500}{27}\right)$:

x	0.3	$\dfrac{1}{3}$	0.4
$\dfrac{dy}{dx}$	$(-3)(0.3)^2 - 8(0.3) + 3 =$ positive	0	$(-3)(0.4)^2 - 8(0.4) + 3 =$ negative
direction of tangent	/		\
shape of curve	⌒		

x	-3.1	-3	-2.9
$\dfrac{dy}{dx}$	$(-3)(-3.1)^2 - 8(-3.1) + 3 = \text{negative}$	0	$(-3)(-2.9)^2 - 8(-2.9) + 3 = \text{positive}$
direction of tangent	╲	—	╱
shape of curve	╲___╱		

So $\left(\dfrac{1}{3}, \dfrac{500}{27}\right)$ is a maximum point and $(-3, 0)$ is a minimum point.

Method 2

$\dfrac{dy}{dx} = -3x^2 - 8x + 3$

$\dfrac{d^2y}{dx^2} = -6x - 8$ .... Use the second derivative.

When $x = -3$, $\dfrac{d^2y}{dx^2} = -6(-3) - 8 > 0$

When $x = \dfrac{1}{3}$, $\dfrac{d^2y}{dx^2} = -6\left(\dfrac{1}{3}\right) - 8 < 0$

$\therefore (-3, 0)$ is a minimum point and $\left(\dfrac{1}{3}, \dfrac{500}{27}\right)$ is a maximum point.

EXERCISE 8B

1 Find the coordinates of the stationary points on the graphs of the following functions, and find whether these points are maxima or minima. Sketch the corresponding graphs. (You do not need to determine the coordinates of the axis intercepts).

   a $2x^3 + 3x^2 - 72x + 5$

   b $x^3 - 3x^2 - 45x + 7$

   c $2x + x^2 - 4x^3$

   d $x^3 + 3x^2 + 3x + 1$

P 2 Prove that the curve $y = x^3 - 3x^2 + 4x - 1$ has no stationary points.

3 $f(x) = \dfrac{9x^2 + 1}{x}$

   a Find the x-coordinates of the stationary points on the curve $y = f(x)$.

   b Determine whether each is a maximum or minimum point.

4 Find the coordinates of the stationary point on the curve $y = x - \sqrt{x}$ and determine its nature.

5 a Find the coordinates of the stationary points on the curve with equation $y = x^2\left(6\sqrt[3]{x} - 7\right)$.

   b Establish whether each is a maximum or minimum point.

6 The curve $y = x^3 + 10x^2 + kx - 2$ has a stationary point at $x = -8$.

  a Find the x-coordinate of the other stationary point.

  b Determine the nature of both stationary points.

7 The curve $y = ax^2 + bx - 2$ has a minimum point at $x = -2$ and passes through the point $(1, 13)$. Find a and b.

8 Find and classify in terms of k the stationary points on the curve $y = kx^3 + 6x^2$.

9 For the graphs of each of the following functions:

  i find the coordinates of the stationary point

  ii say, with reasoning, whether this is a maximum or a minimum point

  iii check your answer by using the method of 'completing the square' to find the vertex

  iv state the range of values which the function can take.

  a $x^2 - 8x + 4$ b $3x^2 + 12x + 5$ c $5x^2 + 6x + 2$

  d $4 - 6x - x^2$ e $x^2 + 6x + 9$ f $1 - 4x - 4x^2$

8.3 Practical maximum and minimum problems

WORKED EXAMPLE 8.3

A closed right circular cylinder of base radius r cm and height h cm has a volume of 54π cm³.

  a Show that the total surface area of the cylinder is given by $S = \dfrac{108\pi}{r} + 2\pi r^2$.

  b Hence find the radius and the height that make the surface area a minimum.

  c Calculate the minimum surface area giving your answer in terms of π.

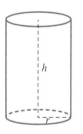

Answer

a $V = \pi r^2 h$ .... Volume of a cylinder (1).

   $S = 2\pi r h + 2\pi r^2$ .... Total surface area of a closed cylinder (2).

   $V = 54\pi$ .... Given. Now equate expressions for the volume.

   $\pi r^2 h = 54\pi$ .... Rearrange.

   $h = \dfrac{54}{r^2}$ .... Substituting into (2).

TIP

This formula for S is an example of one which appears to depend on two different variables (r and h). However, these two variables are related by a particular condition that allows one of the variables to be eliminated. This is common to these types of question.

$$S = 2\pi r\left(\frac{54}{r^2}\right) + 2\pi r^2$$ Simplify.

$$S = \frac{108\pi}{r} + 2\pi r^2$$

b   The maximum/
     minimum area occurs
     when $\frac{dS}{dr} = 0$

$$S = 108\pi r^{-1} + 2\pi r^2$$ Differentiate with respect to r.

$$\frac{dS}{dr} = -108\pi r^{-2} + 4\pi r$$

$$\frac{dS}{dr} = -\frac{108\pi}{r^2} + 4\pi r$$ $\frac{dS}{dr} = 0$

$$4\pi r^3 = 108\pi$$

$$r^3 = 27$$

$$r = 3$$

$$h = \frac{54}{3^2} = 6$$ The height is 6 cm.

As $\frac{dS}{dr} = -108\pi r^{-2} + 4\pi r$ Find $\frac{d^2S}{dr^2}$.

$$\frac{d^2S}{dr^2} = 216\pi r^{-3} + 4\pi$$ When $r = 3$.

$$\frac{d^2S}{dr^2} = \frac{216\pi}{3^3} + 4\pi$$ This is positive so $\frac{d^2S}{dr^2} > 0$ when $r = 3$. This corresponds to a minimum S.

$$\frac{d^2S}{dr^2} = 12\pi$$

So the surface area is
a minimum when the
height is 6 cm and the
radius is 3 cm.

c $$S = \frac{108\pi}{r} + 2\pi r^2$$ Substituting $r = 3$ (or use (2)).

$$S = \frac{108\pi}{3} + 2\pi(3)^2$$

$$S = 36\pi + 18\pi$$

$$S = 54\pi\,\text{cm}^2$$

Minimum surface
area is $54\pi\,\text{cm}^2$

 TIP

Substitute the value
of r that minimises
the quantity back
into the **original
expression** to find
the minimum value
of that quantity.

EXERCISE 8C

1 A rectangle has width x metres and length $30 - x$ metres.

   a Find the maximum area of the rectangle.

   b Show that as x changes the perimeter stays constant and find the value of this perimeter.

2 A square sheet of card of side 12 cm has four squares of side x cm cut from the corners. The sides are then folded to make a small open box.

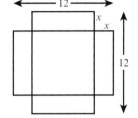

   a Show that the volume, V, is given by $V = x(12 - 2x)^2$.

   b Find the value of x for which the volume is the maximum possible, and prove that it is a maximum.

P 3 Prove that the minimum possible value of the sum of a positive real number and its reciprocal is 2.

4 A solid cylinder has radius r and height h.

   The total surface area of the cylinder is 450 cm^2.

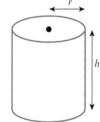

   a Find an expression for the volume of the cylinder in terms of r only.

   b Hence find the maximum possible volume, justifying that the value found is a maximum.

5 A closed carton is in the shape of a cuboid. The base is a square of side x.

   The total surface area is 486 cm^2.

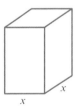

   a Find an expression for the volume of the carton in terms of x only.

   b Hence find the maximum possible volume, justifying that the value found is a maximum.

P 6 A certain type of chocolate is sold in boxes that are in the shape of a triangular prism. The cross-section is an equilateral triangle of side x cm. The length is y cm.

   The volume of the box needs to be 128 cm^3.

   The manufacturer wishes to minimise the surface area.

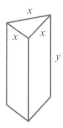

   a Show that $A = \sqrt{3}\left(\dfrac{512}{x} + \dfrac{x^2}{2}\right)$.

   b Find the minimum value of A.

   c Prove that the value found is a minimum.

7   The sum of two numbers x and y is 6, and $x, y \geqslant 0$. Find the two numbers if the sum of their squares is the:

   a   minimum possible

   b   maximum possible.

8   A 20 cm piece of wire is bent to form an isosceles triangle with base b.

   a   Show that the area of the triangle is given by $A = \dfrac{1}{2}\sqrt{100b^2 - 10b^3}$.

   b   Show that the area of the triangle is the largest possible when the triangle is equilateral.

P   9   The sum of the squares of two positive numbers is a. Prove that their product is the maximum possible when the two numbers are equal.

10   A cylinder of radius 6 cm and height 6 cm fits perfectly inside a cone, leaving a constant ring of width x around the base of the cylinder.

   a   Show that the height, h, of the cone is $h = \dfrac{36}{x} + 6$.

   b   Find the volume of the cone in terms of x.

   c   Hence find the minimum value of the volume, justifying that the value you have found is a minimum.

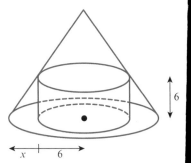

8.4 Rates of change

WORKED EXAMPLE 8.4

Find the rate of change of the function $f(x) = 2x^2 + x - 3$ at the instant when $x = 4$.

Answer

$f(x) = 2x^2 + x - 3$	For the instantaneous rate of change, calculate $f'(x)$.
$f'(x) = 4x + 1$	The instantaneous rate of change at $x = 4$ is found by substituting $x = 4$ into $f'(x)$.
$f'(4) = 4(4) + 1$	
$\quad = 17$	

EXERCISE 8D

1 A point with coordinates (x, y) moves along the curve $y = 2x + \sqrt{4x + 1}$ in such a way that the rate of increase of x has the constant value 0.09 units per second. Find the rate of increase of y at the instant when $x = 2$. State whether the y-coordinate is increasing or decreasing.

PS 2 A point is moving along the curve $y = \dfrac{6}{\sqrt{x}} - 2\sqrt{x}$ in such a way that the x-coordinate is increasing at a constant rate of 0.01 units per second. Find the rate of change of the y-coordinate when $x = 1$.

3 In each of the following cases, find an expression for $\dfrac{\mathrm{d}z}{\mathrm{d}x}$ in terms of x:

    a $z = 4y^2,\ y = 3x^2$ **b** $z = y^2,\ y = x^3 + 1$

4 **a** **i** Given that $z = y^2 + 1$ and $\dfrac{\mathrm{d}y}{\mathrm{d}x} = 5$, find $\dfrac{\mathrm{d}z}{\mathrm{d}x}$ when $y = 5$.

      ii Given that $z = 2y^3$ and $\dfrac{\mathrm{d}y}{\mathrm{d}x} = -2$, find $\dfrac{\mathrm{d}z}{\mathrm{d}x}$ when $y = 1$.

   b **i** Given that $V = 12r^3$, $\dfrac{\mathrm{d}r}{\mathrm{d}t} = 1$ and $\dfrac{\mathrm{d}V}{\mathrm{d}t} = 4$, find the possible values of r.

      ii Given that $H = 3S^{-2}$, find the value of S for which $\dfrac{\mathrm{d}H}{\mathrm{d}x} = 3$ and $\dfrac{\mathrm{d}S}{\mathrm{d}x} = 4$.

5 **a** **i** Given that $A = xy$, find $\dfrac{\mathrm{d}A}{\mathrm{d}t}$ when $x = 4$, $y = 5$, $\dfrac{\mathrm{d}x}{\mathrm{d}t} = 2$ and $\dfrac{\mathrm{d}y}{\mathrm{d}t} = 3$.

      ii Given that $S = ab$, find $\dfrac{\mathrm{d}S}{\mathrm{d}t}$ when $a = 12$, $b = 5$, $\dfrac{\mathrm{d}a}{\mathrm{d}t} = -2$ and $\dfrac{\mathrm{d}b}{\mathrm{d}t} = 4$.

   b **i** Given that $V = 3r^2h$, find $\dfrac{\mathrm{d}V}{\mathrm{d}t}$ when $r = 3$, $h = 2$, $\dfrac{\mathrm{d}r}{\mathrm{d}t} = 2$ and $\dfrac{\mathrm{d}h}{\mathrm{d}t} = -1$.

      ii Given that $N = kx^4$, find $\dfrac{\mathrm{d}N}{\mathrm{d}t}$ when $x = 2$, $k = 5$, $\dfrac{\mathrm{d}k}{\mathrm{d}t} = 1$ and $\dfrac{\mathrm{d}x}{\mathrm{d}t} = 1$.

   c **i** Given that $m = \dfrac{S}{N}$ and that $S = 100$, $\dfrac{\mathrm{d}S}{\mathrm{d}t} = 20$, $N = 50$ and $\dfrac{\mathrm{d}N}{\mathrm{d}t} = 4$, find $\dfrac{\mathrm{d}m}{\mathrm{d}t}$.

      ii Given that $\rho = \dfrac{m}{V}$ and that $m = 24$, $\dfrac{\mathrm{d}m}{\mathrm{d}t} = 2$, $V = 120$ and $\dfrac{\mathrm{d}V}{\mathrm{d}t} = 6$, find $\dfrac{\mathrm{d}\rho}{\mathrm{d}t}$.

PS 6 A point is moving in the plane so that its coordinates are both functions of time, $(x(t), y(t))$. When the coordinates of the point are $(5, 7)$, the x-coordinate is increasing at the rate of 16 units per second and the y-coordinate is increasing at the rate of 12 units per second. At what rate is the distance of the point from the origin changing at this instant?

7 The sum of two real numbers x and y is 12. Find the maximum value of their product xy.

8 The product of two positive real numbers x and y is 20. Find the minimum possible value of their sum.

8.5 Practical applications of connected rates of change

WORKED EXAMPLE 8.5

A spherical balloon is being inflated at a constant rate of $5\,\text{m}^3\text{sec}^{-1}$.

At a particular instant the balloon's radius is 4 metres.

Find how fast the radius of the balloon is increasing at that instant.

Answer

$V =$ volume of air in the balloon in m^3 •••••• Define the variables.

$r =$ the radius of the balloon in m

$t =$ time in seconds

$$\frac{dV}{dt} = \frac{dV}{dr} \times \frac{dr}{dt} \quad \text{------- (1)}$$ The 3 variables are connected by the chain rule.

$\dfrac{dV}{dt} = 5$ is the rate of change of volume of the spherical balloon

$\dfrac{dr}{dt}$ is required

$V = \dfrac{4}{3}\pi r^3$ •••••• Differentiating to find $\dfrac{dV}{dr}$.

$\dfrac{dV}{dr} = 4\pi r^2$ •••••• Substitute into (1).

$5 = 4\pi r^2 \times \dfrac{dr}{dt}$ •••••• Substitute $r = 4$ and $\dfrac{dV}{dt} = 5$.

$5 = 4\pi(4)^2 \times \dfrac{dr}{dt}$

$5 = 64\pi \times \dfrac{dr}{dt}$ •••••• Rearrange.

$\dfrac{dr}{dt} = 5 \times \dfrac{1}{64\pi}$

The radius is increasing at $\dfrac{5}{64\pi}\,\text{m sec}^{-1}$.

EXERCISE 8E

1 The length of the side of a square is increasing at a constant rate of $1.2\,\text{cm s}^{-1}$. At the moment when the length of the side is 10 cm, find:

   a the rate of increase of the perimeter

   b the rate of increase of the area.

2 The length of the edge of a cube is increasing at a constant rate of $0.5\,\text{mm}\,\text{s}^{-1}$. At the moment when the length of the edge is $40\,\text{mm}$, find:

   a the rate of increase of the surface area

   b the rate of increase of the volume.

3 The area of a square is increasing at the constant rate of $50\,\text{cm}^2\,\text{s}^{-1}$. Find the rate of increase of the side of the square when the length of the side is $12.5\,\text{cm}$.

4 A spherical ball is inflated so that its radius increases at the rate of $3\,\text{cm}$ per second. Find the rate of change of the volume when the radius is $12\,\text{cm}$.

5 A rectangle has length a and width b. Both the length and the width are increasing at a constant rate of $3\,\text{cm}$ per second. Find the rate of increase of the area of the rectangle at the instant when $a = 10\,\text{cm}$ and $b = 15\,\text{cm}$.

6 The surface area of a closed cylinder is given by $A = 2\pi r^2 + 2\pi rh$, where h is the height and r is the radius of the base. At the time when the surface area is increasing at the rate of $20\pi\,\text{cm}^2\,\text{s}^{-1}$, the radius is $4\,\text{cm}$, the height is $1\,\text{cm}$ and is decreasing at the rate of $2\,\text{cm}\,\text{s}^{-1}$. Find the rate of change of the radius at this time.

7 The radius of a cone is increasing at the rate of $0.5\,\text{cm}\,\text{s}^{-1}$ and its height is decreasing at the rate of $0.3\,\text{cm}\,\text{s}^{-1}$. Find the rate of change of the volume of the cone at the instant when the radius is $20\,\text{cm}$ and the height is $30\,\text{cm}$.

8 A spherical star is collapsing in size, while remaining spherical. When its radius is one million kilometres, the radius is decreasing at the rate of $500\,\text{km}\,\text{s}^{-1}$. Find:

   a the rate of decrease of its volume

   b the rate of decrease of its surface area.

9 The surface area of a cube is increasing at a constant rate of $24\,\text{cm}^2\,\text{s}^{-1}$. Find the rate at which the volume is increasing at the moment when the volume is $216\,\text{cm}^3$.

10 An underground oil storage tank $ABCDEFGH$ is part of an inverted square pyramid, as shown in the diagram. The complete pyramid has a square base of side $12\,\text{m}$ and height $18\,\text{m}$. The depth of the tank is $12\,\text{m}$.

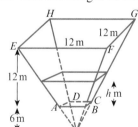

   a When the depth of oil in the tank is h metres, show that the volume $V\,\text{m}^3$ is given by $V = \dfrac{4}{27}(h+6)^3 - 32$.

   Oil is being added to the tank at the constant rate of $4.5\,\text{m}^3\text{s}^{-1}$.

   b At the moment when the depth of oil is $8\,\text{m}$, find the rate at which the depth is increasing.

1   $y = x^2 + ax - 7$ is increasing for $x > 5$. Find a.

2   The diagram shows the graph of $y = f'(x)$.

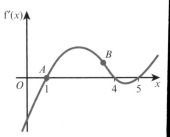

    a   State the value of the gradient of the graph of $y = f(x)$ at the point marked A.

    b   Is the function $f(x)$ increasing or decreasing at the point marked B?

    c   Sketch the graph of $y = f(x)$.

PS   3   A rectangle is drawn inside the region bounded by the curve $y = 4 - x^2$ and the x-axis, so that two of the vertices lie on the axis and the other two on the curve.

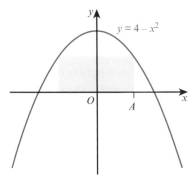

Find the coordinates of vertex A so that the area of the rectangle is the maximum possible.

4   $y = \dfrac{1}{3}x^3 - ax^2 + 3ax + 1$ where $a \neq 0$ has one stationary point. What is the value of a?

5   The curve $y = ax^3 + bx^2 + 8x - 1$ has stationary points at $x = \dfrac{1}{3}$ and $x = 4$. Find a and b.

6   A gardener is planting a lawn in the shape of a sector of a circle joined to a rectangle.

The sector has radius r and angle $\dfrac{2\pi}{3}$ radians.

He needs the area, A, of the lawn to be $200\,\text{m}^2$.

A fence is to be built around the perimeter of the lawn.

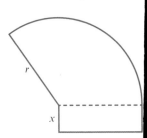

    a   Show that the length of the fence, P, is given by $P = 2r + \dfrac{400}{r}$.

    b   Hence find the minimum length of fence required, justifying that this value is a minimum.

7   A water tank has a rectangular base $1.5\,\text{m}$ by $1.2\,\text{m}$. The sides are vertical and water is being added to the tank at a constant rate of $0.45\,\text{m}^3$ per minute. At what rate is the depth of water in the tank increasing?

124

8   Air is being lost from a spherical balloon at a constant rate of $0.6\,\mathrm{m^3\,s^{-1}}$. Find the rate at which the radius is decreasing at the instant when the radius is $2.5\,\mathrm{m}$.

9   A funnel has a circular top of diameter $20\,\mathrm{cm}$ and a height of $30\,\mathrm{cm}$. When the depth of liquid in the funnel is $12\,\mathrm{cm}$, the liquid is dripping from the funnel at a rate of $0.2\,\mathrm{cm^3\,s^{-1}}$. At what rate is the depth of the liquid in the funnel decreasing at this instant?

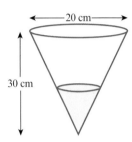

Chapter 9
Integration

- Understand integration as the reverse process of differentiation, and integrate $(ax + b)^n$ (for any rational n except -1), together with constant multiples, sums and differences.
- Solve problems involving the evaluation of a constant of integration.
- Evaluate definite integrals.
- Use definite integration to find the:
  - area of a region bounded by a curve and lines parallel to the axes, or between a curve and a line or between two curves
  - a volume of revolution about one of the axes.

9.1 Integration as the reverse of differentiation

WORKED EXAMPLE 9.1

Find the following integrals:

a $\dfrac{dy}{dx} = \dfrac{7x^2}{10\sqrt{x}}$

b $f'(x) = \dfrac{1}{2x^{\frac{3}{2}}}$

c $\displaystyle\int (x^2 - 1)^2 \, dx$

Answer

a $\dfrac{dy}{dx} = \dfrac{7x^2}{10x^{\frac{1}{2}}}$

$\dfrac{dy}{dx} = \dfrac{7}{10}x^{\frac{3}{2}}$

$y = \dfrac{7}{25}x^{\frac{5}{2}} + c$

b $f'(x) = \dfrac{x^{-\frac{3}{2}}}{2}$

$f'(x) = \dfrac{1}{2}x^{-\frac{3}{2}}$

$f(x) = -x^{-\frac{1}{2}} + c$

$f(x) = -\dfrac{1}{\sqrt{x}} + c$

c $\displaystyle\int (x^4 - 2x^2 + 1) \, dx$

$\displaystyle\int (x^4 - 2x^2 + 1x^0) \, dx$

$\dfrac{1}{5}x^5 - \dfrac{2}{3}x^3 + x + c$

EXERCISE 9A

1 Find a general expression for the function $f(x)$ in each of the following cases.

a $f'(x) = 4x^3$

b $f'(x) = 6x^5$

c $f'(x) = 2x$

d $f'(x) = 3x^2 + 5x^4$

e $f'(x) = 10x^9 - 8x^7 - 1$

f $f'(x) = -7x^6 + 3x^2 + 1$

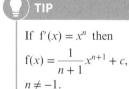

TIP

If $f'(x) = x^n$ then

$f(x) = \dfrac{1}{n+1}x^{n+1} + c$,

$n \neq -1$.

2 Find the following integrals.

$$\int [f(x) \pm g(x)]\,dx =$$

$$\int f(x)\,dx \pm \int g(x)\,dx$$

a i $\int x^{\frac{2}{3}}\,dx$ ii $\int x^{\frac{1}{3}}\,dx$

b i $\int 5x^{\frac{2}{3}}\,dx$ ii $\int 14x^{\frac{3}{4}}\,dx$

c i $\int \frac{5}{4}x^{\frac{1}{4}}\,dx$ ii $\int -\frac{3}{2}x^{\frac{1}{2}}\,dx$

d i $\int -\frac{7x^{\frac{4}{3}}}{6}\,dx$ ii $\int \frac{14x^{\frac{2}{5}}}{15}\,dx$

e i $\int 5x - 7x^{\frac{5}{2}}\,dx$ ii $\int 6 + \frac{x}{3} - 12x^{\frac{1}{2}}\,dx$

f i $\int x^{-2}\,dx$ ii $\int x^{-3}\,dx$

g i $\int x^{-\frac{1}{3}}\,dx$ ii $\int x^{-\frac{1}{4}}\,dx$

h i $\int -4x^{-\frac{2}{3}}\,dx$ ii $\int -5x^{-\frac{3}{2}}\,dx$

i i $\int x^{-\frac{1}{2}} - \frac{6x^{-4}}{5}\,dx$ ii $\int 3x^{-5} + 7x^{-\frac{1}{6}}\,dx$

3 If $f'(x) = \frac{x^3}{2} - 6x^{-\frac{5}{3}} + 2$, find $f(x)$.

4 Find the following integrals.

a i $\int (2x + 3)(x + 1)\,dx$ ii $\int 3x^2(x - 2)\,dx$

b i $\int \sqrt{x}(5x + 4)\,dx$ ii $\int \sqrt[3]{x}(2x^2 + 3)\,dx$

c i $\int (\sqrt[4]{x} + 3x)^2\,dx$ ii $\int (\sqrt{x} - x^2)^2\,dx$

d i $\int \left(x - \frac{1}{x}\right)^2\,dx$ ii $\int \left(2x + \frac{1}{x^2}\right)\left(2x - \frac{1}{x^2}\right)\,dx$

5 Find the following integrals.

a i $\int \frac{7x - 2}{x^3}\,dx$ ii $\int \frac{2 + 5x}{4x^3}\,dx$

b i $\int \frac{\sqrt{x} - 3}{x^2}\,dx$ ii $\int \frac{x^2 - 6x}{\sqrt{x}}\,dx$

6 $y = \frac{(x + 2)(x - 2)}{2\sqrt{x}}$

a Show that $y = ax^{\frac{3}{2}} + bx^{-\frac{1}{2}}$, where a and b are constants to be found.

b Hence find $\int y\,dx$.

7   Show that $\int 12\sqrt{x} - \dfrac{4}{\sqrt{x}} \, dx = 8\sqrt{x}(x-1) + c$.

8   Find $\int \dfrac{(x+4)^2}{8x\sqrt{x}} \, dx$.

9.2 Finding the constant of integration

WORKED EXAMPLE 9.2

A curve is such that $\dfrac{dy}{dx} = 12x^3 - \dfrac{1}{x^2}$, and $(1, 2)$ is a point on the curve.

Find the equation of the curve.

Answer

$\dfrac{dy}{dx} = 12x^3 - \dfrac{1}{x^2}$ .... Write in index form ready for integration.

$\quad = 12x^3 - x^{-2}$ .... Don't forget the $+ c$. It is a part of the answer.

$y = \dfrac{12}{4}x^4 + x^{-1} + c$

$\quad = 3x^4 + \dfrac{1}{x} + c$ .... Use the point $(1, 2)$ to find the value of c.

When $x = 1, y = 2$

$2 = 3(1)^4 + \dfrac{1}{1} + c$

$2 = 3 + 1 + c$

$c = -2$

The equation of the curve is

$y = 3x^4 + \dfrac{1}{x} - 2$.

EXERCISE 9B

1   Find the equation of the curve if:

   a **i** $\dfrac{dy}{dx} = x$ and the curve passes through $(-2, 7)$

      ii $\dfrac{dy}{dx} = 6x^2$ and the curve passes through $(0, 5)$

   b **i** $\dfrac{dy}{dx} = \dfrac{1}{x^2}$ and the curve passes through $(1, -1)$

      ii $\dfrac{dy}{dx} = \dfrac{1}{x^2}$ and the curve passes through $(1, 3)$

c i $\dfrac{dy}{dx} = 3x - 5$ and the curve passes through $(2, 6)$

ii $\dfrac{dy}{dx} = 3 - 2x^3$ and the curve passes through $(1, 5)$

d i $\dfrac{dy}{dx} = 3\sqrt{x}$ and the curve passes through $(9, -2)$

ii $\dfrac{dy}{dx} = \dfrac{1}{\sqrt{x}}$ and the curve passes through $(4, 8)$

2 A curve has gradient $\dfrac{dy}{dx} = x - \dfrac{1}{x^2}$ and passes through the point $(1, 3)$. Find the equation of the curve.

3 $f'(x) = \dfrac{2x - 1}{\sqrt{x}}$ and $f(4) = 2$. Find $f(x)$.

4 $f'(x) = \sqrt{x}(5x - 4)$ and $f(1) = \dfrac{19}{3}$. Find $f(4)$.

5 The gradient of a curve at any point is directly proportional to the x-coordinate of the point. The curve passes through point A with coordinates $(3, 2)$. The gradient of the curve at A is 12. Find the equation of the curve.

6 The gradient of a curve is $\dfrac{dy}{dx} = x^2 - 4$.

a Find the x-coordinate of the maximum point, justifying that it is a maximum.

b Given that the curve passes through the point $(0, 2)$ show that the y-coordinate of the maximum point is $7\frac{1}{3}$.

7 The gradient of the normal to a curve at any point is equal to the square of the x-coordinate at that point. If the curve passes through the point $(2, 3)$, find the equation of the curve in the form $y = f(x)$.

8 A tree is growing so that, after t years, its height is increasing at a rate of $\dfrac{30}{\sqrt[3]{t}}$ cm per year. Assume that, when $t = 0$, the height is 5 cm.

a Find the height of the tree after 4 years.

b After how many years will the height be 4.1 metres?

9 The function $f(x)$ is such that $f'(x) = 9x^2 + 4x + c$, where c is a particular constant. Given that $f(2) = 14$ and $f(3) = 74$, find the value of $f(4)$.

9.3 Integration of expressions of the form $(ax + b)^n$

WORKED EXAMPLE 9.3

Find:

a $\displaystyle\int (2 - 3x)^4\, dx$

b $\displaystyle\int \dfrac{12}{(2x - 3)^5}\, dx$

c $\displaystyle\int \dfrac{2}{\sqrt[3]{3x + 7}}\, dx$

Answer

a $\quad \int (2-3x)^4\,dx = \dfrac{1}{-3(4+1)}(2-3x)^{4+1} + c$

$\qquad\qquad = -\dfrac{1}{15}(2-3x)^5 + c$

b $\quad \displaystyle\int \dfrac{12}{(2x-3)^5}\,dx = 12\int (2x-3)^{-5}\,dx$

$\qquad\qquad = \dfrac{12}{(2)(-5+1)}(2x-3)^{-5+1} + c$

$\qquad\qquad = -\dfrac{3}{2}(2x-3)^{-4} + c$

$\qquad\qquad = -\dfrac{3}{2(2x-3)^4} + c$

c $\quad \displaystyle\int \dfrac{2}{\sqrt[3]{3x+7}}\,dx = 2\int (3x+7)^{-\frac{1}{3}}\,dx$

$\qquad\qquad = \dfrac{2}{3\left(-\dfrac{1}{3}+1\right)}(3x+7)^{-\frac{1}{3}+1} + c$

$\qquad\qquad = \sqrt[3]{(3x+7)^2} + c$

EXERCISE 9C

1 Find the following indefinite integrals.

a i $\quad \displaystyle\int 5(x+3)^4\,dx$
ii $\quad \displaystyle\int (x-2)^5\,dx$

b i $\quad \displaystyle\int (4x-5)^7\,dx$
ii $\quad \displaystyle\int \left(\dfrac{1}{8}x+1\right)^3\,dx$

c i $\quad \displaystyle\int 4\left(3-\dfrac{1}{2}x\right)^6\,dx$
ii $\quad \displaystyle\int (4-x)^8\,dx$

d i $\quad \displaystyle\int \sqrt{2x-1}\,dx$
ii $\quad \displaystyle\int 7(2-5x)^{\frac{3}{4}}\,dx$

e i $\quad \displaystyle\int \dfrac{1}{\sqrt[4]{2+\dfrac{x}{3}}}\,dx$
ii $\quad \displaystyle\int \dfrac{6}{(4-3x)^2}\,dx$

2 Integrate the following with respect to x.

a $\quad (2x+1)^6$
b $\quad (3x-5)^4$
c $\quad (1-7x)^3$
d $\quad \left(\dfrac{1}{2}x+1\right)^{10}$

e $\quad (5x+2)^{-3}$
f $\quad 2(1-3x)^{-2}$
g $\quad \dfrac{1}{(x+1)^5}$
h $\quad \dfrac{3}{2(4x+1)^4}$

i $\quad \sqrt{10x+1}$
j $\quad \dfrac{1}{\sqrt{2x-1}}$
k $\quad \left(\dfrac{1}{2}x+2\right)^{\frac{2}{3}}$
l $\quad \dfrac{8}{\sqrt[4]{2+6x}}$

3 Find the equation of the curve, given $\dfrac{dy}{dx}$ and a point P on the curve.

   a $\dfrac{dy}{dx} = (x - 2)^3 \qquad P = (3, 4)$

   b $\dfrac{dy}{dx} = \sqrt{4 - x} \qquad P = (0, 2)$

   c $\dfrac{dy}{dx} = \dfrac{1}{\sqrt{3x - 5}} \qquad P = (2, 1)$

   d $\dfrac{dy}{dx} = \dfrac{3}{(1 - 3x)^3} \qquad P = \left(0, \dfrac{1}{2}\right)$

4 A curve is such that $\dfrac{dy}{dx} = k(2x - 1)^2$, where k is a constant. The gradient of the normal to the curve at the point $(1, 5)$ is $-\dfrac{1}{6}$. Find the equation of the curve.

5 A curve is such that $\dfrac{dy}{dx} = k - x^{-\frac{1}{2}}$, where $x > 0$. Given that the curve passes through the points $A(1, -2)$ and $B(4, 5)$ find:

   a the value of k

   b the equation of the normal to the curve at A.

6 A curve is such that $\dfrac{dy}{dx} = 10x^{\frac{3}{2}} - 2x^{-\frac{1}{2}}$, where $x \geqslant 0$. Given that the curve passes through the point $(0, 7)$ find the equation of the curve.

(PS) **7** A spot of ink is dropped on a cloth and the resulting stain begins increasing in area at the rate of $\dfrac{2}{\sqrt{t}}$ cm² per minute. Assuming that it grows as an irregular shape, how long (in minutes) will it take for the stain to have an area of $40\,\text{cm}^2$?

8 A curve is such that $\dfrac{dy}{dx} = 3x^2 - 4x - 1$. Given that the tangent to the curve at a point A with x-coordinate 2 passes through the origin, find the equation for this curve.

9.4 Further indefinite integration

WORKED EXAMPLE 9.4

   a Show that $\dfrac{d}{dx} = \left[(3x^2 - 4)^5\right] = 30x\,(3x^2 - 4)^4$.

   b Hence find $\displaystyle\int 6x(3x^2 - 4)^4 dx$.

Answer

   a Let $y = (3x^2 - 4)^5$ ··········   Chain rule.

        $\dfrac{dy}{dx} = (6x)(5)(3x^2 - 4)^{5-1}$

        $= 30x(3x^2 - 4)^4$

b $\displaystyle\int 6x(3x^2 - 4)^4\,dx = \frac{1}{5}\int 30x(3x^2 - 4)^5\,dx$

$$= \frac{1}{5}(3x^2 - 4)^5 + c$$

EXERCISE 9D

1 a Differentiate $(x^2 + 3)^5$ with respect to x.

   b Hence find $\displaystyle\int 2x(x^2 + 2)^4\,dx$.

2 a Differentiate $(2 - 3x^2)^5$ with respect to x.

   b Hence find $\displaystyle\int x(2 - 3x^2)^4\,dx$.

3 a Given that $y = \dfrac{1}{3x^2 - 1}$, show that $\dfrac{dy}{dx} = \dfrac{kx}{(3x^2 - 1)^2}$ and state the value of k.

   b Hence find $\displaystyle\int \frac{4x}{(3x^2 - 1)^2}\,dx$.

4 a Differentiate $\dfrac{1}{(1 - 2x^2)^3}$ with respect to x.

   b Hence find $\displaystyle\int \frac{3x}{(1 - 2x^2)^4}\,dx$.

5 a Differentiate $(x^2 - 4)^4$ with respect to x.

   b Hence find $\displaystyle\int 4x(x^2 - 4)^3\,dx$.

6 a Differentiate $(\sqrt{x} + 1)^5$ with respect to x.

   b Hence find $\displaystyle\int \frac{(\sqrt{x} + 1)^4}{\sqrt{x}}\,dx$.

9.5 Definite integration

WORKED EXAMPLE 9.5

Evaluate:

a $\displaystyle\int_1^3 \frac{3x^3 - 1}{x^2}\,dx$
      b $\displaystyle\int_0^4 \sqrt{2x + 1}\,dx$
      c $\displaystyle\int_{-3}^2 \frac{4}{(5 - x)^3}\,dx$

Answer

a $\displaystyle \int_1^3 \frac{3x^3 - 1}{x^2}\,\mathrm{d}x = \int_1^3 (3x - x^{-2})\,\mathrm{d}x$

$\displaystyle = \left[\frac{3}{2}x^2 + x^{-1}\right]_1^3$

Use square brackets to indicate that the integration has taken place but the limits are still to be applied.

$\displaystyle = \left(\frac{3}{2}(3)^2 + (3)^{-1}\right) - \left(\frac{3}{2}(1)^2 + (1)^{-1}\right)$

$\displaystyle = \left(\frac{27}{2} + \frac{1}{3}\right) - \left(\frac{3}{2} + 1\right)$

$\displaystyle = 11\frac{1}{3}$

b $\displaystyle \int_0^4 \sqrt{2x+1}\,\mathrm{d}x = \int_0^4 (2x+1)^{\frac{1}{2}}\,\mathrm{d}x$

$\displaystyle = \left[\frac{1}{(2)\left(\frac{3}{2}\right)}(2x+1)^{\frac{3}{2}}\right]_0^4$

$\displaystyle = \left[\frac{1}{3}(2x+1)^{\frac{3}{2}}\right]_0^4$

$\displaystyle = \left(\frac{1}{3}\times 9^{\frac{3}{2}}\right) - \left(\frac{1}{3}\times 1^{\frac{3}{2}}\right)$

$\displaystyle = 9 - \left(\frac{1}{3}\right)$

$\displaystyle = 8\frac{2}{3}$

c $\displaystyle \int_{-3}^2 \frac{4}{(5-x)^3}\,\mathrm{d}x = \int_{-3}^2 4(5-x)^{-3}\,\mathrm{d}x$

$\displaystyle = \left[\frac{4}{(-1)(-2)}(5-x)^{-2}\right]_{-3}^2$

$\displaystyle = \left[\frac{2}{(5-x)^2}\right]_{-3}^2$

$\displaystyle = \left(\frac{2}{9}\right) - \left(\frac{2}{64}\right)$

$\displaystyle = \frac{55}{288}$

1 Evaluate the following definite integrals, giving exact answers.

TIP

$$\int_a^b [f(x) \pm g(x)]\,dx =$$

$$\int_a^b f(x)\,dx \pm \int_a^b g(x)\,dx$$

a i $\displaystyle\int_2^6 x^3\,dx$　　　　　ii $\displaystyle\int_4^5 x^4\,dx$

b i $\displaystyle\int_{-2}^2 3x^5\,dx$　　　　ii $\displaystyle\int_{-3}^3 2x^2\,dx$

c i $\displaystyle\int_{-3}^{-1} 6x^2 - 3\,dx$　　ii $\displaystyle\int_{-4}^{-2} 3x^2 - 4\,dx$

d i $\displaystyle\int_1^4 x^2 + x\,dx$　　　ii $\displaystyle\int_{-2}^1 3x^2 - 5x\,dx$

e i $\displaystyle\int_4^9 2\sqrt{x}\,dx$　　　　ii $\displaystyle\int_8^{27} 6\sqrt[3]{x}\,dx$

f i $\displaystyle\int_1^{16} \frac{6}{\sqrt{x}}\,dx$　　　　ii $\displaystyle\int_{-3}^{-1} \frac{3}{x^2}\,dx$

g i $\displaystyle\int_{-4}^{-2} 1 + \frac{2}{x^2}\,dx$　　ii $\displaystyle\int_{-3}^{-1} 2x - \frac{1}{x^2}\,dx$

2 Evaluate the following definite integrals.

a $\displaystyle\int_0^8 12\sqrt[3]{x}\,dx$　　　b $\displaystyle\int_1^2 \frac{3}{x^2}\,dx$　　　c $\displaystyle\int_1^4 \frac{10}{\sqrt{x}}\,dx$

d $\displaystyle\int_1^2 \left(\frac{8}{x^3} + x^3\right)dx$　　e $\displaystyle\int_4^9 \frac{2\sqrt{x}+3}{\sqrt{x}}\,dx$　　f $\displaystyle\int_1^8 \frac{1}{\sqrt[3]{x^2}}\,dx$

3 Evaluate the following integral, giving your answer in the form
$$a + b\sqrt{2}: \int_2^8 3\sqrt{x} - 2x\,dx.$$

4 Show that $\displaystyle\int_1^3 9\sqrt{x} - \frac{4}{\sqrt{x}}\,dx = a + b\sqrt{3}$, where a and b are integers to be found.

5 Find the following in terms of k: $\displaystyle\int_1^k 2 - \frac{1}{x^2}\,dx$.

6 Find the following in terms of a: $\displaystyle\int_{-a}^2 x^2(4x - 3)\,dx$.

7 Find the value of a such that $\displaystyle\int_1^a \sqrt{t}\,dt = 42$.

8 $\displaystyle\int_{-2}^p 1 - \frac{10}{3x^2}\,dx = -\frac{2}{3}$

Find all possible values of p.

9.6 Area under a curve

TIP

Remember when areas are above and below the x-axis in the same question, you evaluate each area separately.

WORKED EXAMPLE 9.6

Find the total area of the shaded regions.

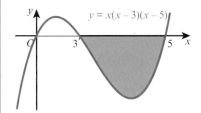

Answer

$$\int_0^3 x(x-3)(x-5)\,\mathrm{d}x = \int_0^3 (x^3 - 8x^2 + 15x)\,\mathrm{d}x$$

$$= \left[\frac{1}{4}x^4 - \frac{8}{3}x^3 + \frac{15}{2}x^2\right]_0^3$$

$$= \left(\frac{1}{4}(3)^4 - \frac{8}{3}(3)^3 + \frac{15}{2}(3)^2\right) - \left(\frac{1}{4}(0)^4 - \frac{8}{3}(0)^3 + \frac{15}{2}(0)^2\right)$$

$$= \left(15\tfrac{3}{4}\right) - (0)$$

$$= 15\tfrac{3}{4}$$

$$\int_3^5 x(x-3)(x-5)\,\mathrm{d}x = \int_3^5 (x^3 - 8x^2 + 15x)\,\mathrm{d}x$$

$$= \left[\frac{1}{4}x^4 - \frac{8}{3}x^3 + \frac{15}{2}x^2\right]_3^5$$

$$= \left(\frac{1}{4}(5)^4 - \frac{8}{3}(5)^3 + \frac{15}{2}(5)^2\right) - \left(\frac{1}{4}(3)^4 - \frac{8}{3}(3)^3 + \frac{15}{2}(3)^2\right)$$

$$= \left(\frac{125}{12}\right) - \left(\frac{63}{4}\right)$$

$$= -5\tfrac{1}{3}$$

Hence, the total area of the shaded regions $= 5\tfrac{1}{3} + 15\tfrac{3}{4} = 21\tfrac{1}{12}$ units^2.

1 Find the shaded areas.

a i

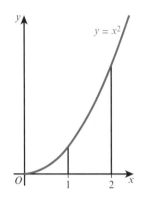

ii

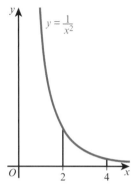

b i

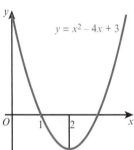

ii

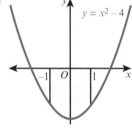

c i

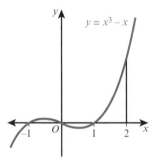

ii

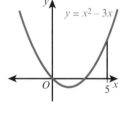

2 Find the following areas. You may want to sketch the graph first.

a i Between the curve $y = x^2 + 2$, the x-axis and the lines $x = 2$ and $x = 5$.

ii Between the curve $y = 2x^2 + 1$, the x-axis and the lines $x = 1$ and $x = 2$.

b i Enclosed between the graph of $y = 4 - x^2$ and the x-axis.

ii Enclosed between the graph of $y = x^2 - 1$ and the x-axis.

c i Enclosed between the curve $y = x^2 - 9x$ and the x-axis.

ii Enclosed between the curve $y = x^3 - 3x^2 + 2x$ and the x-axis.

 TIP

Always sketch the graph first (if it is not given) when asked to find an area.

3 The diagram shows the graph of $y = \sqrt{x}$. The shaded area is 18.

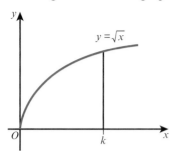

Find the value of k.

4 a Write down the coordinates of the points where the graph of $y = x^2 - kx$ crosses the x-axis.

b The area shaded in the diagram is bounded by the curve $y = x^2 - kx$, the x-axis and the lines $x = 0$ and $x = 3$. The area below the x-axis equals the area above the x-axis. Find the value of k.

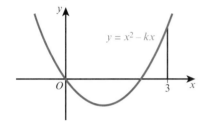

5 The diagram shows the curve $y = \sqrt{3x + 1}$. The shaded region is bounded by the curve, the y-axis and the line $y = 4$. Find the area of the shaded region.

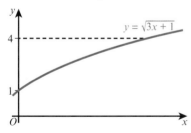

6 Find the exact area of the region bounded by the curve $y = 2x^2 + 2$, the line $y = 10$ and the y-axis.

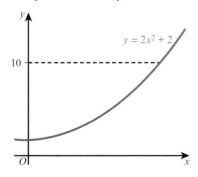

137

7 a Show that $\dfrac{d}{dx}(\sqrt{2x^2 + 3}) = \dfrac{2x}{\sqrt{2x^2 + 3}}$.

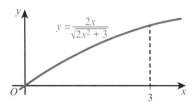

b Use your result from part **a** to evaluate the area of the shaded region.

PS 8

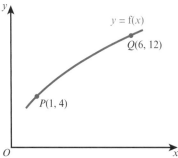

The figure shows part of the curve $y = f(x)$. The points $P(1, 4)$ and $Q(6, 12)$ lie on the curve. Given that $\displaystyle\int_1^6 y\,dx = 30$, find the value of $\displaystyle\int_4^{12} x\,dy$.

PS 9 Given that $f(x)$ and $g(x)$ are two functions such that $\displaystyle\int_0^4 f(x)\,dx = 17$ and $\displaystyle\int_0^4 g(x)\,dx = 11$, find, where possible, the value of each of the following.

a $\displaystyle\int_0^4 (f(x) - g(x))\,dx$ b $\displaystyle\int_0^4 (2f(x) + 3g(x))\,dx$ c $\displaystyle\int_0^2 f(x)\,dx$

d $\displaystyle\int_0^4 (f(x) + 2x + 3)\,dx$ e $\displaystyle\int_0^1 f(x)\,dx + \int_1^4 f(x)\,dx$ f $\displaystyle\int_{-4}^0 g(x)\,dx$

g $\displaystyle\int_1^5 f(x - 1)\,dx$ h $\displaystyle\int_{-4}^0 g(-t)\,dt$

9.7 Area bounded by a curve and a line or by two curves

 TIP

$A = \displaystyle\int_a^b f(x)\,dx - \int_a^b g(x)\,dx$ is equivalent to $A = \displaystyle\int_a^b [f(x) - g(x)]\,dx$

WORKED EXAMPLE 9.7

The diagram shows the curve $y = -x^2 + 11x - 24$ and the line $y = 12 - 2x$, which intersect when $x = 4$ and $x = 9$.

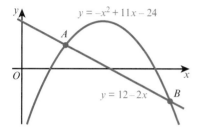

$y = -x^2 + 11x - 24$

$y = 12 - 2x$

Find the area of the shaded region.

Answer

$$\text{Area} = \int_4^9 (-x^2 + 11x - 24)\,dx - \int_4^9 (12 - 2x)\,dx$$

$$= \int_4^9 (-x^2 + 13x - 36)\,dx$$

$$= \left[-\frac{1}{3}x^3 + \frac{13}{2}x^2 - 36x \right]_4^9$$

$$= \left(-\frac{1}{3}(9)^3 + \frac{13}{2}(9)^2 - 36(9) \right) - \left(-\frac{1}{3}(4)^3 + \frac{13}{2}(4)^2 - 36(4) \right)$$

$$= 20\frac{5}{6}\,\text{units}^2$$

EXERCISE 9G

1 The curve in the diagram has equation $y = \sqrt{x}$.

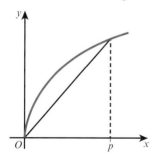

Find the shaded area in terms of p.

139

2 The diagram shows a part of the parabola $y = a^2 - x^2$. Point p has x-coordinate $\dfrac{a}{2}$.

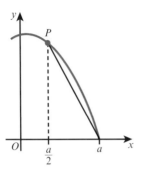

Find the shaded area in terms of a.

3 The diagram shows the graphs of $y = 36 - x^2$ and $y = 18x - x^2$. The shaded region is bounded by the two curves and the x-axis.

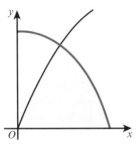

Find the area of the shaded region.

4 Find the area enclosed between the straight line $y = 12x + 14$ and the curve $y = 3x^2 + 6x + 5$.

5 The diagram shows the graphs of $y = 16 + 4x - 2x^2$ and $y = x^2 - 2x - 8$. Find the area of the region, shaded in the diagram, between the curves.

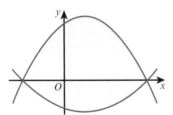

6 Find the area between the curves $y = (x - 4)(3x - 1)$ and $y = (4 - x)(1 + x)$.

7 The diagram shows the curve $y = x^3$. The point P has coordinates $(3, 27)$ and PQ is the tangent to the curve at P. Find the area of the region enclosed between the curve, PQ and the x-axis.

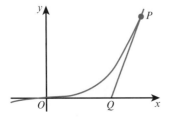

8 The diagram shows the curve $y = (x - 2)^2 + 1$ with minimum point P. The point Q on the curve is such that the gradient of PQ is 2. Find the area of the region, shaded in the diagram, between PQ and the curve.

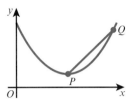

9 Show that the area enclosed between the curves $y = 9 - x^2$ and $y = x^2 - 7$ is $\dfrac{128\sqrt{2}}{3}$.

9.8 Improper integrals

WORKED EXAMPLE 9.8

Show that the improper integral $\displaystyle\int_1^\infty \frac{2}{x^3}\,dx$ has a finite value and find this value.

Answer

$$\int_1^X \frac{2}{x^3}\,dx = \int_1^X 2x^{-3}\,dx \qquad \text{Write the integral with an upper limit } X.$$

$$= \left[-x^{-2} \right]_1^X$$

$$= \left(-\frac{1}{X^2} \right) - \left(-\frac{1}{1^2} \right)$$

$$= 1 - \frac{1}{X^2}$$

As $X \to \infty$, $\dfrac{1}{X^2} \to 0$

$$\therefore \int_1^\infty \frac{2}{x^3}\,dx = 1 - 0 = 1$$

Hence, the improper integral $\displaystyle\int_1^\infty \frac{2}{x^3}\,dx$ has a finite value of 1.

WORKED EXAMPLE 9.9

Find the value, if it exists, of $\int_0^2 \dfrac{2}{x^3}\,\mathrm{d}x$.

Answer

The function $f(x) = \dfrac{2}{x^3}$ is not defined when $x = 0$.

$$\int_X^2 \dfrac{2}{x^3}\,\mathrm{d}x = \int_X^2 2x^{-3}\,\mathrm{d}x$$

Write the integral with a lower limit X.

$$= \left[-1x^{-2}\right]_X^2$$

$$= \left(-\dfrac{1}{2^2}\right) - \left(-\dfrac{1}{X^2}\right)$$

$$= \dfrac{1}{X^2} - \dfrac{1}{4}$$

As $X \to 0$, $\dfrac{1}{X^2}$ has no finite value.

Hence, $\int_0^2 \dfrac{2}{x^3}\,\mathrm{d}x$ has no finite value.

EXERCISE 9H

1 Find the values of the improper integrals.

a $\displaystyle\int_0^{16} \dfrac{1}{\sqrt[4]{x}}\,\mathrm{d}x$

b $\displaystyle\int_0^{16} \dfrac{1}{\sqrt[4]{x^3}}\,\mathrm{d}x$

c $\displaystyle\int_0^1 x^{-0.99}\,\mathrm{d}x$

2 Find the values of the infinite integrals.

a $\displaystyle\int_2^{\infty} \dfrac{6}{x^4}\,\mathrm{d}x$

b $\displaystyle\int_4^{\infty} \dfrac{6}{x\sqrt{x}}\,\mathrm{d}x$

c $\displaystyle\int_1^{\infty} x^{-1.01}\,\mathrm{d}x$

3 The diagram shows part of the curve $y = \dfrac{10}{(3x+2)^2}$.

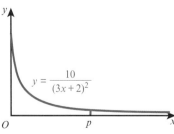

Show that as $p \to \infty$, the shaded area approaches the value $\dfrac{5}{3}$.

4 Show that each of the following improper integrals does not exist.

a $\displaystyle\int_3^\infty \frac{1}{2\sqrt{x}}\,dx$

b $\displaystyle\int_0^\infty \frac{3}{x^2\sqrt{x}}\,dx$

c $\displaystyle\int_0^\infty \frac{10}{x^2}\,dx$

d $\displaystyle\int_1^\infty \frac{2}{3x+2}\,dx$

e $\displaystyle\int_{\frac{1}{3}}^2 \frac{2}{(3x-1)^2}\,dx$

f $\displaystyle\int_0^5 \left(2\sqrt{x}+\frac{1}{x^3}\right)dx$

9.9 Volumes of revolution

WORKED EXAMPLE 9.10

The diagram shows part of the curve $y = 9 - x^2$ and the line $y = 5$.

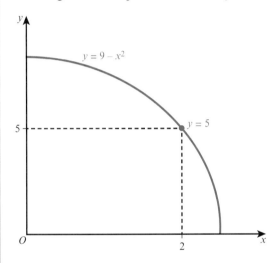

Find the volume in terms of π obtained when the shaded region is rotated through 2π radians about the x-axis.

$$\text{Volume of solid} = \pi\int_0^2 (9 - x^2)^2\,dx - \pi\int_0^2 5^2\,dx$$

$$= \pi\int_0^2 \left[(9 - x^2)^2 - 5^2\right]dx$$

$$= \pi\int_0^2 [81 - 18x^2 + x^4 - 25]\,dx$$

$$= \pi\left[81x - 6x^3 + \frac{1}{5}x^5 - 25x\right]_0^2$$

$$= \pi\left[\left(162 - 48 + \frac{32}{5} - 50\right) - 0\right]$$

$$= \frac{352\pi}{5}\ \text{units}^3$$

For rotations about the y-axis:

$$V = \int_a^b \pi x^2 \, dy$$

For rotations about the x-axis:

$$V = \int_a^b \pi y^2 \, dx$$

EXERCISE 9I

1 Find the volume formed when the region under the graph of $y = f(x)$ between $x = a$ and $x = b$ is rotated through $360°$ about the x-axis.

   a $f(x) = x + 3$; $a = 3, b = 9$ b $f(x) = x^2 + 1$; $a = 2, b = 5$

   c $f(x) = \sqrt{x + 1}$; $a = 0, b = 3$ d $f(x) = x(x - 2)$; $a = 0, b = 2$

2 Find the volume generated when the region bounded by the graph of $y = f(x)$, the y-axis and the lines $y = c$ and $y = d$ is rotated about the y-axis to form a solid revolution.

   a $f(x) = x^2$; $c = 1, d = 3$ b $f(x) = x + 1$; $c = 1, d = 4$

   c $f(x) = \sqrt{x}$; $c = 2, d = 7$ d $f(x) = \dfrac{1}{x}$; $c = 2, d = 5$

   e $f(x) = \sqrt{9 - x}$; $c = 0, d = 3$ f $f(x) = x^2 + 1$; $c = 1, d = 4$

   g $f(x) = x^{\frac{2}{3}}$; $c = 1, d = 5$ h $f(x) = \dfrac{1}{x} + 2$; $c = 3, d = 5$

3 The region enclosed by both axes, the line $x = 2$ and the curve $y = \dfrac{1}{8}x^2 + 2$ is rotated about the y-axis to form a solid. Find the volume of this solid.

4 The part of the curve $y = kx^2$, where k is a constant, between $y = 1$ and $y = 3$ is rotated through $360°$ about the y-axis. Given that the volume generated is 12π, calculate the value of k.

5 Sketch the graph of $y = \dfrac{9}{2x + 3}$ for positive values of x.

The part of the curve between $x = 0$ and $x = 3$ is rotated through 2π radians about the x-axis. Calculate the volume of the solid of revolution formed.

6 a Sketch the graphs of $y = x^2$ and $y = (x - 4)^2$, and find the coordinates of the point p where they intersect. Check your answer using technology.

   b The region bounded by the x-axis between $x = 0$ and $x = 4$, the graph of $y = x^2$ between the origin and p, and the graph of $y = (x - 4)^2$ between p and the x-axis is rotated through 2π radians about the x-axis. Calculate in terms of π the volume of the solid of revolution formed.

7   The diagram shows the curve $y = \dfrac{1}{\sqrt[3]{4x+3}}$.

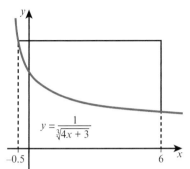

Find the area of the shaded region.

PS   8   **a**   Explain why the coordinates (x, y) of any point on a circle, centre O, radius a, shown in the diagram, satisfy the equation $x^2 + y^2 = a^2$.

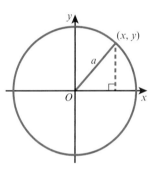

   b   The semicircle above the x-axis is rotated about the x-axis through $360°$ to form a sphere of radius a. Explain why the volume V of this sphere is given by $V = 2\pi \displaystyle\int_0^a (a^2 - x^2)\,\mathrm{d}x$.

   c   Hence show that $V = \dfrac{4}{3}\pi a^3$.

145

END-OF-CHAPTER REVIEW EXERCISE 9

1   A curve has gradient $\dfrac{\mathrm{d}y}{\mathrm{d}x} = 3x - \sqrt{x}$ and passes through the point $(4, -1)$. Find the equation of the curve.

2   **a**   Find the exact value of $\displaystyle\int_2^{2\sqrt{3}} 3 - \dfrac{12}{x^2}\,\mathrm{d}x$.

   Give your answer in the form $a + b\sqrt{3}$, where a and b are integers.

   b   The curve in the diagram has equation $y = 3 - \dfrac{12}{x^2}$. The curve crosses the x-axis at $x = 2$.

   The shaded region is bounded by the curve, the y-axis and the lines $y = 0$ and $y = 2$.

   Find the area of the shaded region.

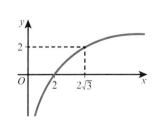

3 a Find the positive value of a for which $\int_0^a x^3 - x \, dx = 0$.

b For this value of a, find the total area enclosed between the x-axis and the curve $y = x^3 - x$ for $0 \leqslant x \leqslant a$.

4 The diagram shows a parabola with equation $y = a^2 - x^2$. The parabola crosses the x-axis at points A and B, and the y-axis at point C.

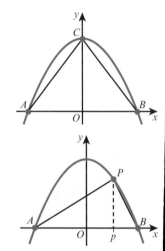

a i Write down the coordinates of A, B and C.

ii Find, in terms of a, the area of the shaded region.

b Point P lies on the parabola. The x-coordinate of P is p.

The value of p varies between the x-coordinates of A and B.

Find the minimum value of the shaded area.

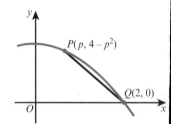

(PS)

5 A part of the curve with equation $y = 4 - x^2$ is shown in the diagram. Point P has coordinates $(p, 4 - p^2)$ and point Q has coordinates $(2, 0)$.

The shaded region is bounded by the curve and the chord PQ.

Show that the area of the shaded region is $\dfrac{1}{6}(2 - p)^3$.

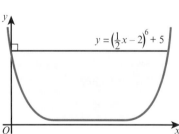

6 The diagram shows the curve $y = \left(\dfrac{1}{2}x - 2\right)^6 + 5$. Find the area of the shaded region.

7 The diagram shows the curve $y = x^{-\frac{2}{3}}$.

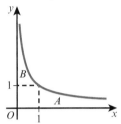

a Show that the shaded area A is infinite.

b Find the shaded area B.

c Area A is rotated through 360° about the x-axis. Find the volume generated.

d Area B is rotated through 360° about the y-axis. Find the volume generated.

8 Sketch the curve $y = 9 - x^2$. The finite region bounded by the curve and the x-axis is denoted by R.

a Find the area of R and hence or otherwise find $\displaystyle\int_0^9 \sqrt{9 - y}\,\mathrm{d}y$.

b Find the volume of the solid of revolution obtained when R is rotated through 360° about the x-axis.

c Find the volume of the solid of revolution obtained when R is rotated through 360° about the y-axis.

9 The diagram shows the curve $y = 4x^3 - 4x^2 - 10x + 12$ and the tangent at the point A where $x = 1$.

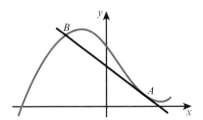

a Find the equation of this tangent.

b Verify that this tangent meets the curve again at the point B with x-coordinate -1.

c Calculate the area of the region that lies between the curve and the tangent AB.

10 A solid is made by rotating the part of the curve with equation $y = (3x - 1)^{\frac{3}{2}}$ from $x = \frac{1}{3}$ to $x = \frac{2}{3}$ through four right-angles about the x-axis. Find the volume of the solid, giving your answer in terms of π.

Answers

Answers to proof-style questions are not included.

1 Quadratics

Exercise 1A

1   **a**   **i** $2, -\dfrac{3}{2}$ **ii** $5, \dfrac{2}{3}$

     b   **i** $\dfrac{4}{3}$ **ii** $-\dfrac{5}{4}$

     c   **i** $5, -4$ **ii** $\dfrac{5}{2}, -3$

     d   **i** $6, -\dfrac{1}{2}$ **ii** $\dfrac{4}{3}, 1$

2   **a** $-2, 5$ **b** $-6, 1$ **c** $-3, \dfrac{1}{2}$

     d $-4, 3$ **e** $1, -\dfrac{8}{3}$ **f** $-7, 2$

     g $5, -\dfrac{11}{3}$ **h** $\dfrac{1}{2}, -\dfrac{4}{11}$

3 $x = 1, 6$

4 $x = 2k, 4k$

5 $x = \dfrac{-\sqrt{10} \pm \sqrt{22}}{2}$

6 $x = 1$

7   12 and 14

8   6 days

9   **a** $-1, 2$ **b** $-3, -1$

     c $\dfrac{-5}{2}, 2$ **d** 6

10 $-35, \dfrac{-7}{2}$

Exercise 1B

1   **a** $(x + 1)^2 + 1$ **b** $(x - 4)^2 - 19$

     c $\left(x + 1\tfrac{1}{2}\right)^2 - 9\tfrac{1}{4}$ **d** $(x-3)^2 - 4$

     e $(x + 7)^2$ **f** $2(x + 3)^2 - 23$

     g $3(x - 2)^2 - 9$ **h** $11 - 4(x + 1)^2$

     i $2\left(x + 1\tfrac{1}{4}\right)^2 - 6\tfrac{1}{8}$

2   **a** $(x - 7)(x + 5)$

     b $(x - 22)(x + 8)$

     c $(x + 24)(x - 18)$

     d $(3x + 2)(2x - 3)$

     e $(2 + 7x)(7 - 2x)$

     f $(4x + 3)(3x - 2)$

3   **a** $3 \pm \sqrt{3}$ **b** $0, -4$

     c $-3 \pm \dfrac{1}{2}\sqrt{5}$ **d** $\dfrac{1}{3}(7 \pm 2\sqrt{2})$

     e $-p \pm \sqrt{q}$ **f** $-b \pm \sqrt{\dfrac{c}{a}}$

4   \$4800, 100

5   Proof

6 $a = -3, b = 2, c = 48$

7   **a** $(x - 5)^2 + 10$ **b** $\dfrac{1}{1000}$

8   **a**   Proof   **b**   6 km

Exercise 1C

1   **a**   **i** $x = \dfrac{3 \pm \sqrt{5}}{2}$

        ii $x = \dfrac{1 \pm \sqrt{5}}{2}$

     b   **i** $x = \dfrac{-3 \pm \sqrt{11}}{2}$

        ii $x = \dfrac{9 \pm \sqrt{21}}{10}$

     c   **i** $x = -2 \pm \sqrt{6}$

        ii $x = -1, \dfrac{4}{3}$

     d   **i** $x = \dfrac{3 \pm \sqrt{7}}{2}$

        ii $x = 2 \pm \sqrt{7}$

2   **a** $\dfrac{1}{2}(-3 \pm \sqrt{29})$ **b** $2 \pm \sqrt{11}$

     c -3 (repeated)   **d** $\dfrac{1}{2}(-5 \pm \sqrt{17})$

     e   No solution   **f** $\dfrac{1}{6}(5 \pm \sqrt{97})$

     g -3 and $-\dfrac{1}{2}$ **h** $\dfrac{1}{2}(-3 \pm \sqrt{41})$

     i $\dfrac{1}{6}(2 \pm \sqrt{34})$

3   1.5 m

4   20.5 cm

5   5.98 seconds

Exercise 1D

1   **a** $x = 3, y = 4$ or $x = -4, y = -3$

     b $x = 3, y = 4$ or $x = 4, y = 3$

     c $x = 5, y = 2$ or $x = -1, y = -4$

d $x = 3, y = -1$

e $x = 0, y = 5$ or $x = 4, y = -3$

f $x = 1, y = 0$ or $x = \frac{1}{2}, y = \frac{1}{2}$

g $x = 0, y = 7$

h $x = 3, y = -2$ or $x = \frac{1}{7}, y = -10\frac{4}{7}$

2 **a** $(-4, -8), (-1, -5)$

    b $3\sqrt{2}$

    c $y = -x - 9$

3 **a** $(2, 5)$ and $(1, 3)$

    b $(1, 5)$ and $(-2.2, -4.6)$

    c $(3, 4)$ and $(-1, -4)$

    d $(1, 1)$ and $\left(-4, 3\frac{1}{2}\right)$

    e $(4, 3)$

    f $(2, -1)$ and $\left(-\frac{7}{8}, 4\frac{3}{4}\right)$

    g $(5, -2)$ and $(27, 42)$

    h $\left(\frac{1}{2}, -1\right)$ and $\left(-1\frac{5}{8}, -1\frac{17}{20}\right)$

4 **a** $4x^2 - 32x + 39 = 0$

    b $1.5, 6.5$

5 $\left(-\frac{3}{4}, 6\right)$

6 $p = q = 13$

7 $(2 + \sqrt{2}, 13 + 6\sqrt{2})$

8 $(0, 2), (0, -2), (-\sqrt{3}, -1), (\sqrt{3}, -1)$

9 Proof

10 $a = -7, b = -2$

Exercise 1E

1 **a** **i** $a = \pm 1.73, \pm 2.65$

       ii $x = \pm 2, \pm 1.73$

    b **i** $x = -1.71, 1.14$

       ii $a = -2, 1$

    c **i** $x = \pm 2.11$

       ii $x = \pm 2.45$

    d **i** $x = 4, 16$

       ii $x = 16, 36$

    e **i** $x = 1, 2$

       ii $x = 0, 4$

2 $x = \pm 3, \pm 1$

3 $x = 0, -\frac{4}{15}$

4 $x = 4, 1$

5 $x = 0, 2$

6 $x = 0, 1$

7 $x = -1, 3$

8 $x = 16$

9 **a** 16 **b** $25, 9$

    c 49 **d** 25

    e $-8, 27$ **f** $-1, 64$

Exercise 1F

1 **a** **i** $(3, 4)$ **ii** $(5, 1)$

    b **i** $(7, -1)$ **ii** $(1, -5)$

    c **i** $(-1, 3)$ **ii** $(-7, -3)$

    d **i** $(-2, -4)$ **ii** $(-1, 5)$

2 **a** **i** A   **ii** C   **iii** B

    b **i** C   **ii** A   **iii** B

3 $y = -2x^2 - 2x + 4$

4 **a** **i**

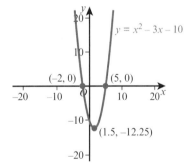

       ii

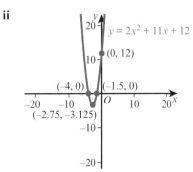

149

b i

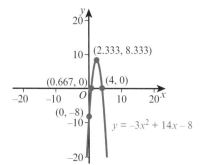

ii

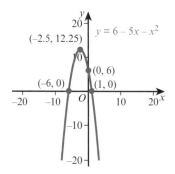

c i

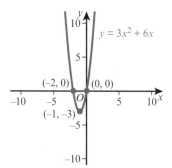

ii

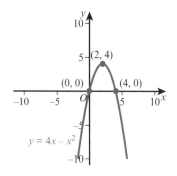

d i

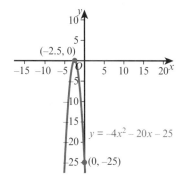

ii

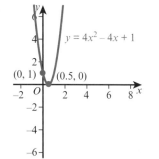

5 **a** $3\left(x + \dfrac{1}{3}\right)^2 + \dfrac{2}{3}$ **b** Proof

  c $x = -\dfrac{1}{3}$

6 **a** A, B, G, H **b** B, D, F
  c F, G, H **d** D
  e G **f** I
  g B, E **h** A, C, E

7 $(x + 3)^2 - 5; -5$ at $x = -3$

8 **a** Minimum

  b $a = 3, b = 7$

9 **a** $p = 1, q = 4$

  b $x = 1.5$

Exercise 1G

1 **a** **i** $-2\sqrt{2} \leqslant x \leqslant 2\sqrt{2}$

    ii $-\sqrt{5} < x < \sqrt{5}$

  b **i** $x < -\sqrt{6}$ or $x > \sqrt{6}$

    ii $x \leqslant -2\sqrt{3}$ or $x \geqslant 2\sqrt{3}$

  c **i** $x < -1$ or $x > 4$

    ii $-\dfrac{2}{3} < x < \dfrac{5}{2}$

  d **i** $x < -1$ or $x > 3$

    ii $2 < x < 4$

  e **i** $x < 3$ or $x > 12$

    ii $-2 < x < 2$

2 **a** $x < \frac{1}{2}(-3 - \sqrt{29})$ or $x > \frac{1}{2}(-3 + \sqrt{29})$

    b True for no x

    c $\frac{1}{2}(5 - \sqrt{17}) < x < \frac{1}{2}(5 + \sqrt{17})$

    d True for all x

    e $-3 < x < 3$

    f $x = -1$ only

    g $\frac{1}{4}(3 - \sqrt{17}) < x < \frac{1}{4}(3 + \sqrt{17})$

    h $\frac{1}{2}(-3 - \sqrt{41}) < x < \frac{1}{2}(-3 + \sqrt{41})$

    i $x \leqslant \frac{1}{4}(-7 - \sqrt{41})$ or $x \geqslant \frac{1}{4}(-7 + \sqrt{41})$

3 **a** $x < 2$

    b $-3 < x < -2, \ x > 1$

    c $-2 < x < 1, \ x > 10$

    d $0 < x < 3, \ x > 4$

    e $-2 < x < -1, \ 1 < x < 2$

    f $-4 < x \leqslant -1, \ 2 < x \leqslant 4$

4 $x < -2$ or $x > 1.5$

5 $-\frac{5}{3} \leqslant x \leqslant 2$

6 $0.904\,\text{s}$

7 **a** **i** $x < 2.5$ **ii** $0.5 < x < 5$

    b $0.5 < x < 2.5$

8 $x \leqslant -1$ or $1 \leqslant x < 2$ or $x > 3$

9 $-0.4 \leqslant x \leqslant 0$ or $2 \leqslant x \leqslant 3$

10 $5 \leqslant n \leqslant 38$

Exercise 1H

1 **a** **i** 36   **ii** 68

    b **i** -47 **ii** -119

    c **i** 0   **ii** 0

    d **i** 49   **ii** 49

2 **a** **i** Two   **ii** Two

    b **i** None   **ii** None

    c **i** One   **ii** One

    d **i** Two   **ii** Two

3 **a** **i** $k < \frac{1}{24}$ **ii** $k > -\frac{25}{12}$

    b **i** $k = \frac{3}{5}$ **ii** $k = -\frac{17}{24}$

    c **i** $k \geqslant -\frac{13}{4}$ **ii** $k \leqslant \frac{1}{16}$

    d **i** $k > \frac{3}{8}$ **ii** $k < -\frac{25}{12}$

    e **i** $k = \frac{17}{4}$ **ii** $k = \frac{55}{32}$

    f **i** $k = 1$ **ii** $k = \frac{1}{32}$

    g **i** $k < 0$ **ii** $k < 0$

4 $m = \pm\sqrt{2}$

5 $k = \frac{11 \pm 2\sqrt{30}}{2}$

6 $c \geqslant \frac{1}{16}$

7 $0 < k < 6$

8 $-9 < k < -1$

9 $m \leqslant -8$ or $m \geqslant 0$

10 Proof

Exercise 1I

1 Proof

2 $-1 \pm 2\sqrt{6}$

3 $\pm 6\sqrt{2}$

4 $a < 0$ or $a > 2$

5 Proof that $k^2 + 12 > 0$ for all k

6 $2, -2$

7 -1

8 ± 5

9 **a** Proof

    b **i** Line is tangent to the curve.

        ii Line and curve do not intersect.

    c Proof

End-of-chapter review exercise 1

1 $x = 3, 2$

2 $k = \pm 9$

3 $m = 0$

4 $x = 1, x = 16$

5 **a** $6\left(x + \frac{5}{6}\right)^2 + \frac{5}{6}$

    b $(6x^2 + 10x + 5)^2 \geqslant \frac{25}{36}$

6 **a** Proof   **b** Proof

    c Proof

7 **a** $\dfrac{1}{2} < x \leqslant 2$ **b** $-\dfrac{1}{2} < x < \dfrac{7}{2}$

  c $x > 6.3$

8 Proof; 6

9 $x = 1, y = 1$ or $x = 4, y = -1$

10 $-2, 0$

2 Functions

Exercise 2A

1 **a** one-one **b** many-one
  c one-one **d** one-one
  e one-one **f** one-one
  g one-one **h** one-many

2 **a** function **b** function
  c not a function **d** not a function
  e function **f** function

3 a, d, f, g, k

4 a, c, e, f, g, h, j

5 **a** 0 **b** -1 **c** $\dfrac{2}{3}$
  d 4 **e** -5 **f** -1
  g $1\frac{1}{2}$ **h** 1 **i** 4

Exercise 2B

1 **a** function **b** function
  c function **d** function
  e function **f** function

2 **a** $f(x) \geqslant 1$ **b** $f(x) \geqslant -2$
  c $-8 \leqslant f(x) \leqslant 8$ **d** $f(x) \geqslant 1$

3 **a** $f(x) \geqslant -5$ **b** $f(x) \geqslant 1$

4 **a** $4 - (x+1)^2; f(x) \leqslant 4$
  b $10 - (x+3)^2; f(x) \leqslant 10$

5 $g(x) \leqslant 6 + \dfrac{3a^2}{4}$

6 $a = 3$

7 **a** $4(x-1)^2 - 2$
  b $k = 2$
  c $-2 \leqslant f(x) \leqslant 2$

8 **a** domain: $x \in \mathbb{R}$
   range: $f(x) \in \mathbb{R}$
  b domain: $x \in \mathbb{R}$
   range: $f(x) \in \mathbb{R}, f(x) \geqslant 1$

  c domain: $x \in \mathbb{R}$
   range: $f(x) \in \mathbb{R}, f(x) > 0,$
  d domain: $x \in \mathbb{R}, x \neq 0$
   range: $f(x) \in \mathbb{R}, f(x) \neq 0$
  e domain: $x \in \mathbb{R}, x \neq 3$
   range: $f(x) \in \mathbb{R}, f(x) \neq 0$
  f domain: $x \in \mathbb{R}, x \geqslant -0.5$
   range: $f(x) \in \mathbb{R}, f(x) \geqslant -1$

9 **a** $\mathbb{R}, f(x) \in \mathbb{R}$
  b $x \neq 0, f(x) \neq 0$
  c $x \neq -\dfrac{2}{3}, f(x) \neq 0$
  d $x \neq 3, f(x) > 0$

10 **a** $\mathbb{R}, f(x) \geqslant 0$
  b $\mathbb{R}, -1 \leqslant f(x) \leqslant 1$
  c $x \geqslant 3, f(x) \geqslant 0$
  d $\mathbb{R}, f(x) \geqslant 5$
  e $x > 0, f(x) > 0$
  f $\mathbb{R}, f(x) \leqslant 4$
  g $0 \leqslant x \leqslant 4, 0 \leqslant f(x) \leqslant 2$
  h $\mathbb{R}, f(x) \geqslant 6$
  i $x \geqslant 3, f(x) \geqslant 0$

Exercise 2C

1 **a** 7 **b** -19
  c 1 **d** $\dfrac{1}{2}$
  e $\dfrac{1}{2}$ **f** -1
  g $3\frac{2}{3}$ **h** 2

2 **a** $x \mapsto 2x^2 + 5$ **b** $x \mapsto (2x+5)^2$
  c $x \mapsto \dfrac{2}{x} + 5$ **d** $x \mapsto \dfrac{1}{2x+5}$
  e $x \mapsto 4x + 15$ **f** $x \mapsto x$
  g $x \mapsto \left(\dfrac{2}{x} + 5\right)^2$ **h** $x \mapsto \dfrac{1}{(2x+5)^2}$

3 **a** $x \mapsto \sin x° - 3$ **b** $x \mapsto \sin(x-3)°$
  c $x \mapsto \sin(x^3 - 3)°$ **d** $x \mapsto \sin(x^3)°$
  e $x \mapsto x - 9$ **f** $x \mapsto (\sin x°)^3$

4 **a** fh **b** fg
  c hh **d** hg or ggh
  e gf or fffg **f** gffh
  g fgfg or ffffgg **h** hf
  i hffg

152

5   **a** $x \geqslant 0$, $gf(x) \geqslant -5$

     b $x \geqslant -3$, $gf(x) \geqslant 0$

     c $x \neq 2$, $gf(x) \neq 0$

     d $\mathbb{R}$, $0 \leqslant gf(x) \leqslant 1$

     e $\mathbb{R}$, $gf(x) \geqslant 0$

     f $-4 \leqslant x \leqslant 4$, $0 \leqslant gf(x) \leqslant 2$

     g $x \leqslant -2$ or $x \geqslant 3$, $gf(x) \geqslant 0$

     h $x < -2$, $gf(x) > 0$

6   **a** $-2\frac{2}{3}$ or 4   **b**   7

     c   1

7 $a = 4, b = 11$ or $a = 4\frac{1}{2}, b = 10$

8   **a**   2   **b**   1

9 $f(x) = \pm(3x + 1)$

10   2

Exercise 2D

1   **a** $f^{-1}(x) = \dfrac{x-5}{6}$ **b** $f^{-1}(x) = 5x - 4$

     c $f^{-1}(x) = 2 - \dfrac{1}{2}x$ **d** $f^{-1}(x) = \dfrac{3x-7}{2}$

     e $f^{-1}(x) = \sqrt[3]{\dfrac{x-5}{2}}$

     f $f^{-1}(x) = \dfrac{1}{x-4}$, $x \neq 4$

     g $f^{-1}(x) = \dfrac{5}{x} + 1$, $x \neq 0$

     h $f^{-1}(x) = -2 + \sqrt{x-7}$, $x \geqslant 7$

     i $f^{-1}(x) = \dfrac{3 + \sqrt{x+5}}{2}$, $x \geqslant -5$

     j $f^{-1}(x) = 3 + \sqrt{x+9}$, $x \geqslant -9$

2   Proofs

3   **a** $y \mapsto \dfrac{2y}{y-1}$, $y \neq 1$

     b $y \mapsto \dfrac{4y+1}{y-2}$, $y \neq 2$

     c $y \mapsto \dfrac{5y+2}{y-1}$, $y \neq 1$

     d $y \mapsto \dfrac{3y-11}{4y-3}$, $y \neq \dfrac{3}{4}$

4   6

---

5 $x \mapsto \sqrt{x - 5\frac{3}{4}} - \dfrac{1}{2}$, $x > 6$; $f^{-1}(x) > 0$

6 $x \mapsto 1 - \sqrt{-\dfrac{1}{2}(x+5)}$, $x < -5$; $f^{-1}(x) < 1$

7   **a**   60°   **b**   180°   **c**   30°

8   Proof

9   **a** $k = 0$; $f^{-1}(x) = -\sqrt{x}$, $x \geqslant 0$

     b $k = -1$; $f^{-1}(x) = \sqrt{x-2} - 1$, $x > 2$

     c $k = 1$; $f^{-1}(x) = 1 - \sqrt{6-x}$, $x \leqslant 6$

     d $k = -2$, $\sqrt{x+1} - 2$, $x > -1$

10 $k = -3$

Exercise 2E

1   **a** $x \mapsto \dfrac{1}{4}x$

     b $x \mapsto x - 3$

     c $x \mapsto x^2$, $x \geqslant 0$

     d $x \mapsto \dfrac{1}{2}(x-1)$

     e $x \mapsto \sqrt{x} + 2$, $x \geqslant 0$

     f $x \mapsto \dfrac{1}{3}(1-x)$

     g $x \mapsto \dfrac{3}{x}$, $x \neq 0$

     h $x \mapsto 7 - x$

2   **a** $f(x) > 3$

     b $f^{-1}x \mapsto (x-3)^2 + 2$; $x > 3$, $f^{-1}(x) > 2$

     c

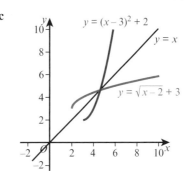

3 $k = -1$

     a $f(x) \geqslant 5$

     b $f^{-1}x \mapsto -1 - \sqrt{x-5}$; $x \geqslant 5$, $f^{-1}(x) \leqslant -1$

c

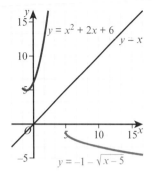

4 a

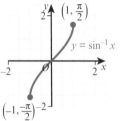

b

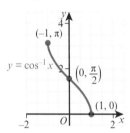

c

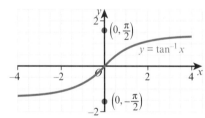

5 $a = \dfrac{1}{8}, b = \dfrac{3}{8}$

6 a

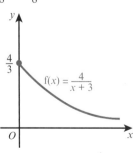

Range $0 < f(x) \leqslant \dfrac{4}{3}$

b $\dfrac{4 - 3x}{x}, x \in \mathbb{R}, x \neq 0$

c 1

7 a i $f(x) \geqslant -3$

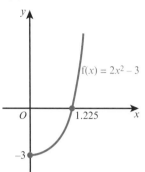

ii f^{-1} exists because f is one-one

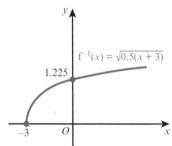

b $x \geqslant -\dfrac{1}{9}$

8 a

b

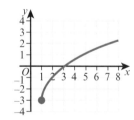

c

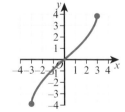

d

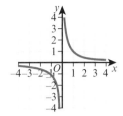

9 Proof

10 a

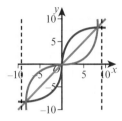

   b Domain: $-9 < x < 9$; range: $y \in \mathbb{R}$

   c $x = -8, 0, 8$

Exercise 2F

1 a i

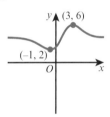

   ii

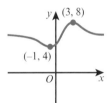

 b i

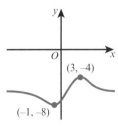

   ii

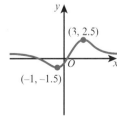

c i

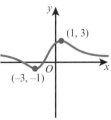

   ii

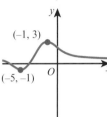

d i

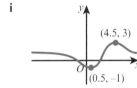

   ii

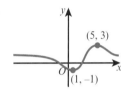

2 a i $y = 3x^2 + 3$ **ii** $y = 9x^3 - 7$

  b i $y = 7x^3 - 3x + 4$

    ii $y = 8x^2 - 7x + 6$

  c i $y = 4(x - 5)^2$

    ii $y = 7(x + 3)^2$

  d i $y = 3(x + 4)^3 - 5(x + 4)^2 + 4$

    ii $y = (x - 3)^3 + 6(x - 3) + 2$

3 a i Vertically down 5 units

    ii Vertically down 4 units

  b i Left 1 unit   **ii** Left 5 units

  c i Left 3 units

    ii Right 2 units

Exercise 2G

1 a i $y = -3x^2$ **ii** $y = -9x^3$

  b i $y = -7x^3 + 3x - 6$

    ii $y = -8x^2 + 7x - 1$

  c i $y = 4x^2$ **ii** $y = -7x^3$

  d i $y = -3x^3 - 5x^2 + 4$

    ii $y = -x^3 + 6x + 2$

2 **a** 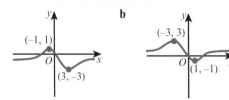 **b**

ii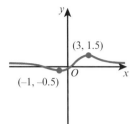

3 **a** **i** Reflection in the x-axis

    ii Reflection in the x-axis

   b **i** Reflection in the y-axis

    ii Reflection in the y-axis

   c **i** Reflection in the y-axis

    ii Reflection in the y-axis

c **i**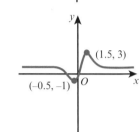

4 **a** $y = -6x^2$

   b $y = -3x^3$

   c $y = 3x^2 + 4x + 2$

   d $y = 2x^2 - x - 5$

5 **a** Reflection in the x-axis

   b Reflection in the y-axis

   c Reflection in the x-axis

   d Reflection in the x-axis

ii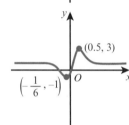

Exercise 2H

1 **a** **i**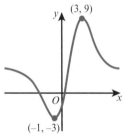

d **i**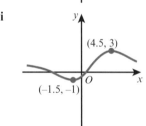

    ii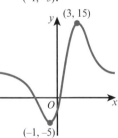

ii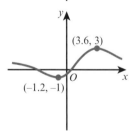

   b **i**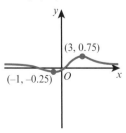

2 **a** **i** $y = 21x^2$

    ii $y = 18x^3$

   b **i** $y = \dfrac{1}{3}(7x^3 - 3x + 6)$

    ii $y = \dfrac{4}{5}(8x^2 - 7x + 1)$

   c **i** $y = x^2$

    ii $y = 7\left(\dfrac{x}{5}\right)^2$

d **i** $y = 3(2x)^3 - 5(2x)^2 + 4$

   ii $y = \left(\dfrac{3x}{2}\right)^3 + 6\left(\dfrac{3x}{2}\right) + 2$

3 **a** **i** Vertical stretch, scale factor 4

   ii Vertical stretch, scale factor 6

 b **i** Horizontal stretch, scale factor $\dfrac{1}{3}$

   ii Horizontal stretch, scale factor $\dfrac{1}{4}$

 c **i** Horizontal stretch, scale factor $\dfrac{1}{3}$

     (or vertical stretch, scale factor $\sqrt{3}$)

   ii Horizontal stretch, scale factor 2

4 **a** $y = 9x^2$

 b $y = 2x^3 - 2$

 c $y = 3^{x-1} + 2$

 d $y = \dfrac{3}{2}x^2 - 3x + 1$

 e $y = 16x^3 - 12x$

5 **a** Stretch parallel to the x-axis with stretch factor $\dfrac{1}{2}$

 b Stretch parallel to the y-axis with stretch factor 3

 c Stretch parallel to the y-axis with stretch factor 4

 d Stretch parallel to the x-axis with stretch factor $\dfrac{1}{3}$

Exercise 2I

1 **a** **i**

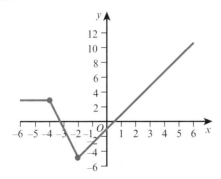

   ii

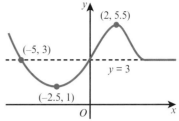

 b **i**

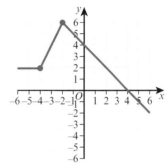

   ii

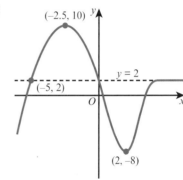

 c **i**

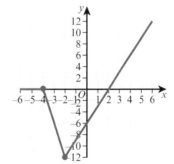

   ii

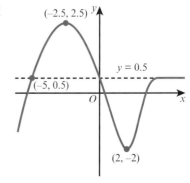

d **i**

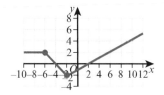

ii

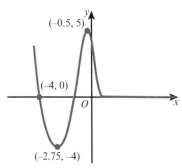

e **i**

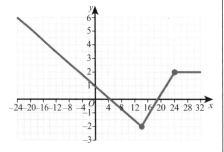

ii

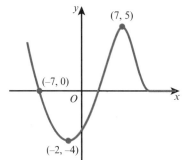

2 **a** $(5, -4)$ **b** $(2, -9)$ **c** $(2, 4)$

d $(1, -4)$ **e** $(2, -8)$

3 **a** $(x + 1)^2 + 7$

b Reflection in the x-axis, followed by a translation $\begin{pmatrix} -1 \\ 7 \end{pmatrix}$

4 **a** **i** $g(x) = 6x^2 - 6$

ii $g(x) = x^2 + 1$

b **i** $g(x) = x^2 + 4$

ii $g(x) = 7x^2 - 4$

c **i** $g(x) = 3 - 2x^2$

ii $g(x) = 6 - 2x^2$

d **i** $g(x) = 5 - x^2$

ii $g(x) = -3 - 3x^2$

5 **a** **i** $g(x) = f(x + 1) = f(-x - 1)$: translation $\begin{pmatrix} 1 \\ 0 \end{pmatrix}$ then reflection in y-axis. Alternatively, reflection in y-axis then translation $\begin{pmatrix} -1 \\ 0 \end{pmatrix}$.

ii $g(x) = f(x - 3) = f(3 - x)$: translation $\begin{pmatrix} -3 \\ 0 \end{pmatrix}$ then reflection in y-axis. Alternatively, reflection in y-axis then translation $\begin{pmatrix} 3 \\ 0 \end{pmatrix}$.

b **i** $k(x) = f(2x + 2)$: translation $\begin{pmatrix} -2 \\ 0 \end{pmatrix}$ then stretch of $\dfrac{1}{2}$ relative to $x = 0$. Alternatively, stretch of $\dfrac{1}{2}$ relative to $x = 0$ then translation $\begin{pmatrix} -1 \\ 0 \end{pmatrix}$.

ii $k(x) = f(3x - 1)$: translation $\begin{pmatrix} 1 \\ 0 \end{pmatrix}$ then stretch of $\dfrac{1}{3}$ relative to $x = 0$. Alternatively, stretch of $\dfrac{1}{3}$ relative to $x = 0$ then translation $\begin{pmatrix} \frac{1}{3} \\ 0 \end{pmatrix}$.

6 **a** $y = p(\sin(x) + c)$

b $y = p \sin x + c$

c $y = \sin\left(\dfrac{x + d}{q}\right)$

d $y = \sin\left(\dfrac{x}{q} + d\right)$

7 **a**

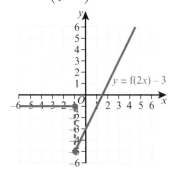

158

b

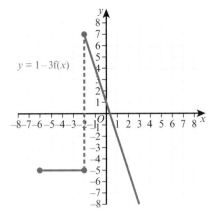

$y = 1 - 3f(x)$

8 $y = -x^2 + 7x - 10$

9 $a = 5, b = -1$

10 $a = 16, b = 0, c = -25$

End-of-chapter review exercise 2

1 **a** $\mathbb{R}, f(x) \leqslant 4$ **b** $\mathbb{R}, f(x) \geqslant -7$

 c $x \geqslant -2, f(x) \geqslant 0$ **d** $\mathbb{R}, \mathbb{R}$

 e $\mathbb{R}, f(x) \geqslant 0$ **f** $x \geqslant 0, f(x) \leqslant 2$

2 **a** $x \mapsto (1 - 2x)^3$ **b** $x \mapsto 1 - 2x^3$

 c $x \mapsto 1 - 2x^9$ **d** $x \mapsto 4x - 1$

 e $x \mapsto \dfrac{1}{2}(1 - x)$

3 **a** 48 **b** 3 **c** -1

 d 4 **e** 4

4 **a** gf **b** ff

 c g^{-1} **d** fgh or fhg

 e hfg **f** f^{-1}

 g $g^{-1}fgh$ or $g^{-1}fhg$ **h** hf^{-1}

5 $a = -2, b = 11$ or $a = 2, b = -13$

6 **a** $x \mapsto \dfrac{1}{2}(x - 7)$ **b** $x \mapsto \sqrt[3]{x + 1}$

 c $x \mapsto \sqrt[3]{\dfrac{1}{2}(x - 5)}$

 d $x \mapsto \dfrac{1}{2}(\sqrt[3]{x + 1} - 7)$

 e $x \mapsto 2x^3 + 5$

 f $x \mapsto (2x + 7)^3 - 1$

 g $x \mapsto \sqrt[3]{\dfrac{1}{2}(x - 5)}$

 h $x \mapsto \dfrac{1}{2}(\sqrt[3]{x + 1} - 7)$

7 **a** 3 **b** 7

 c 3 **d** 7

8 **a** $f(x) \geqslant \dfrac{1}{3}$ **b** 0

 c $\dfrac{1}{2}(x + 1)$

 d Reflections in $y = x$

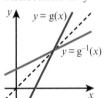

9 **a** $f(x) \leqslant 4$

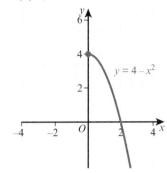

 b Reflect in $y = 2$

 c $\sqrt{4 - x}, x \leqslant 4$

 d 1.56

3 Coordinate geometry

Exercise 3A

1 **a** **i** 13 **ii** 5

 b **i** $\sqrt{5}$ **ii** $\sqrt{10}$

 c **i** $2\sqrt{5}$ **ii** $2\sqrt{2}$

 d **i** $\sqrt{10}$ **ii** $\sqrt{17}$

2 **a** $(4, 13)$ **b** $(1, 8)$

 c $\left(-\dfrac{1}{2}, -4\dfrac{1}{2}\right)$ **d** $\left(-5\dfrac{1}{2}, 4\dfrac{1}{2}\right)$

 e $(2p + 3, 2p - 3)$ **f** $(p + 4, -2)$

 g $(3p, 3q)$ **h** $(a + 3, b + 1)$

3 $3a\sqrt{5}$

4 Proof

5 **a** Both are 5

 b Being the same distance from A and C does not ensure that B lies on AC.

6 $1 \pm \dfrac{2\sqrt{5}}{5}$

159

7 Proof

8 **a** **i** $2\sqrt{5}\sqrt{a^2 + 1}$

    ii $(-1 + 2a, 2 + a)$

  b It is 2:1.

9 $5\sqrt{5}\,\text{m}$

Exercise 3B

1 Right-angle at A, area $= 6.5$

2 $(6 \pm 2\sqrt{2}, 0)$

3 -1

4 5 or -3

5 **a** Gradients PQ and SR both $-\dfrac{1}{3}$, QR 4,

    PS $\dfrac{3}{4}$

  b Trapezium

6 **a** $DE = DG = \sqrt{10}$, $EF = FG = \sqrt{40}$

  b Kite

7 **a** M is $(6, 1)$ **b** Proof

  c N is $\left(8, 5\frac{1}{2}\right)$ **d** Proof

8 **a** Proof

  b $q = \dfrac{14}{3}$, area $= \dfrac{53}{3}$

9 **a** Proof   **b** $k = 2$

10 78

Exercise 3C

1 **a** **i** Perpendicular

    ii Parallel

  b **i** Parallel

    ii Parallel

  c **i** Perpendicular

    ii Neither

  d **i** Neither

    ii Neither

2 **a** Proof

  b $2x + 5y - 22 = 0$

3 **a** $\left(2, \dfrac{9}{2}\right)$ **b** $y = 1.2x + 2.1$

4 **a** $2x + 3y = -5$ **b** $\dfrac{11}{2}$

5 **a** $y = -2x + 4$

  b $2\sqrt{5}$

6 **a** $x + 3y - p - 3q = 0$

  b $x - p = 0$

  c $x - y - p + q = 0$

  d $qx + py - pq = 0$

7 $y = 7$

8 $y = mx - md$

9 Proof

10 For example, if $a = x$ or $b = y$

Exercise 3D

1 **a** **i** $(x - 3)^2 + (y - 7)^2 = 16$

    ii $(x - 5)^2 + (y - 1)^2 = 36$

  b **i** $(x - 3)^2 + (y + 1)^2 = 7$

    ii $(x + 4)^2 + (y - 2)^2 = 5$

2 **a** **i** Centre $(2, -3)$, radius $\dfrac{3}{2}$

    ii Centre $(-1, -5)$, radius $\dfrac{2}{5}$

  b **i** Centre $\left(3, \dfrac{1}{2}\right)$, radius $\sqrt{6}$

    ii Centre $\left(-\dfrac{3}{4}, \dfrac{1}{5}\right)$, radius $\sqrt{3}$

3 **a** **i** Centre $(-2, 3)$, radius 3

    ii Centre $(4, -1)$, radius 3

  b **i** Centre $(1, -3)$, radius 3

    ii Centre $(5, -2)$, radius $\sqrt{30}$

  c **i** Centre $\left(-\dfrac{5}{2}, \dfrac{1}{2}\right)$, radius $\dfrac{3\sqrt{2}}{2}$

    ii Centre $\left(\dfrac{3}{2}, -\dfrac{7}{2}\right)$, radius $\dfrac{\sqrt{70}}{2}$

  d **i** Centre $\left(0, \dfrac{5}{2}\right)$, radius $\dfrac{\sqrt{73}}{2}$

    ii Centre $\left(-\dfrac{3}{2}, 0\right)$, radius $\dfrac{7}{2}$

4 **a** **i** On circumference

    ii On circumference

  b **i** Outside circle

    ii Inside circle

5 **a** $(x + 6)^2 + (y - 3)^2 = 117$

  b $(0, -6)$, $(0, 12)$

6 **a** $\left(\dfrac{5}{2}, -\dfrac{1}{2}\right)$, $r = \dfrac{\sqrt{38}}{2}$

  b Outside

7 $4\sqrt{6}$

8 a Proof **b** $\sqrt{442}$

c $\left(x-\dfrac{5}{2}\right)^2+\left(y+\dfrac{3}{2}\right)^2=\dfrac{221}{2}$

9 a $\sqrt{17}$

b Outside the circle

10 a $90°$ **b** Proof

Exercise 3E

1 a i $y=4$ **ii** $y=\dfrac{3}{5}x+\dfrac{19}{5}$

b i $y=-\dfrac{2}{3}x+\dfrac{5}{3}$ **ii** $y=\dfrac{2}{3}x-\dfrac{4}{3}$

c i $y=-2x+9$ **ii** $y=-x+6$

2 a i Intersect **ii** Intersect

b i Disjoint **ii** Intersect

c i Intersect **ii** Tangent

3 a $(x-2)^2+(y-5)^2=29$

b Proof

c 7.43

4 a 7 or 21

b $(-2.39,-1.99)$ and $(-2.39,12.0)$

5 $\dfrac{200}{3}$

6 $1.04, 6.16$

7 4.11

8 a $(2,-1)$ **b** Proof

9 a Proof **b** Proof

c $150-25\pi$

10 $a^2+b^2=(1\pm r)^2$

End-of-chapter review exercise 3

1 a $x+3y=9$ **b** $(0.9,2.7)$

c $\sqrt{0.9}$

2 a $x+y=1$ **b** $(2,-1),(0,1)$

3 a $k=-\dfrac{5}{2}$ **b** $p=-6$

c $3x-2y-6=0$ **d** $(2,0)$

4 a $(1,5)$ **b** Proof

c $(3.4,3.8)$

5 $k=-19$

6 a Proof

b $(x-6)^2+y^2=13$

c $3x+2y-5=0$

7 $-6-5\sqrt5<k<-6+5\sqrt5$

8 a $\dfrac{256}{3}$ **b** $\dfrac{104}{3}$

9 $2mac=a^2-c^2$

10 $2<r<8$

4 Circular measure

Exercise 4A

1 a $\dfrac{1}{2}\pi$ **b** $\dfrac{3}{4}\pi$ **c** $\dfrac{1}{4}\pi$

d $\dfrac{1}{6}\pi$ **e** $\dfrac{2}{5}\pi$ **f** $\dfrac{1}{10}\pi$

g $\dfrac{2}{3}\pi$ **h** $\dfrac{1}{8}\pi$ **i** 4π

j $\dfrac{10}{3}\pi$ **k** $\dfrac{3}{2}\pi$ **l** $\dfrac{1}{180}\pi$

2 a $60°$ **b** $9°$ **c** $36°$

d $22\frac{1}{2}°$ **e** $20°$ **f** $120°$

g $112\frac{1}{2}°$ **h** $108°$ **i** $4°$

j $1080°$ **k** $-90°$ **l** $50°$

3 a $\frac{1}{2}\sqrt3$ **b** $\frac{1}{2}\sqrt2$ **c** $\frac{1}{3}\sqrt3$

d 0 **e** $-\frac{1}{2}\sqrt2$ **f** $-\frac{1}{2}\sqrt3$

g $-\sqrt3$ **h** $\dfrac{3}{4}$

4 a i 5.59 **ii** 0.349

b i 4.71 **ii** 1.57

c i 1.13 **ii** 2.53

d i 1.75 **ii** 1.45

5 a i $60°$ **ii** $45°$

b i $150°$ **ii** $120°$

c i $270°$ **ii** $300°$

d i $69.9°$ **ii** $265°$

6 a $85.9°$ **b** $126°$ **c** $60.7°$

d $111°$ **e** $39.0°$

7 a 0.932 **b** 0.697 **c** 2.57

d 0.866 **e** 0.809 **f** -1

8 9.97 units

9 1.19 radians. Not safe

Exercise 4B

1 a 0.938   b 53.7°
2 7.5 cm
3 a 2π cm   b $\dfrac{9\pi}{4}$ cm
   c 6π cm   d 10π cm
4 a 14.4 cm   b 2.48 cm
5 a 0.25 radians   b 0.556 radians
6 a 17.0   b 5
   c 2.44 radians
7 1.33 radians (3 sf)
8 6.98 cm
9 28.2 cm

Exercise 4C

1 9.49 cm
2 48.4 cm²
3 11.3 cm
4 5.14 cm²
5 2.54 radians
6 6.72 cm²
7 a Proof
   b Proof
8 a $\dfrac{\pi}{8}$ radians   b $\dfrac{25\pi}{4}+10$ cm
9 2π cm, $2(\pi-\sqrt{3})$ cm²
10 a $A=3r-r^2$ b $\theta=2$

End-of-chapter review exercise 4

1 a $s=8.4, A=29.4$
   b $s=7.35, A=12.9$
   c $\theta=1.5, A=48$
   d $r=20, A=140$
   e $\theta=2.4, s=12$
   f $r=8, \theta=2$
   g $s=8$
   h $\theta=\dfrac{5}{3}$
2 5 cm
3 2 cm or 1.5 cm
4 Proof
5 a Proof   b 70.1°   c 3.67 cm²
6 a 44.9 cm²   b 29.1 cm
7 a 4 cm   b 10 cm²
   c 3.59 cm   d 3.57 cm²

8 a $\dfrac{2\pi}{3}$ radians   b 12π cm²
   c $9\sqrt{3}$ cm²   d 22.1 cm²
   e 24.6 cm
9 15.5 cm, 14.3 cm²

5 Trigonometry

Exercise 5A

1 a i 11   ii $\dfrac{4}{5},\dfrac{3}{5},\dfrac{4}{3}$
   b i 37.5   ii $\dfrac{15}{17},\dfrac{8}{17},\dfrac{15}{8}$
   c i $\sqrt{13}$
      ii $\dfrac{3}{13}\sqrt{13},\dfrac{2}{13}\sqrt{13},\dfrac{3}{2}$
   d i 11
      ii $\dfrac{5}{14}\sqrt{3},\dfrac{11}{14},\dfrac{5}{11}\sqrt{3}$
   e i $17\sqrt{5}$
      ii $\dfrac{22}{85}\sqrt{5},\dfrac{31}{85}\sqrt{5},\dfrac{22}{31}$
   f i $12\sqrt{2}$
      ii $\dfrac{1}{3},\dfrac{2}{3}\sqrt{2},\dfrac{1}{4}\sqrt{2}$
2 a $\dfrac{4}{5}$ b $\dfrac{4}{3}$ c $\dfrac{36}{25}$
   d $\dfrac{27}{16}$ e $\dfrac{9}{20}$ f $\dfrac{1}{9}$
3 a $\dfrac{\sqrt{5}}{3}$ b $\dfrac{2}{3}$ c 1
   d $\dfrac{8\sqrt{5}}{15}$ e 2   f $5\sqrt{5}$
4 a $\dfrac{\sqrt{3}}{4}$ b $\dfrac{3}{4}$
   c $\dfrac{1+\sqrt{3}}{2}$ d $\dfrac{\sqrt{3}}{3}$
   e $\dfrac{6-\sqrt{3}}{11}$ f $\dfrac{4\sqrt{3}}{3}$
5 a 0.75   b $\dfrac{4}{3}$
   c $\dfrac{\sqrt{2}+\sqrt{3}}{2}$ d $\dfrac{1-\sqrt{3}}{2}$
6 Proof
7 Proof
8 $a=2, b=-2$

Exercise 5B

1   **a**   75°   **b**   30°
    c   28°   **d**   10°

2   **a**   Second   **b**   Fourth
    c   Third   **d**   Third
    e   Fourth   **f**   First
    g   Fourth

3   **a**   105°   **b**   −150°

    c   666°   **d** $\dfrac{4\pi}{3}$

    e $\dfrac{11\pi}{4}$ **f** $-\dfrac{11\pi}{5}$

Exercise 5C

1   **a** $-\dfrac{\sqrt{5}}{3}$ **b** $-\dfrac{\sqrt{5}}{2}$

2 $\pm\dfrac{3\sqrt{10}}{10}$

3 $-\sqrt{1-s^2}$

4   **a** $-\dfrac{5}{13}$ **b** $-\dfrac{12}{5}$

5   **a** $-\dfrac{3}{5}$ **b** $-\dfrac{4}{5}$

    c $-\dfrac{1}{2}$ **d** $\sqrt{3}$

6   **a**   **i** $-\dfrac{\sqrt{2}}{2}$ **ii** $-\dfrac{\sqrt{2}}{2}$

    b   **i** $-\dfrac{1}{2}$ **ii** $-\dfrac{\sqrt{3}}{2}$

    c   **i**   −1   **ii**   −1

7   **a** $\dfrac{3}{4}$ **b** $\dfrac{\sqrt{2}+\sqrt{3}}{2}$

    c $\dfrac{1-\sqrt{3}}{2}$

8   Proof

9   Proof

Exercise 5D

1   **a**   Amplitude = 3; period = $\dfrac{\pi}{2}$

    b   Amplitude = 1; period = 4π

    c   Amplitude = 1; period = $\dfrac{2\pi}{3}$

    d   Amplitude = 2; period = 2

2   **a**   **i**

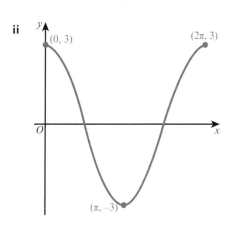

       ii

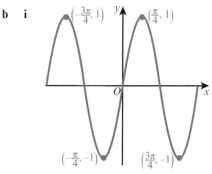

    b   **i**

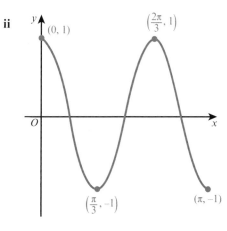

       ii

163

c   i

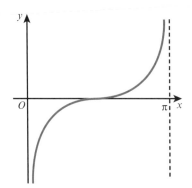

ii

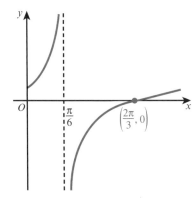

d   i

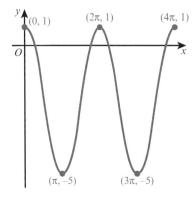

ii

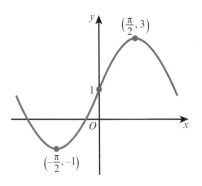

3   **a**   9 m, 23 m   **b**   6 a.m.

4   **a**   4   **b**   2 s

5 $p = 5, q = 2$

6 $a = 2, b = 20°$

7   **a**

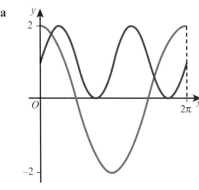

b   2   **c**   8

8 $a = 1.5; b = \dfrac{\pi}{6}; m = 4.5$

9   **a** $h = 14 - 12\cos\theta$

b $\theta = \dfrac{\pi t}{2}$

c $h = 14 - 12\cos\left(\dfrac{\pi t}{2}\right)$; 1 min 20 s

10   **a**   2, 0; 180, 90   **b**   9, 1; 240, 60

c   49, 9; 105, 45   **d**   8, 5; 90, 180

e   6, 3; 180, 360   **f**   60, 30; $7\frac{1}{2}, 52\frac{1}{2}$

Exercise 5E

1   **a**   30°   **b**   45°   **c**   90°

d   60°   **e**   −60°   **f**   −90°

g   −45°   **h**   180°

2   **a** $\dfrac{1}{4}\pi$ **b** $-\dfrac{1}{6}\pi$

c $\dfrac{2}{3}\pi$ **d** $\dfrac{1}{6}\pi$

3   **a**   0.5   **b**   −1

c $\sqrt{3}$ **d**   0

4   **a** $\dfrac{1}{2}\pi$ **b** $\dfrac{1}{6}\pi$

c $\dfrac{1}{6}\pi$ **d**   0

5   **a** $\dfrac{1}{2}$ **b** $\dfrac{1}{2}$

c $\dfrac{1}{2}\sqrt{3}$ **d**   1

6　**a**　Domain $\mathbb{R}$

Range: $-\dfrac{\pi}{2} < y < \dfrac{\pi}{2}$

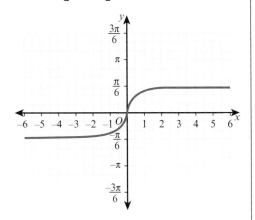

b　Domain: $-1 \leqslant x \leqslant 1$

Range: $-2 \leqslant y \leqslant \pi - 2$

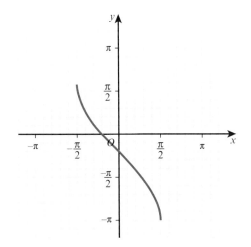

a　$1 \leqslant f(x) \leqslant 5$

b　$f^{-1}(x) = \sin^{-1}\left(\dfrac{x-3}{2}\right)$

$1 \leqslant f(x) \leqslant 7$

a　$\dfrac{3\pi}{2}$

b　$f^{-1}(x) = \sin^{-1}\left(\dfrac{5-x}{2}\right)$, $3 \leqslant x \leqslant 7$

xercise 5F

a　**i**　$\theta = 5.74°, 174°$

　　ii　$\theta = -14.5°, 194°$

b　**i**　$x = 63.6°, 296°$

　　ii　$x = 57.3°, 303°$

c　**i**　$t = -121°, 59.0°$

　　ii　$t = 65.6°, 246°$

2　$23.6°, 135°, 156°, 315°$

3　$x = -276°, -83.6°$

4　$\theta = 205°$

5　$x = -255°, -225°, -75°, -45°, 105°, 135°,$
$285°, 315°$

6　$x = -88.3°, 1.67°, 31.7°$

7　$x = \pm5.48°, \pm12.2°$

8　**a**　**i**　$x = 54.7°, 125°, 235°, 305°$

　　　ii　$x = 52.2°, 128°, 232°, 308°$

　　b　**i**　$x = 71.6°, 117°, 252°, 297°$

　　　ii　$x = 48.2°, 180°, 312°$

　　c　**i**　$x = 41.4°, 319°$

　　　ii　$x = 53.1°, 127°$

　　d　**i**　$x = 0°, 180°, 199°, 341°, 360°$

　　　ii　$x = 0°, 129°, 180°, 309°, 360°$

9　**a**　**i**　$\theta = \pm180°, \pm66.4°, 0°$

　　　ii　$\theta = -127°, -90°, -53.1°, 90°$

　　b　**i**　$\theta = -90°, 14.5°, 90°, 166°$

　　　ii　$\theta = \pm180°, \pm53.1°, 0°$

10　$\theta = 90°, 180°, 270°$

Exercise 5G

1　**a**　3　　　　　　**b**　1

　　c　-2　　　　　**d**　$\dfrac{3}{2}$

2　**a**　$4 - \sin^2 x$　　**b**　$2\cos^2 x - 1$

3　**a**　**i**　Proof　　　**ii**　Proof

　　b　**i**　Proof　　　**ii**　Proof

4　**a**　$5 - \dfrac{2}{\cos^2 x}$　　**b**　$\cos^2 x$

5　1

6　$k = -2$

7　**a**　$\dfrac{1}{1+t^2}$　　　**b**　$\dfrac{t^2}{1+t^2}$

　　c　$\dfrac{1-t^2}{1+t^2}$　　　**d**　$\dfrac{2+3t^2}{t^2}$

8　Proof

9　Proof

10　**a**　$30°, 150°, 210°, 330°$

　　b　$0°, 180°, 360°$

　　c　$36.9°, 143.1°, 199.5°, 340.5°$

　　d　$0°, 51.0°, 180°, 309.0°, 360°$

Exercise 5H

1 **a** **i** $x = 33.7°$ **ii** $x = 59.0°$
   b **i** $x = 66.8°$ **ii** $x = 78.7°$

2 **a** **i** $x = 45°, 135°, 225°, 315°$
      ii $x = 54.7°, 125°, 235°, 305°$
   b **i** $x = 45°, 135°, 225°, 315°$
      ii $x = 0°, 180°, 360°$

3 $x = 67.5°, 158°, 248°, 338°$

4 $x = 0°, 135°, 180°, 315°, 360°$

5 $x = 0°, \pm180°$

6 $\theta = \pm41.8°, \pm138.2°$

7 $\theta = 30°, 150°, 270°$

8 $-14.5°, -90°, -166°$

9 **a** $\dfrac{2}{3}, -\dfrac{1}{2}$

   b $x = 48.2°, 120°, 240°, 312°$

10 **a** Proof
   b $x = -153°, -135°, 26.6°, 45°$

End-of-chapter review exercise 5

1 **a** $-\dfrac{11}{14}$ **b** $\dfrac{20}{29}$

   c $\pm\dfrac{1}{2}\sqrt{3}$

   d $0, \pm78.5$ (to 1 decimal place)

2 **a** $0°, 180°, 360°$
   b $0°, 30°, 150°, 180°, 360°$

   c $67\frac{1}{2}°, 157\frac{1}{2}°, 247\frac{1}{2}°, 337\frac{1}{2}°$

   d $30°, 120°, 210°, 300°$

3 $x = 570°, 690°$

4 Eight

5 $a = 5, b = 45°$

6 Proof

7 $x = -69.1°, -20.9°, 15°, 75°$

8 **a** $k = \pm4$ **b** Proof
   c **i** One
      ii $\theta = \pm60°, \pm300°$
      iii $k = 5$
      iv Seven

9 **a** $90°$ **b** $45°$ **c** $180°$

   d $30°$ **e** $360°$ **f** $11\frac{1}{4}°$

10 **a** 110 cm and 90 cm
   b 0.36 seconds
   c 0.72 seconds
   d 0.468

6 Series

Exercise 6A

1 **a** **i** $32 - 80x + 80x^2 - 40x^3 + 10x^4 - x^5$
      ii $729 + 1458x + 1215x^2 + 540x^3$
            $+ 135x^4 + 18x^5 + x^6$
   b **i** $16 - 96x + 216x^2 - 216x^3 + 81x^4$
      ii $8x^3 - 84x^2 + 294x - 343$
   c **i** $243x^5 + 405x^4y + 270x^3y^2$
      ii $16c^4 - 32c^3d + 24c^2d^2$
   d **i** $8x^6 - 36x^5 + 54x^4 - 27x^3$
      ii $\dfrac{8}{x^3} + \dfrac{60y}{x^2} + \dfrac{150y^2}{x} + 125y^3$
   e **i** $8x^3 + 12x + \dfrac{6}{x} + \dfrac{1}{x^3}$
      ii $x^4 - 12x^2 + 54 - \dfrac{108}{x^2} + \dfrac{81}{x^4}$

2 **a** 4   **b** 35
   c 7   **d** 56

3 **a** $80y^4$ **b** $-80y^3$

4 $y^6 + 18y^7 + 135y^8 + 540y^9$

5 **a** $n = 6$ **b** $a = \pm2$

6 **a** $n = 3$
   b $27x^6y^3 + 135x^5y + 225x^4y^{-1} + 125x^3y^{-3}$

7 -672

8 $-945x^5$

9 $79\,200\,000$

Exercise 6B

1 **a** **i** 8   **ii** 15
   b **i** 1   **ii** 7
   c **i** $n = 10$ **ii** $n = 12$

2 **a** $n = 10$ **b** $a = 180$

3 **a** $n = 12$ **b** $a = 6$

4 **a** $128 - 2240x + 16\,800x^2 - 70\,000x^3$
   b $-36\,400$

5 **a** $81 - 540x + 1350x^2$
   b 80.461

6 **a** $128 + 1344x + 6048x^2$
   b **i** 322.28   **ii** 142.0448
   c Smaller value of x means higher order
         terms are much smaller and therefore less
         important, so the error is less for 2.03^7.

7 **a** $16\,384 - 28\,672x + 21504x^2$
   b $-30\,720$

8 **a** $e^5 + 10e^3 + 40e + \dfrac{80}{e} + \dfrac{80}{e^3} + \dfrac{32}{e^5}$

    b $2e^5 + 80e + \dfrac{160}{e^3}$

9 **a, b** Student's own (reasonable) answers.

Exercise 6C

1 **a** **i** 33   **ii** 29
    b **i** 100   **ii** 226

2 17

3 $a = 2, b = -3$

4 **a** Proof   **b** 456 pages

5 $a = -7, d = 3$

6 Proof

7 $u_n = 6n - 5$

8 $\theta = 20°$

9 **a** 71 071   **b** 429 429

10 24 192

Exercise 6D

1 **a** $2 \times 3^{n-1}$ **b** 39 366

2 **a** $a = 3, r = \pm2$ **b** ±384

3 **a** $-\dfrac{7}{2}, 7$ **b** $\dfrac{137\,781}{2}$, 137 781

4 10th

5 **a** **i** 17 089 842   **ii** 2303.4375
    b **i** 514.75   **ii** 9.487 171
    c **i** 39 368   **ii** 9840
    d **i** 191.953 125 or 63.984 375
       ii 24 414 062.5 or 16 276 041.67

6 **a** **i** $r = 0.15$ **ii** $r = 2.7$
    b **i** $r = -1.3, 0.3$
       ii $r = -0.947$

7 $r = -\dfrac{1}{2} \pm \dfrac{\sqrt{147}}{6}$

8 **a** 1.5   **b** 160

9 $2^{64} - 1 \approx 1.84 \times 10^{19}$

10 Proof

Exercise 6E

1 **a** **i** $\dfrac{27}{2}$ **ii** $\dfrac{196}{3}$
    b **i** $\dfrac{1}{3}$ **ii** $\dfrac{26}{33}$
    c **i** Divergent   **ii** Divergent

    d **i** $\dfrac{25}{3}$ **ii** $\dfrac{18}{5}$
    e **i** Divergent   **ii** $\dfrac{7}{3}$

2 **a** **i** $|x| < 1$ **ii** $|x| < 1$
    b **i** $|x| < \dfrac{1}{3}$ **ii** $|x| < \dfrac{1}{10}$
    c **i** $|x| < \dfrac{1}{5}$ **ii** $|x| < \dfrac{1}{3}$
    d **i** $|x| < 4$ **ii** $|x| < 12$
    e **i** $|x| < 3$ **ii** $|x| < \dfrac{4}{5}$
    f **i** $|x| > 2$ **ii** $|x| > \dfrac{1}{2}$
    g **i** $1 < x < 2$ **ii** $0 < x < 4$
    h **i** $\dfrac{1}{2} < x < 1$ **ii** $x < -\dfrac{1}{2}$
    i **i** $|x| < 1$ **ii** $|x| < \dfrac{1}{\sqrt[3]{4}}$

3 **a** $S_n = \dfrac{18\left(1 - \left(-\frac{1}{3}\right)^n\right)}{\frac{4}{3}}$

    b $S_\infty = \dfrac{27}{2}$

4 **a** $\dfrac{2}{3}$ **b** 9

5 $\dfrac{1}{8}$

6 **a** $|x| < \dfrac{3}{2}$ **b** 5

7 9

8 **a** $x < 0$ **b** $x = -3$

9 19 m

10 **a** Edge of table   **b** 8

Exercise 6F

1 **a** $a + d, a + 5d$ **b** Proof
    c 660, 715 827 882

2 $d = 0, -\dfrac{1}{4}$

3 $\dfrac{-1 + \sqrt{5}}{2}$

4 **a** $0.5x^2$ **b** $5x - 8$
    c $x = 8$ **d** 3775

5 2.5, 5, 7.5, 10

6 **a** 1, 0.5   **b** 2

7 $a = -2, b = 4$

8 $m = 7$

167

End-of-chapter review exercise 6

1. $232 - 164\sqrt{2}$

2. $-\dfrac{1}{3}$

3. -5

4. 80

5. $a = 2, n = 5$

6. $\dfrac{2}{3}$

7. a $-3, 7$ b 54

8. $19\,264$

9. $270x^2 + 250;\ \pm\dfrac{4}{3}$

10. Proof

7 Differentiation

Exercise 7A

1. a i $y' = \dfrac{1}{3}x^{-\frac{2}{3}}$ ii $y' = \dfrac{1}{5}x^{-\frac{4}{5}}$

   b i $y' = 2x^{-\frac{3}{4}}$ ii $y' = \dfrac{1}{6}x^{-\frac{1}{2}}$

   c i $y' = x^{-2}$ ii $y' = -4x^{-5}$

   d i $y' = -6x^{-3}$ ii $y' = 4x^{-11}$

   e i $y' = -\dfrac{1}{2}x^{-\frac{3}{2}}$ ii $y' = -\dfrac{1}{3}x^{-\frac{4}{3}}$

   f i $y' = -2x^{-\frac{6}{5}}$ ii $y' = -\dfrac{2}{3}x^{-\frac{5}{4}}$

2. a i $f'(x) = 4x + 5$
   ii $f'(x) = 6x - 15$

   b i $f'(x) = 6x^{\frac{1}{2}} + \dfrac{3}{2}x^{-\frac{1}{2}}$

   ii $f'(x) = \dfrac{4}{3}x^{\frac{1}{3}} - \dfrac{1}{3}x^{-\frac{2}{3}}$

   c i $f'(x) = 1 + 8x + 6x^{\frac{1}{2}}$

   ii $f'(x) = \dfrac{1}{2}x^{-\frac{1}{2}} - 2x^{-\frac{3}{4}}$

   d i $f'(x) = 2x - 2x^{-3}$
   ii $f'(x) = 2x + 8x^{-3}$

3. a $\dfrac{1}{\sqrt{x}}$ b $\dfrac{1}{\sqrt{x}} + 1$

   c $1 - \dfrac{1}{4\sqrt{x}}$ d $1 - \dfrac{1}{\sqrt{x}}$

---

e $1 + \dfrac{1}{x^2}$ f $2x + 1 - \dfrac{1}{x^2}$

g $1 - \dfrac{2}{x^2}$ h $1 + \dfrac{1}{\sqrt{x}}$

4. $f'(x) = \dfrac{15}{2}x^{\frac{2}{3}} - \dfrac{1}{2}x^{-\frac{4}{3}}$

5. $\dfrac{dy}{dx} = -12x^2 + 24x + 1$

6. a $f'(x) = \dfrac{3}{2}x^{-\frac{1}{2}} + x^{-\frac{3}{2}}$

   b $\dfrac{7}{8}$

7. $b = 8, c = -7$

8. $\left(-\dfrac{1}{3},\ -4\frac{17}{27}\right), (2, 13)$

Exercise 7B

1. a i $15(3x + 4)^4$ ii $35(5x + 4)^6$

   b i $\dfrac{3}{2\sqrt{3x - 2}}$ ii $\dfrac{1}{2\sqrt{x + 1}}$

   c i $\dfrac{1}{(3 - x)^2}$ ii $-\dfrac{4}{(2x + 3)^3}$

2. a $30(5x + 3)^5$ b $\dfrac{5}{2}(5x + 3)^{-\frac{1}{2}}$

   c $\dfrac{-5}{(5x + 3)^2}$

3. a $-20(1 - 4x)^4$ b $12(1 - 4x)^{-4}$

   c $\dfrac{-2}{\sqrt{1 - 4x}}$

4. a $15x^2(1 + x^3)^4$

   b $-12x^2(1 + x^3)^{-5}$

   c $\dfrac{x^2}{(1 + x^3)^{\frac{2}{3}}}$

5. a $24x(2x^2 + 3)^5$ b $\dfrac{-4x}{(2x^2 + 3)^2}$

   c $\dfrac{-2x}{\sqrt{(2x^2 + 3)^3}}$

6. a $-\dfrac{4}{25}$ b 0

7. $\dfrac{3}{8}$

8. a $6(x^2 + 3x + 1)^5(2x + 3)$

   b $\dfrac{-3(2x + 5)}{(x^2 + 5x)^4}$

Exercise 7C

1 $y = x + 2$

2 $y = \frac{1}{4}x + 1$

3 $x = 1$

4 Proof

5 $y = -2x - 6$

6 $3y - x = 4, y + 3x = 28$

7 $(0, 12), \left(\frac{3}{4}, 0\right)$

8 $y = 12x - 25$

9 $x + 4y = 8$

10 $x + 6y = 23$

Exercise 7D

1 **a** 4 **b** $36x^2 - 42x$

c $-\frac{72}{x^5}$ **d** $108(3x + 1)^2$

e $-\frac{1}{(1 - 2x)^{\frac{3}{2}}}$ **f** $\frac{15}{4(x + 1)^{\frac{5}{2}}}$

g $\frac{6x - 30}{x^4}$ **h** 4

i $\frac{3x + 12}{4x^{\frac{5}{2}}}$

2 **a** $\frac{2}{3x^3}$ **b** $\frac{2x + 12}{x^4}$

c $\frac{-3}{(1 - 3x^2)^{\frac{3}{2}}}$ **d** $\frac{12 - 9x}{x^5}$

e $\frac{35x^{\frac{3}{2}}}{4} - 18x$ **f** $6x - 2$

3 $2 - 9(3x - 1)^2, 54 - 162x$

4 **a** -2 **b** 4 **c** -8

5 **a** **i** 54 **ii** 384

b **i** 8 **ii** $\frac{1}{108}$

6 **a** $x = -3$ **b** $x = 2$

7 $x = \pm\sqrt{2}$

8 **a** **i** $12x^2$ **ii** $24x$ **b** Proof

9 Proof

10 $a = 2, b = \pm 1$

End-of-chapter review exercise 7

1 -54

2 $a = 4.8, b = -1.8$

3 $x = 1, 25$

4 **a** **i** $2ax + 1 - a$ **ii** $3x^2$

b **i** $\frac{1}{2}\sqrt{\frac{b}{a}}$ **ii** $6a^2v$

5 $80y = 32x - 51$

6 $\left(-3, -\frac{1}{3}\right)$

7 2

8 -183

9 $mn = -1$

10 $\left(\frac{67}{32}, \frac{5}{8}\right)$

8 Further differentiation

Exercise 8A

1 **a** $2x + 4, x \leqslant -2$

b $2x - 3, x \leqslant \frac{3}{2}$

c $-3 + 2x, x \leqslant \frac{3}{2}$

d $4x - 8, x \leqslant 2$

e $7 - 4x, x \geqslant \frac{7}{4}$

f $-5 - 14x, x \geqslant -\frac{5}{14}$

2 **a** **i** $x > \frac{1}{2}$ **ii** $x < -1$

b **i** $x < -1$ or $x > 1$ **ii** $-\frac{4}{3} < x < 0$

c **i** $x < 0$ **ii** $x > \frac{1}{6}$

3 **a** $-\frac{1}{18}$ **b** increasing

4 Proof

5 $a = -6, b = 2$

6 $2 < x < 3$

7 **a** $\frac{9}{4}$

b Positive gradient; increasing

8 D

Exercise 8B

1   a $(-4, 213)$, maximum; $(3, -130)$, minimum

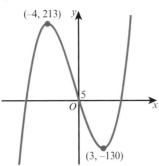

b $(-3, 88)$, maximum; $(5, -168)$, minimum

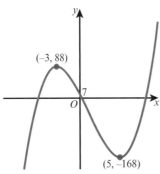

c $\left(-\frac{1}{3}, -\frac{11}{27}\right)$, minimum; $\left(\frac{1}{2}, \frac{3}{4}\right)$, maximum

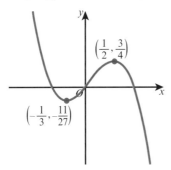

d $(-1, 0)$, neither

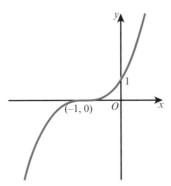

2   Consider discriminant of the derivative expression

3   a $x = \pm\frac{1}{3}$

b $\left(\frac{1}{3}, 6\right)$ local minimum;

$\left(-\frac{1}{3}, -6\right)$ local maximum

4   $\left(\frac{1}{4}, -\frac{1}{4}\right)$ local minimum

5   a $(0, 0)$ and $(1, -1)$

b $(0, 0)$ local maximum; $(1, -1)$ local minimum

6   a $x = \frac{4}{3}$

b   Local maximum at $x = -8$

Local minimum at $x = \frac{4}{3}$

7   $a = 3, b = 12$

8   $(0, 0)$ local minimum; $\left(-\frac{4}{k}, \frac{32}{k^2}\right)$ local maximum if $k \neq 0$

9   a   i $(4, -12)$ ii   minimum

iv $f(x) \geqslant -12$

b   i $(-2, -7)$ ii   minimum

iv $f(x) \geqslant -7$

c   i $\left(-\frac{3}{5}, \frac{1}{5}\right)$ ii   minimum

iv $f(x) \geqslant \frac{1}{5}$

d   i $(-3, 13)$ ii   maximum

iv $f(x) \leqslant 13$

e   i $(-3, 0)$ ii   minimum

iv $f(x) \geqslant 0$

f   i $\left(-\frac{1}{2}, 2\right)$ ii   maximum

iv $f(x) \leqslant 2$

Exercise 8C

1   a $225\,\mathrm{m}^2$ b $60\,\mathrm{m}$

2   a   Proof   b $x = 2$

3   Proof

4   a $V = 225r - \pi r^3$ b $733\,\mathrm{cm}^3$

5   a $V = \dfrac{x(243 - x^2)}{2}$ b $729\,\mathrm{cm}^3$

6   **a**   Proof   **b** $166\,\text{cm}^2$

     c   Proof

7   **a** $3, 3$ **b** $0, 6$

8   **a**   Proof   **b**   Proof

9   Proof

10   **a**   Proof

     b $V = \pi(6 + x)^2\left(\dfrac{12}{x} + 2\right)$

     c 486π

Exercise 8D

1   Increasing at 0.24 units per second

2   Decreasing at 0.04 units per second

3   **a** $144x^2$ **b** $6x^2(x^3 + 1)$

4   **a**   **i** 50 **ii** -12

     b   **i** $\pm\dfrac{1}{3}$ **ii** -2

5   **a**   **i** 22 **ii** 38

     b   **i** 45 **ii** 176

     c   **i** 0.24 **ii** 0.00667

6 $20\,\text{units/sec}$

7 36

8 $4\sqrt{5}$

Exercise 8E

1   **a** $4.8\,\text{cm}\,\text{s}^{-1}$ **b** $24\,\text{cm}^2\,\text{s}^{-1}$

2   **a** $240\,\text{mm}^2\,\text{s}^{-1}$ **b** $2400\,\text{mm}^3\,\text{s}^{-1}$

3 $2\,\text{cm}\,\text{s}^{-1}$

4 $1728\pi\,\text{cm}^3\,\text{s}^{-1}$

5 $75\,\text{cm}^2\,\text{s}^{-1}$

6 $2\,\text{cm}\,\text{s}^{-1}$

7 $160\pi\,\text{cm/s}$

8   **a** $2\pi \times 10^{15}\,\text{km}^3\,\text{s}^{-1}$

     b $4\pi \times 10^9\,\text{km}^2\,\text{s}^{-1}$

9 $36\,\text{cm}^3\,\text{s}^{-1}$

10   **a**   Proof   **b** $0.052\,\text{m}\,\text{s}^{-1}$

End-of-chapter review exercise 8

     $a = -10$

   a 0

   b   Increasing

c

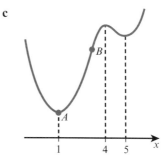

3 $\left(\dfrac{2\sqrt{3}}{3}, 0\right)$

4 $a = 3$

5 $a = 2, b = -13$

6   **a**   Proof   **b** $40\sqrt{2}\,\text{m}$

7 $0.25\,\text{m}\,\text{min}^{-1}$

8 $0.0076\,\text{m}\,\text{s}^{-1}$

9 $0.0040\,\text{cm}\,\text{s}^{-1}$

9 Integration

Exercise 9A

1   **a** $x^4 + c$ **b** $x^6 + c$

     c $x^2 + c$ **d** $x^3 + x^5 + c$

     e $x^{10} - x^8 - x + c$

     f $-x^7 + x^3 + x + c$

2   **a**   **i** $\dfrac{3}{5}x^{\frac{5}{3}} + c$ **ii** $\dfrac{3}{4}x^{\frac{4}{3}} + c$

     b   **i** $3x^{\frac{5}{3}} + c$ **ii** $8x^{\frac{7}{4}} + c$

     c   **i** $x^{\frac{5}{4}} + c$ **ii** $-x^{\frac{3}{2}} + c$

     d   **i** $-\dfrac{x^{\frac{7}{3}}}{2} + c$ **ii** $\dfrac{2x^{\frac{7}{5}}}{3} + c$

     e   **i** $\dfrac{5}{2}x^2 - 2x^{\frac{7}{2}} + c$ **ii** $6x + \dfrac{x^2}{6} - 8x^{\frac{3}{2}} + c$

     f   **i** $-x^{-1} + c$ **ii** $-\dfrac{1}{2}x^{-2} + c$

     g   **i** $\dfrac{3}{2}x^{\frac{2}{3}} + c$ **ii** $\dfrac{4}{3}x^{\frac{3}{4}} + c$

     h   **i** $-12x^{\frac{1}{3}} + c$ **ii** $10x^{-\frac{1}{2}} + c$

     i   **i** $2x^{\frac{1}{2}} + \dfrac{2x^{-3}}{5} + c$

           ii $-\dfrac{3x^{-4}}{4} + \dfrac{42x^{\frac{5}{6}}}{5} + c$

3 $f(x) = \dfrac{1}{8}x^4 + 9x^{-\frac{2}{3}} + 2x + c$

4   **a**   **i** $\dfrac{2}{3}x^3 + \dfrac{5}{2}x^2 + 3x + c$

         ii $\dfrac{3}{4}x^4 - 2x^3 + c$

     b   **i** $2x^{\frac{5}{2}} + \dfrac{8}{3}x^{\frac{3}{2}} + c$

         ii $\dfrac{3}{5}x^{\frac{10}{3}} + \dfrac{9}{4}x^{\frac{4}{3}} + c$

     c   **i** $\dfrac{2}{3}x^{\frac{3}{2}} + 3x^3 + \dfrac{8}{3}x^{\frac{9}{4}} + c$

         ii $\dfrac{1}{2}x^2 + \dfrac{1}{5}x^5 - \dfrac{4}{7}x^{\frac{7}{2}} + c$

     d   **i** $\dfrac{1}{3}x^3 - x^{-1} - 2x + c$

         ii $\dfrac{4}{3}x^3 + \dfrac{1}{3}x^{-3} + c$

5   **a**   **i** $-7x^{-1} + x^{-2} + c$

         ii $-\dfrac{1}{4}x^{-2} - \dfrac{5}{4}x^{-1} + c$

     b   **i** $-2x^{-\frac{1}{2}} + 3x^{-1} + c$

         ii $\dfrac{2}{5}x^{\frac{5}{2}} - 4x^{\frac{3}{2}} + c$

6   **a** $a = \dfrac{1}{2}, b = -2$ **b** $\dfrac{1}{5}x^{\frac{5}{2}} - 4x^{\frac{1}{2}} + c$

7   Proof

8 $\dfrac{1}{12}x^{\frac{3}{2}} + 2x^{\frac{1}{2}} - 4x^{-\frac{1}{2}} + c$

Exercise 9B

1   **a**   **i** $y = \dfrac{x^2}{2} + 5$ **ii** $y = 2x^3 + 5$

     b   **i** $y = \dfrac{-1}{x}$ **ii** $y = -\dfrac{1}{x} + 4$

     c   **i** $y = \dfrac{3}{2}x^2 - 5x + 10$

         ii $y = 3x - \dfrac{1}{2}x^4 + \dfrac{5}{2}$

     d   **i** $y = 2x^{\frac{3}{2}} - 56$ **ii** $y = 2\sqrt{x} + 4$

2 $y = \dfrac{x^2}{2} + \dfrac{1}{x} + \dfrac{3}{2}$

3 $f(x) = \dfrac{4}{3}x^{\frac{3}{2}} - 2x^{\frac{1}{2}} - \dfrac{14}{3}$

4 $\dfrac{149}{3}$

5 $y = 2x^2 - 16$

6   **a** $x = -2$ **b**   Proof

7 $y = \dfrac{1}{x} + \dfrac{5}{2}$

8   **a** $118\,\text{cm}$ (to 3s.f.)

     b   27

9   192

Exercise 9C

1   **a**   **i** $(x + 3)^5 + c$

         ii $\dfrac{1}{6}(x - 2)^6 + c$

     b   **i** $\dfrac{1}{32}(4x - 5)^8 + c$

         ii $2\left(\dfrac{1}{8}x + 1\right)^4 + c$

     c   **i** $-\dfrac{8}{7}\left(3 - \dfrac{1}{2}x\right)^7 + c$

         ii $-\dfrac{1}{9}(4 - x)^9 + c$

     d   **i** $\dfrac{1}{3}(2x + 1)^{\frac{3}{2}} + c$

         ii $-\dfrac{4}{5}(2 - 5x)^{\frac{7}{4}} + c$

     e   **i** $4\left(2 + \dfrac{x}{3}\right)^{\frac{3}{4}} + c$

         ii $2(4 - 3x)^{-1} + c$

2   **a** $\dfrac{1}{14}(2x + 1)^7 + c$

     b $\dfrac{1}{15}(3x - 5)^5 + c$

     c $-\dfrac{1}{28}(1 - 7x)^4 + c$

     d $\dfrac{2}{11}\left(\dfrac{1}{2}x + 1\right)^{11} + c$

     e $-\dfrac{1}{10}(5x + 2)^{-2} + c$

     f $\dfrac{2}{3}(1 - 3x)^{-1} + c$

g $-\dfrac{1}{4}(x+1)^{-4}+c$

h $-\dfrac{1}{8}(4x+1)^{-3}+c$

i $\dfrac{1}{15}(10x+1)^{\frac{3}{2}}+c$

j $\sqrt{2x-1}+c$

k $\dfrac{6}{5}\left(\dfrac{1}{2}x+2\right)^{\frac{5}{3}}+c$

l $\dfrac{16}{9}(2+6x)^{\frac{3}{4}}+c$

3 a $\dfrac{(x-2)^4}{4}+\dfrac{15}{4}$

b $y=-\dfrac{2}{3}(4-x)^{\frac{3}{2}}+\dfrac{22}{3}$

c $y=\dfrac{2}{3}\sqrt{3x-5}+\dfrac{1}{3}$

d $y=\dfrac{1}{2(1-3x)^2}$

4 $y=(2x-1)^3+4$

5 a $k=3$

b $y=-\dfrac{x}{2}-\dfrac{3}{2}$

6 $y=4x^{\frac{5}{2}}-4x^{\frac{1}{2}}+7$

7 $100\,\mathrm{min}$

8 $y=x^3-2x^2-x+8$

Exercise 9D

1 a $10x(x^2+3)^4$ **b** $\dfrac{1}{5}(x^2+2)^5+c$

2 a $-30x(2-3x^2)^4$

b $-\dfrac{1}{30}(2-3x^2)^5+c$

3 a $k=-6$ **b** $\dfrac{2}{3-9x^2}+c$

4 a $\dfrac{12x}{(1-2x^2)^4}$ **b** $\dfrac{1}{4(1-2x^2)^3}+c$

5 a $8x(x^2-4)^3$ **b** $\dfrac{1}{2}(x^2-4)^4+c$

6 a $\dfrac{5(\sqrt{x}+1)^4}{2\sqrt{x}}$ **b** $\dfrac{2}{5}(\sqrt{x}+1)^5+c$

Exercise 9E

1 a i 320 **ii** 420.2
 b i 0 **ii** 36
 c i 46 **ii** 48
 d i 28.5 **ii** $\dfrac{33}{2}$
 e i $\dfrac{76}{3}$ **ii** $\dfrac{585}{2}$
 f i 36 **ii** 2
 g i $\dfrac{5}{2}$ **ii** $-\dfrac{26}{3}$

2 a 144 **b** $1\frac{1}{2}$
 c 20 **d** $6\frac{3}{4}$
 e 16 **f** 3

3 $-60+28\sqrt{2}$

4 $a=2,b=10$

5 $2k+\dfrac{1}{k}-3$

6 $8-a^4-a^3$

7 $a=16$

8 $p=-\dfrac{10}{3}$ or $p=-1$

Exercise 9F

1 a i $\dfrac{7}{3}$ **ii** $\dfrac{1}{4}$
 b i $\dfrac{2}{3}$ **ii** $\dfrac{22}{3}$
 c i $\dfrac{11}{4}$ **ii** $\dfrac{79}{6}$

2 a i 45 **ii** $\dfrac{17}{3}$
 b i $\dfrac{32}{3}$ **ii** $\dfrac{4}{3}$
 c i $\dfrac{243}{2}$ **ii** $\dfrac{1}{2}$

3 $k=9$

4 a $(0,0),(k,0)$ **b** $k=2$

5 6

6 $\dfrac{32}{3}$

7 a Proof **b** $\sqrt{3}(\sqrt{7}-1)$

8 38

9 a 6 **b** 67 **c** Not possible.
 d 45 **e** 17 **f** Not possible.
 g 17 **h** 11

173

Exercise 9G

1 $\dfrac{1}{6}p\sqrt{p}$

2 $\dfrac{a^3}{48}$

3 108

4 32

5 108

6 $42\dfrac{2}{3}$

7 $6\dfrac{3}{4}$

8 $1\dfrac{1}{3}$

9 Proof

Exercise 9H

1 **a** $10\dfrac{2}{3}$ **b** 8   **c** 100

2 **a** $\dfrac{1}{4}$ **b** 6   **c** 100

3 Proof

4 Proof

Exercise 9I

1 **a** 504π **b** $\dfrac{3498}{5}\pi$

    c $\dfrac{15}{2}\pi$ **d** $\dfrac{16}{15}\pi$

2 **a** 4π **b** 9π **c** 3355π

    d $\dfrac{3}{10}\pi$ **e** $\dfrac{648}{5}\pi$ **f** $\dfrac{9}{2}\pi$

    g 156π **h** $\dfrac{2}{3}\pi$

3 9π

4 $\dfrac{1}{3}$

5

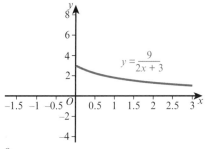

    9π

6 **a** $(2, 4)$

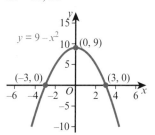

b $\dfrac{64}{5}\pi$

7 $3\dfrac{1}{2}$

8 Proof

End-of-chapter review exercise 9

1 $y = \dfrac{3}{2}x^2 - \dfrac{2}{3}x^{\frac{3}{2}} - \dfrac{59}{3}$

2 **a** $-12 + 8\sqrt{3}$ **b** $12 - 4\sqrt{3}$

3 **a** $a = \sqrt{2}$ **b** $\dfrac{1}{2}$

4 **a** **i** $A(-a, 0),\ B(a, 0),\ C(0, a^2)$

      ii $\dfrac{1}{3}a^3$

    b $\dfrac{1}{3}a^3$

5 Proof

6 $438\dfrac{6}{7}$

7 **a** Proof   **b** 2

    c 3π **d** $\dfrac{1}{2}\pi$

8 **a** $R = 36, 18$

b $\dfrac{1296}{5}\pi$ **c** $\dfrac{81}{2}\pi$

9 **a** $y + 6x = 8$ **b** Proof

    c $\dfrac{16}{3}$

10 $\dfrac{1}{12}\pi$